MARÍA SABINA: Her Life and Chants

photo by LISA LAW ©1980

MARÍA SABINA: Her Life and Chants

written by Álvaro Estrada

translation and commentaries by Henry Munn

with a retrospective essay by R. Gordon Wasson

preface by Jerome Rothenberg

Ross-Erikson Inc., *Publishers*, Santa Barbara

First English Language Edition
Translation copyright © 1981 by Henry Munn.
All rights reserved. Manufactured in the United States of America.
Cover/jacket/interior design by Frederick A. Usher

Library of Congress Cataloging in Publication Data

Estrada, Álvaro
María Sabina, Her Life and Chants.

(New wilderness poetics)
Translation of Vida de María Sabina.
Includes bibliographical references.
1. María Sabina, 1894-   2. Mazatec Indians—Biography.
3. Mazatec Indians—Religion and mythology.
4. Mushrooms, Hallucinogenic—Mexico.   5. Indians of
Mexico—Religion and mythology.
I. Title. II. Series.
F1221. M35M37413   970.004'97[B]   80-20866
ISBN 0-915520-33-8
ISBN 0-915520-32-X (pbk.)

To my parents, Evaristo G. Estrada and Maximina Pineda,
who have demonstrated to me that faith
is a human being's greatest strength.

Contents

PREFACE

In Mazatec, María Sabina's calling is, literally, that of "wise woman"—a term that we may choose to translate as "shaman" or, by a further twist, as "poet." But that's to bring it and her into our own generalized kind of reckoning and naming. In much the same way, this book, which first appeared in Spanish in 1977, and French by 1979, translates her from the particularities of local Mazatec culture to the generalities of a book and media technology that can travel almost anywhere. (Or so we like to think.)

When I visited Mexico in the summer of 1979, the film, *María Sabina: Mujer Espíritu,* a documentary by Nicolas Echevaria, was playing under government sponsorship at the large Cine Regis in downtown Mexico City. María Sabina herself had been brought to Mexico City the previous month—a small, elderly Indian woman, dressed in the traditional bird and flower *huipil,* and with only a touch of Spanish at her service—and had been much patronized (even lionized I think the word is) before her return to native Huautla. (All this in contrast to the attempt, a dozen years before, to arrest her for practice of the sacred mushroom ceremonies that existed in the Mazatecan sierras long before the first Conquerors set foot there.)

I hope, in calling attention to the degree of fame that she has, that I don't frustrate the reader's enthusiasm for things Indian and remote. She's certainly aware of being famous ("the Judge knows me, the Government knows me," she sings), though by our standards it has had little effect on her life *per se*. She lives still in her old tin-roofed house—though a new pre-fabricated home supplied by the government is going up nearby. She still walks barefoot up the hillside, still speaks Mazatec not Spanish, still cures and shamanizes, still smokes cigarettes and drinks beer from the bottle, still celebrates her own life of labor and her ability to make a clean bed, along with those other powers, language foremost among them, that have won her local and international repute. A poet, in short, with a sense of both a real physical world and a world beyond what the mind may sense, or the mouth proclaim.

Before her name reached us clearly, her image and words had already come into our world. By the late 1950s, Gordon Wasson's recording, *The Mushroom Ceremony of the Mazatec Indians of Mexico*, was in circulation, and travelers in Mexico spoke of side-trips to see and to be illumined by the "mushroom woman" of Oaxaca. (Her own view of these matters awaits the reader, within.) And in the strange way in which ideas about language may travel in advance of the language itself, the American poet Anne Waldman, having come across the liner notes to Wasson's *Ceremony*, used them, circa 1970, to model a work called *Fast Speaking Woman* that she performed in poetry readings and even, if memory doesn't fail me, as part of Dylan's short-lived *Rolling Thunder Movie*:

> *I'm a shouting woman*
> *I'm a speech woman*
> *I'm an atmosphere woman*
> *I'm an airtight woman*

in distinct reflection of the other's:

> *I am a spirit woman, says*
> *I am a lord eagle woman, says*

—which the North American poet acknowledges formally as her "indebtedness to the Maztatec Indian Shamaness in Mexico." Yet she fails to name her—with a sense, one guesses, that the "shamaness" is of the anonymous tribal/oral sort. But María Sabina was already in "the world" by then—beyond the boundaries of her own place, to be given a fame and the western trappings of immortality-through-written-language that she herself could hardly have sought.

The confusion, as such, is easy enough to understand. María Sabina is Mazatec without question, and the mode of her chants (the way the words go, etc.) isn't merely personal but common to other Mazatec shamans. Among them she stands out—not alone but sharing a language with the other great ones, including those "tiger shamans" we hear of in the hills, who rarely make themselves visible in the town environs of Huautla.

This book, then, is centrally hers.

But it is as well a book of transmissions, of which Waldman's is a curious and distant instance. The songs, the words, come to María Sabina through the agency of what Henry Munn has elsewhere called "the mushrooms of language." (Her qualification of each line with the word *tzo*, "says," is a testimony to that: that it isn't María Sabina but the unspoken he/she/it whose words these are.) Then, sometime past the middle of her life, R. Gordon Wasson begins the other transmission that carries her words over great distances: an offshoot of his studies of mushroom history and lore but one that has continued to affect him to the present.

The transmission most crucial to this book is that between María Sabina and Alvaro Estrada. A Mazatec speaker and fellow townsman, Estrada engaged her in a series of recorded conversations, which he translated into Spanish and made the basis of her "oral autobiography." To this he added a new translation of Wasson's 1956 recording and a series of footnotes and commentaries, not as an outside observer but with a native feel for Mazatec particulars and with testimony from older members of his own family and from other Mazatecs, local shamans among them, still deeply involved in the native religion. He is in that sense no innocent Castaneda nor is María Sabina a shadowy Don Juan, but both stand open before us. The poetry and the vision are none the less intense.

In the present version Henry Munn has continued the process begun by Estrada, adding a second chanting session (the only recorded one in which only Mazatecs were present), with additional observations from both "inside" and "outside" points of view. Munn's connection is itself a part of the recent history of Huautla. His entry, circa 1965, was as one of those "oddballs" labeled by Wasson in his retrospective essay [see below], but he was a genuine seeker as well, and after the "great bust of 1967," he returned to Huautla, married into the Estrada family, and has since become his own witness and a devoted student of Mazatec culture. An early essay of his, "The Mushrooms of Language,"* is a brilliant introduction to the verbal side of Mazatec shamanism: a first recognition of the shaman's work as an essentially poetic act and, in the Surrealist master André Breton's definition of *poesis* quoted therein, "a sacred action." Munn's translations (drawing on both Mazatec and Spanish) are equally attentive, and his commentaries direct us to a range of mythopoetic connections (local and universal) informing the Mazatec chants.

The presence, alongside María Sabina, of Estrada, Munn, and Wasson makes of this a multi-levelled book of testimony—and something more: a book of exiles and losses. This will seem surprising only if one sentimen-

---

*Published in Michael Harner's anthology, *Hallucinogens and Shamanism*, 1974.

talizes or primitivizes the Mazatec present, for the present is perenially a time of loss and change. Viewed in this way, Estrada may appear as the acculturated Mazatec, whose adolescence coincided with the arrival in Huautla of anonymous hippies and world-famous superstars in search of God, and who early withdrew to work in Mexico as a writer and engineer. However, Estrada's yearning here (as it came across to me in conversation with him) is for something that draws him backward, fascinates and troubles him, and that he cannot possess; he honors it, but mostly lives apart from it. With Munn, the stance—of exile and escape—seems different: a flight-from-time in search of mysteries/illuminations that brings him to the place left vacant by Estrada: the town, the family, and so on.

But overshadowing them both is the culturally authentic, strangely marginal figure of María Sabina, whose personal history (never "erased" in the Castanedian sense) is always precarious and whose spiritual universe begins to change (she tells us) with the coming of the blond strangers, a few at first, then in great waves in the 1960s. It's with a sense of what was at stake and of his own part in it that Wasson, accused, responds as poignant witness: "[Her] words make me wince. I, Gordon Wasson, am held responsible for the end of a religious practice in Mesoamerica that goes back far, for millennia. 'The little mushrooms won't work any more. There is no helping it.' I fear she spoke the truth, exemplifying her *sabiduría*." And, still more strikingly, the words of another shaman count the losses for Estrada: "What is terrible, listen, is that the divine mushroom no longer belongs to us. Its sacred language has been profaned. The language has been spoiled and it is indecipherable for us."

The word "language" hits here with tremendous force; for this is crucially a book of language, a reflection of the great Book of Language that María Sabina saw in her initiatory vision:

> On the Principal Ones' table a book appeared, an open book that went on growing until it was the size of a person. In its pages there were letters. It was a white book, so white it was resplendent.
>
> One of the Principal Ones spoke to me and said: "María Sabina, this is the Book of Wisdom. It is the Book of Language. Everything that is written in it is for you. The Book is yours, take it so that you can work." I exclaimed with emotion: "That is for me. I receive it."

And she does and is thereafter a woman of language—what we would dare to translate, by a comparison to those most deeply into it among us, as "poet."

Her own words and her highly tuned chants (the improvised and collaged "sessions" that function like long, driving poems) make this clear. Munn's commentaries bring the message home. And hearing her voice on tape or reading her here in translation, we catch the presence of a great oral poet, one whom we can now see working and changing over the course of time—in two full sessions, 1956 and 1970. The Language revealed is awesome, not because it allows her to control the world around her (it doesn't) but because it lets her survive the sufferings of a world in which the spirit of Language itself has been "profaned," in which "it wanders without direction in the atmosphere...not only the divine spirit...but our own spirit, the spirit of the Mazatecs, as well."

A devastatingly human book and testimony, hers is the appropriate opener for a series on poetics over a broad human range. This broadening and expansion was the motive for those of us who entered some years ago into the pursuit of a virtual "ethnopoetics"—a term which the poet David Antin expanded still further to mean "Human Poetics...People's Poetics or the poetics of natural language." And other-than-human as well, if we take her word for it: "Language belongs to the *saint children*"—the sacred mushrooms—"They speak and I have the power to translate." Or Antin further: "What I take the 'poetics' part of ETHNOPOETICS to be is the structure of those liguistic acts of invention and discovery through which the mind explores the transformational power of language and discovers and invents the world and itself."

In that sense we aren't dealing with something merely alien/exotic, but we are all potential witnesses and transmitters, all suffering exiles and losses, are all in an encounter with language and vision. María Sabina's Language bears the traces of such an encounter and presents them in a form in no way incomplete: a language-centered poetics and a guide that encompasses even that writing which we would still speak of, in our arrogance, as the final instrument of langauge that separates her and us. But she has seen the book as well—the Book of Language—and that makes of this a Book about the Book. And, if we let it, it is also a book of healing: a language directed against that *sparagmos*—that classic split in consciousness—that tears us all asunder. The wounds are deep and are probably irremediable, but the dream, while we're alive, is that of wholeness. Here is language as a medicine, its ancient function; for, as she chants, "with words we live and grow," and (again speaking of the mushrooms with a familiar Mazatec word): "I cured them with the Language of the *children*."

Jerome Rothenberg

July 1980

A RETROSPECTIVE ESSAY

On the night of 29/30 June 1955, when I first attended a "velada" sung by María Sabina in Huautla de Jiménez and when on her invitation I first ingested the divine mushrooms, I was bowled over by the performance. It took place in the lower floor of the home of Cayetano García and his wife Guadalupe. The simple hospitality of our hosts and their children and relatives, all clothed in their best attire, the chanting of María Sabina and her daughter María Apolonia, María Sabina's percussive artistry and her solo dancing in the pitch darkness—combined with the distant worlds I was viewing with a clarity of vision never approached by eyesight in daylight—my body lying there on the *petate* responding to my touch as though it belonged to another—all these effects, shared with my photographer Allan Richardson, shook us both to the core of our beings. My ethnomycological inquiries had led me far but never had I expected an unearthly experience like this.

Here was a religious office, as I said to myself at the time and for months thereafter, that had to be presented to the world in a worthy manner, not sensationalized, not cheapened and coarsened, but soberly and truthfully.

We alone could do justice to it, my wife Valentina Pavlovna and I, in the book that we were writing and in responsible magazines. But given the nether reaches of vulgarity in the journalism of our time, inevitably there would follow all kinds of debased accounts erupting into print around the world. All this we foresaw and all this took place, to a point where the "Federales" had to make a clean sweep of certain Indian villages in the highlands of Mesoamerica in the late 1960s, deporting the assortment of oddballs misbehaving there.

My wife and I, we both continued on our programme, and after my wife's death at the end of 1958 I alone. Our book, *Mushrooms, Russia, and History*, came out in May 1957 at a staggering price and sold out at once, never to be reprinted. We published articles in *LIFE* and *LIFE en español*, in *This Week*, and in various learned journals.

Our need of mycological help was urgent and we immediately turned to Professor Roger Heim, then Directeur de la Laboratoire de Cryptogamie de le Musée National d'Histoire Naturelle de Paris. He grasped at once the scope of our discovery. He lent himself wholeheartedly to our programme of field work, coming over to Mexico repeatedly and joining us in the remote mountain villages of southern Mexico. His able assistant Roger Cailleux by good fortune succeeded in growing several species of the divine mushrooms, most of them new to science, in his laboratory. Professor Heim turned them over to Dr. Albert Hofmann of Bale, the discoverer of LSD, and his colleagues Drs. Arthur Brack and Hans Kobel, for chemical analysis; for their pharmacological aspects to Dr. Aurelio Cerletti; and Professor Jean Delay of Paris initiated the psychiatric studies. Thus Valentina Pavlovna and I had gratifying success in assembling a first class team to cooperate in our work, and in 1958 the Museum published a large and handsomely illustrated volume, *Les Champignons hallucinogènes du Mexique*, Roger Heim and I appearing on the title page and the others contributing their respective chapters.

We were amazed at the interest shown in our activities, not only in the press (including comic books and comic strips) but among mycologists, one of whom flattered us by making a week's whirlwind trip down to Mexico, where he had never been, interviewing our very informants, hanging anxiously on the appearance of Roger Heim's publications, and then rushing hastily into print to gain a spurious priority.

In 1958 we taped a complete velada, a dramatic one, of María Sabina, and a team of us worked on the tapes until 1974, when we finally brought out our *María Sabina and her Mazatec Mushroom Velada*. The Cowans, George and Florence, reduced the tapes to a text written in Mazatec in characters that a linguist understands; they translated the text into Spanish and English, publishing the three in parallel columns; George added a chapter on the Mazatec language; the musical notation of the whole velada was prepared under the supervision of Willard Rhodes, the renowned ethnomusicologist, and he added a chapter on the music; we all contributed to the footnotes, and I also wrote the Prologue and an Analytical Index; the whole illustrated with maps and with the photographs of the same velada taken by Allan Richardson; Harcourt Brace Jovanovich showing their breadth of vision and enterprise by bringing it out along with the music on cassettes and discs, the printing being done by the unrivaled Mardersteigs of Verona.

I felt that we had achieved at last the goal we set for ourselves in 1955, to treat María Sabina's velada worthily—except for one major matter. We and María Sabina felt good will in plenty for each other, but for us she was locked behind an impenetrable, an insuperable linguistic barrier. Her *persona* remained beyond our reach. I was perforce resigned to this gap in our presentation to the world of our superb exponent of the Old Religion, there being no way known to me to overcome it.

Imagine then my surprise and joy on meeting in Mexico in 1975 Alvaro Estrada, Mazatec Indian, born to the Mazatec language, and learning from him that he had already embarked on taking down from María Sabina's lips her own account of her life! Here in Sr. Estrada's book this "Wise Woman" in her eighties, unlettered,* tells us how life has been for her, of her ancestry and hard childhood, of her two husbands who came and went, how she got to know the mushrooms and how they revealed themselves to her in an event as dramatic as Saul's on the road to Damascus; how we (the Wassons) came into her life, and all that followed, until today when at last her pilgrimage in this world approaches its end. The narrative that María Sabina has given to Sr. Estrada and that he has translated for all of us is, so far as I can judge (and this is considerable), accurate, accurate in the sense that any unlettered person's memory can be considered accurate. María Sabina belongs to prehistory, to proto-history, where there are almost no documentary sources for checking her unaided memory. What she says (insofar as I am in a position to judge) is accurate in the main, but everything is a bit frayed around the edges—that is, slightly inaccurate. Considering her advanced age and that she is unlettered, I find this a noteworthy achievement indeed. What is more, there emerges from these pages something precious for all of us, the portrait of a person who has had a genuine religious calling and who has pursued that calling to the end of her days. Who knows? Perhaps María Sabina bids fair to become the most famous Mexican of her time. Long after the personages of contemporary Mexico sink back into the forgotten slough of the dead past, her name and what she stood for may remain etched in men's minds. She richly deserves it. She is probably not unique except that she, alone among the shamans of first rank in Mexico, has allowed herself to become known beyond the confines of her personal following in the Mazatec land. I wish that the eminent painters and sculptors of Mexico would seek her out and give us her portrait, and that composers would take note of her traditional chants. The drama of her

---

*The reader should note that María Sabina is *unlettered*, not *illiterate*. The poets who composed the Iliad and Odyssey, the Vedic Hymns, the Song of Deborah, were all unlettered. The whole world was unlettered then, and immense areas still are. María Sabina was never exposed to the written word in the society where she grew up. The pejorative illiterate applies to those who, in a world where writing reaches everywhere, have not had the wit to learn to read and write.

sojourn in this world needed to be set down in the printed word. This last, at least, is what our friend Sr. Estrada has here done admirably.

In the story of her life María Sabina has not a word to say about the source of her verses, her chants. For us of the modern world such questions are compelling. For her they do not exist. When anyone asks her about this, her reply is simple: the little things (the sacred mushrooms) tell her what to say, how to sing.

María Sabina's grandfather and her great grandfather were notable shamans, as also were her great aunt and great uncle. Recently, on reviewing my collection of slides taken during the many veladas that I have attended, I was struck by the omnipresence of children of all ages, as they cling to her with awe and adoration. They go to sleep, they sleep, with her chants ringing in their ears. María Apolonia sings her part in the 1958 velada with an infant in her rebozo, held tight against her mother's body: the baby from the start *feels* her mother sing as well as hears her. There is no mistaking where the Wise Woman learned her chants, without effort. Her melodies, her verses are the warp, the woof of her being, from infancy.

In 1955, after I had attended two veladas (my first two) with María Sabina, my programme called for me to go down to the Sierra Costera, to San Agustín Loxicha, south of Miahuatlan, in the company of the anthropologist Roberto Weitlaner. There we passed some days with Aristeo Matías, Wise Man of the first rank, and on Thursday 21 July we attended a velada that he conducted. He sang feebly but I thought it unmistakable: the chants were the same as María Sabina's. His chants were in Zapotec, linguistically unrelated to Mazatec, as far removed as two languages can be, but both cultures are in the Mesoamerican area. In my diary I wrote down what I thought was the musical resemblance and made public this impression of mine in *Mushrooms, Russia, & History.*

But this is not all. In 1967 Lic. Alfredo López Austin, distinguished Nahuatlato, in *Historia Mexicana* (July-September vol. 42, No. 1) published his *Términos del nahuallatolli*, in which he presented to his readers a list of the terms assembled by Hernando Ruiz de Alarcón in 1629 in his *Tratado de las supersticiones de los naturales de esta Nueva España*. What was my surprise to discover in this *Tratado*, dealing with the Nahuatl culture, remarkable correspondences with María Sabina's veladas, as shown in the velada text that I brought out in 1974. Here are some of the parallels:

1. Both María Sabina and the Nahuatl Wise One engage in an elaborate self-presentation (to use the word of López Austin), beginning in María Sabina's case with professions of humility and working up to assertions of power and even ability to talk with the supernatural beings almost on terms of equality.

2. Ruiz de Alarcón points out how the Nahuatl Wise One stresses the

amoxtli, "book," as the means of arriving at the secret knowledge that he uses. María Sabina uses the Spanish word "libro," there being today in Mazatec no word for book. It figures large in her mystical world. The *amoxtli* of Ruiz de Alarcón are the hand painted *Códices* of the Nahua, which everyone viewed with immense reverence at the moment of the Conquest. As Henry Munn has pointed out, the Bible and other liturgical books in the Huautla parish church have replaced the *Códices* of former times as the focus of adoration, but there has also evolved in the mind of María Sabina a mystical "book" that belongs specifically to her and that may come down to her from the *amoxtli* of pre-Conquest times.

3. María Sabina refers admiringly twice to a Young Man, a Youth, vigorous, athletic, virile, a kind of Mesoamerican Apollo, but whom she calls Jesus Christ. (An astonishing confluence of ideas!) Her Nahuatl confrère more than three centuries earlier introduced a similar divinity into his singing, but we learn that this divinity was Piltzintecuhtli, the Noble Infant, who as Dr. Alfonso Caso tells us in his essay, *Representaciones de Hongos en los Códices, Estudios de Nahuatl*, vol. 4, is receiving from the hands of Quetzalcóatl the gift of the Divine Mushrooms in the *Códice Vindobonensis*, a *Códice* especially important for us because it gives us the mythical origin of the miraculous mushrooms. In María Sabina's consciousness, and probably in the consciousness of other Wise Ones flourishing today, there is a complete synthesis of the Christian and pre-Conquest religions.

If we discover in María Sabina's words features that Ruiz de Alarcón picked out in the Nahuatl texts of his time, more than three centuries ago, features that already must have been translinguistic in Mesoamerica then, the chants that our tapes offer to us in Mazatec and that we also heard* in the Zapotec of San Agustín Loxicha must have been traditional at that time and were a legacy from long, long before the Conquest. How long before? For this calculation we possess three *points de repère* from which to triangulate back into the distant past, two of our tripodal bases being contemporary with us but distant in space from each other—San Agustín Loxicha and Huautla—and the third being distant from the other two both in space and time—the Nahuatl culture in the early seventeenth century. We must bear in mind how slowly, at a snail's pace, human cultures evolved in proto- and prehistory, before the art of writing was perfected. We must remember how ancient must have been the cult of the divinatory mushrooms in Mesoamerica: the Indians' skill as herbalists was no novelty when Cortés burst in on them. They knew the empirical properties of all plants accessible to them with an accuracy that puts us to shame. Early man depended for his very life on this knowledge. As for

---

*I am convinced that the chants were musically identical, but as I did not tape them and therefore cannot prove it, I point out that this taping remains to be done.

Siberia, where mushroom veladas among the most remote tribes survived down into our own days, there are two striking resemblances in specific features between the respective mushroom cults: (1) in both, the mushroom "speaks" through the mouth of the Sabio ["Wise One"], he only serving as the vehicle for the mushroom's voice, and (2) the mushrooms are visualized as little beings, male or female or both, the size of mushrooms, "elves", duendes, "clowns" up to all manner of endearing and mischievous tricks—in the vocabulary of the anthropologists, "tricksters." Sure the Mesoamerican cult goes back in direct genetic lineage to Siberia, back to the migration across the Bering Strait or the landbridge of the last Ice Age.

María Sabina has always been in good standing with the church. Though she herself does not know her age, thanks to the diligence of Sr. Estrada, we learn from the parish records of the church in Huautla that she was born on 17 March 1894 and duly baptized as María Sabina eight days later.* It seems that as far back as memory now reaches there has been no conflict between the Church and the customary practices of the native healers. Father Alfonso Aragón, whose incumbency in the parish lasted for almost twenty years up to 1960 and who gave to the Church in Huautla a vigorous impetus, maintained throughout a certain contact with the Wise Ones in his parish. Father Antonio Reyes Hernández in 1970, speaking of his Huautla parish, in an interview with Sr. Estrada [see chap. 15, note 2, on page 76], said:

> The Wise Ones and Curers don't compete with our religion; not even the Sorcerers do. All of them are very religious and come to mass. They don't proselytize; therefore they aren't considered heretics and it's not likely that anathemas will be hurled at them.

How far we have progressed from the days of Motolinía and the Holy Office of the Inquisition of the early seventeenth century!

There are rare insights in this little book that Alvaro Estrada has given us. Take for example chapter 15. It relates in detail how María Sabina and one Apolonia Terán, some thirty years ago, were concerned with organizing the Sisterhood of the Sacred Heart of Jesus, on the one hand, and the first Association of Stewards on the other. They were both Wise Ones; each knew about the other's vocation. But she makes a point of the fact that when working together they were silent about their "wisdom," even as between themselves. They spoke only on matters of the Sisterhood and of the Stewards. "The wise shouldn't go around advertising what they are, because it is a delicate matter." Here then we find in her own words the

---

*Her mother always called her "Bi" and her first husband "Sabi," thus confirming the name given in the parish register and demolishing the legend that assumed "Sabina" when she became a "Sabia" [Wise Woman].

difficulty that I had to overcome more than twenty years ago when I, a blond foreigner, a stranger had to break into that secret circle. Though she says that she obeys the Church and obeys the municipal authorities, and though she says that when she responded favorably to my request she was simply complying with the request of the *sindico municipal*, Cayetano García, I remain in doubt. She adds that she would even have granted me a velada without the endorsement of the Authorities. I would never have met her but for Cayetano; and if by rare chance I had met her, would she really have performed for me a velada? This is surely open to question.

"It's true," she says, "that before Wasson nobody spoke so open about the *children*. No Mazatec revealed what he knew about this matter . . . The *children* are the blood of Christ. When we Mazatecs speak of the vigils we do it in a low voice, and in order not to pronounce the name that they have in Mazatec (/nti¹xi³tjo³)* we call them *little things* or *little saints*. That is what our ancestors called them" (chap. 15).

The account of her life that María Sabina has given us, Sr. Estrada serving as midwife, is extraordinary. In 1971 Irmgard Weitlaner Johnson and I visited Huautla once more. We had heard what had happened there since my last visit in 1962 and we were fearful that the hurly-burly of the great world would have changed María Sabina radically. We were both dumbfounded to see that, contrary to our expectations, María Sabina was unchanged. This is amply confirmed in the little book that we are now introducing to the public. She shows no vainglory. The Governor of Oaxaca has given her two mattresses for the first bed that she has ever owned. She has visited the Principal Ones in the city of Oaxaca and in Mexico, and in turn the great of the world have waited on her in her humble hut high in the pass going from Huatla to San Miguel. A bishop has called on her; there is not the slightest reason to doubt this. He wished to take the mushrooms, but it was not the mushroom season. He asked her to teach the younger generation of her own offspring her wisdom, and her reply, unlettered as she is, was memorable:

> I told him that the color of the skin or the eyes can be inherited, including the manner of crying or of smiling, but the same can't be done with wisdom. Wisdom can't be inherited. Wisdom one brings with one from birth. My wisdom can't be taught; that's why I say that nobody taught me my Language, because it is the Language the *saint children* speak upon entering my body. Whoever isn't born to be wise can't attain the Language although they do many vigils.

Not once does María Sabina reproach me for having made known to the

---

*This name in Mazatec is obviously in its turn a euphemism for a still earlier word now lost. It simply means "the dear little ones that leap forth."

world both the mushrooms and her gift as their ministrant. But not
without anguish do I read her words:

> Before Wasson, I felt that the *saint children* elevated me. I don't feel
> like that anymore. The force has diminished. If Cayetano hadn't
> brought the foreigners...the saint children would have kept their
> power...From the moment the foreigners arrived, the *saint children*
> lost their purity. They lost their force; the foreigners spoiled them.
> From now on they won't be any good. There's no remedy for it.

These words make me wince: I, Gordon Wasson, am held responsible for
the end of a religious practice in Mesoamerica that goes back far, for a
millenia. I fear she spoke the truth, exemplifying her wisdom. A practice
carried on in secret for centuries has now been aerated and aeration spells
the end.

At the time of my first velada with María Sabina, in 1955, I had to make
a choice: suppress my experience or resolve to present it worthily to the
world. There was never a doubt in my mind. The sacred mushrooms and
the religious feeling concentrated in them through the Sierras of Southern
Mexico had to be made known to the world, and worthily so, at whatever
cost to me personally. If I did not do this, "consulting the mushroom"
would go on for a few years longer, but its extinction was and is inevitable.
The world would know vaguely that such a thing had existed but not the
importance of its role. On the other hand, worthily presented, its prestige,
María Sabina's prestige, would endure. Alvaro Estrada has contributed
the final chapter to this massive effort that I have made and I am grateful to
him, and to María Sabina also, for her cooperation.

R. Gordon Wasson

Danbury, Connecticut
1 December 1976

"The survey of the mystical use of the most important drugs in the medical stock of the colonial curer is an exciting task that, sooner or later, will without doubt be realized..."

—Gonzalo Aguirre Beltrán
Medicine and Magic

INTRODUCTION

It was not only the gold and natural riches of Anahuac, the culture and art of Mesoamerica that astonished the Spanish priests and conquistadors who arrived in this land in the sixteenth century: the native medicines (comprising a "marvellous collection" of hallucinogenic plants) were also the objects of attention, study, and condemnation on the part of European writers, botanists, and doctors during the colonial epoch in Mexico.

First the repressions exercised by the Tribunal of the Holy Office against those who resorted to the ingestion of *ololiuhqui, peyotl,* or *teonanácatl* ("seeds, cactus, or mushrooms," all of them hallucinogenic), then centuries of condemnations from the pulpit, forced native doctors to shift the rites and worship of the magical plants onto a private, even secret, plane.

In our day, these "demoniacal" practices of the Indians have been disappearing with the advance of Western culture in Mexico. The same phenomenon has extinguished similar customs among other Asiatic and American peoples. Yet in Huautla—a town situated in the Sierra Mazatec of the Mexican state of Oaxaca—investigators have found a mine for the study of this type of native practice. There the mushroom—to which the investigators have added the adjective "hallucinogenic"—is central to the indigenous religion in which it is said that the ancient *teonanácatl*—"Flesh of the Gods" in the pre-hispanic epoch—not only has the power to cure all sicknesses but gives the mystical force that creates the elevated, esoteric language of the shaman.

During trance, the *Wise One* (the name the Mazatecs give to the sha-man) speaks, invoking tribal deities as well as Christian ones (testimony to the inescapable syncretism of our time).

Did anyone write about the hallucinogenic plants and their use before their recent rediscovery? The ethnomycologist R. Gordon Wasson writes: "The references that we find in Mexico to the specific use of *teonanácatl* by the Mexican Indians are valuable but incomplete. Sahagún, Motolinía, Diego Durán, Father de la Serna, the learned Ruiz de Alarcón, Tezozomoc and don Francisco Hernández, the botanist and doctor of Philip II, all wrote about the subject. Without doubt the informants of the chroniclers didn't tell all they knew about the various hallucinogenic plants they were aware of and used, because they were impeded by the principle of not revealing religious secrets to anyone from outside the community. Now it is known that the ingestion of such plants in the past was always connected with religion. Every religion has secrets; even the Christian religion speaks of *mysteries* (personal communication).

In his book, *Medicine and Magic*, Dr. Gonzalo Aguirre Beltrán writes: "The distorted vision displayed by such famous writers as Hernando Ruiz de Alarcón, Jacinto de la Serna, and Pedro Ponce, when they touch this fundamental aspect of native medicine, is easy to explain in individuals whose religious principles prevent them from seeing anything but the work of the devil—the helpless and maligned devil—in Indian mysticism."

In brief, we find that the natives neither revealed all that they knew nor were the chroniclers able to divest themselves of their prejudices suffi-ciently to leave an impartial, objective testimony to the cult with which the ancient Mexicans surrounded the Flesh of the Gods.

The motives which prompted my decision to write *The Life of María Sabina* were: (1) the intention of leaving a testimony to the thought and life of the Mazatec *Wise Woman* whom journalists and writers from various countries have not known how to appreciate fully; (2) the hope that it may be a useful document for ethnologists, ethnomycologists, students of folklore, and other specialists; and (3) to give the general public a better idea of the native customs, and to encourage young people in particular to treat the elements of the native religion with more respect. It is my hope, too, that this work may stimulate young writers—above all Indians—to study such native customs in order to rescue them from their approaching definitive extinction.

The present manuscript is the result of a series of interviews that I conducted sporadically from September 1975 to August 1976. During this time my professional duties as an engineer, which make it necessary for me to live in Mexico City, alternated with visits to Huautla to converse with María Sabina. Mine has not been an easy task even though I am a native of Huautla and speak Mazatec.

To make it easier for the reader, I have omitted the questions that I asked María Sabina, although I have kept the tapes on which the Mazatec *Wise Woman's* words were recorded.

In the final writing of the text, as throughout this project, I have been conscious of the responsibility incurred in writing down the autobiography of a person who, because she can neither read nor write and does not even speak Spanish, could never herself know with exactitude whether what has been written about her is correct or not.

I cannot pass over the assistance that was given me in one form or another by family and friends. Nor should I forget to mention the disinterested aid of Robert Gordon Wasson and Henry Munn, persons who have dedicated a part of their lives to obtaining, by means of assiduous research, a greater understanding of that *homo religiosus* who in the past used the divine mushroom.

To all of them, my infinite gratitude.

Alvaro Estrada

Mexico, D.F.
September 4, 1976

THE LIFE

THE LIFE

1

I don't know in what year I was born, but my mother, María Concepción, told me that it was in the morning of the day they celebrate the Virgin Magdalene, there in Rio Santiago, an *agencia* of the municipality of Huautla. None of my ancestors knew their age.

My mother was born and raised in a place near Huautla on the way to San Andres Hidalgo. My father, Crisanto Feliciano, was born and raised in Rio Santiago. When they started to live together—they didn't get married—she was around fourteen and he twenty. My mother had lived three years with her man when I was born. I was baptised right away. My baptismal godfathers were Juan Manuel and María Sebastiana, a campesino couple who felt a lot of affection for my father. My mother gave birth to María Ana, my sister, when I was two years old. We were the only two children born to them. I didn't know my father very well, since he died when I was three years old. I know that he was a very hard worker. He planted maize and beans on land he had succeeded in buying with his work. He sold what he harvested at the market in Huautla or in neighboring towns. Our home in Rio Santiago was a little hut with walls of mud plastered over a bamboo framework, and a thatched roof of sugarcane leaves. My mother made the tortillas and put the pot of beans, which she later served to each of us, on the fire. With our meals, we drank *pinole* water sweetened with cane sugar. It was drunk hot. At that time there was no coffee; few people grew it. We went to bed before it got dark. My father left to work the land very early, a little after the first rooster crowed. We slept on the ground, on mats, with our clothes on. That's how we all slept.

At the birth of my sister, María Ana, my father was already sick. There was no remedy for his sickness because the origin of his illness wasn't a matter of this world, but a punishment of the powerful Lord of Thunder who takes care of and gives fertility to what is sown. The thing is that my father, when he was still a bachelor, had aroused the anger of this great and powerful Lord. The story is as follows:

One dawn the young Crisanto Feliciano started for his field to clear it; it was necessary to get rid of the leaves and bushes on the land. He took his hoe and his machete. Like all the men of his time, he wore white pants and shirt of pure cotton. On festival days, a poncho was worn that reached the knees and that was tied with a silk belt at the waist.

For two days Crisanto Feliciano worked on his land to gather together the leaves and weeds and all the garbage that impeded a good planting; then he formed a pile with it all in a place near someone else's field. Finally he set the pile on fire. The sticks, the dry leaves, and the weeds burned easily. It was late afternoon and the end of the day was near. The wind blew strong, the day had been very hot, and one could feel the dryness. But the flames of the pile got lively, and the wind played with them until they got near the neighboring field; so much so that they burned some corn plants. Seeing that, Crisanto rushed to put out the flames burning in the other's cornfield. Not much was burned, but Crisanto knew that damaging the field, even though the damage was slight, could cause his death. A crop protected by the Lord of Thunder grows pretty and abundant. Crisanto was condemned to death: he had burned a sacred cornfield. Only some plants, but it was enough to receive the curse of the Lord of Thunder. People who deliberately or imprudently harm a sacred crop suffer from lumps that come out on the chest and neck. The lumps burst when they've matured and turn into pustulous and repugnant pimples. Then the people die. The damage that is done to a sacred crop can't be paid for with anything: neither by replacing the destroyed plants, nor by paying the damage in money to the owner.

Crisanto knew that he was lost but he had one hope. His grandfather and his father were Wise Men: they used *saint children* to speak with the Lords of the Mountains. The Wise Ones can speak with the beings who are the masters of all the things in the world. And they could speak with the Lord of Thunder. They could ask him to pardon Crisanto who from imprudence had burned the plants of a protected cornfield.

So thought Crisanto and that gave him hope for his life. Meanwhile he didn't want to alarm his family. He preferred for the moment to keep quiet about his pain. "Later I'll tell them . . ." he said to himself.

Months passed and young Crisanto went on hiding his pain.

But on a certain occasion, his father, Pedro Feliciano, stayed awake to eat the *saint children*. There, during the night, the Wise One saw that his son would soon die from the pimples. The following morning, he said: "Crisanto, my son, I've had a terrible vision. I've seen you turned into a turkey. The *Little-One-Who-Springs-Forth* has revealed to me that you are condemned to die. I know the reason as well, the *Little-One-Who Springs-Forth* himself has told me . . ."

In that way, Crisanto found himself obliged to tell his father about the burned cornfield.

His father consoled him, saying: "We will fight against the force of the Lord of Thunder. We will stay awake with *Little-One-Who-Springs-Forth*. We will ask the Lords that you be pardoned." Later the Wise Man, Pedro Feliciano, accompanied by his father, Juan Feliciano, stayed awake several times with the *saint children*, but they didn't obtain anything. They also called in Sorcerers and Sucking Doctors without achieving anything.   6

Later, one night, as Crisanto tried to sleep, he passed a hand over his chest, and his fingers stopped at the feel of little bumps above his nipples. "What can that be?" he asked himself. With a shock, he realized everything: they were the lumps from the curse that were beginning to break out. He felt fear and deep worry. That night he thought about his life. He thought that he was very young (he would have been around twenty years old), and worry didn't let him sleep for the rest of the night.

The following morning, Crisanto said decisively to his father: I desire a woman for myself. I've seen a girl on the way to Huautla. She lives with her parents just beyond San Andres. You could ask for her to come and live with me."

With time the parents asked for the girl, and one day Crisanto went for his woman, María Concepción. He took her to live in Rio Santiago.

My father suffered from his illness and my mother understood him. The first lumps burst, forming purulous pimples that later covered his neck and part of his chest.

With the passing years, my father got worse. When I was around three years old, I imagine, and my sister, María Ana, barely four or five months old, he died. Neither the Sorcerers nor the Curers nor the Wise Ones could heal him. Poor man, he died, turned into a turkey. Because the mortal curse of the Lord of Thunder makes one sick little by little. The cursed person lasts years suffering: it can be four, five, six or seven, in which time the lumps turn into purulous pimples. Some

persons condemned to suffer like that resign themselves to die, others
fight against the curse of the Lord of Thunder. The Sorcerers speak to
where the echo is, to the mountains and the slopes. There they ask for
help from the Lord of the Holy Mountain. But little can be done
against the curse of the Lord of Thunder. The neck of the sick person
looks like that of a turkey. Exactly like that of a turkey. And that is
because the Lord of Thunder has at his service a sacred turkey. This
turkey is the one who is charged with punishing the persons and
animals who dare to damage the crops. The turkey turns the people or
animals into turkeys. That's why they die with pimples on their neck.
The Sorcerers sacrifice chickens, they give cacao beans and turkey
eggs to Chicon Nindó.

2

My mother, upon being left a widow, seeing that there was nothing to hope for from her in-laws, decided to return to her parents. She had lived with Crisanto Feliciano for six years. At that time she was still young, somewhere around twenty. My father must have died at twenty-five or twenty-six; I don't know the exact age at which he died.

My maternal grandparents were very poor. My mother brought us to live with them and forgot Rio Santiago completely.

My grandfather, Manuel Cosme, already quite an old man, worked as a peon for the landholders. My grandmother, María Estefanía, did the tasks of the house and took care of the land around the little hut, where corn and beans were planted. Gourds and chayotes grew there as well. The place where we came to live—and where I'm still living— is called Fortress Mountain, above the Mixtec section of town, very near Nindó Tocosho. My grandparents had abandoned the hut along the path to San Andres to which, one day, Crisanto Feliciano went for his wife. Now they lived on this high place from where one could see, down there below, the little town of Huautla. There were only a few houses of thatch and shingle at that time. Trees and bushes covered everything, but the church was already built.

My grandparents told me that in their youth they had worked as servants for the priest, Catarino García. This priest lived many years in Huautla. He had children by several Indian women. At his death he asked—and it was granted—to be buried underneath the altar of the Huautla church.

Life with my grandparents was difficult. By custom we got up at dawn, when by the light of a burning *ocote* torch, grandmother, my mother, and my aunt Juanita worked wool, silk, or cotton. The grandparents raised silkworms inside the hut; the worms took almost a year to raise. First the little butterflies laid their eggs on mats, they laid them in the month of March. At five months, the little worms came out of their little eggs and we gave them food, *mora* leaves that they ate noisily. We picked out the little worms and separated them from the bigger ones so that those didn't do them harm. The worms grew to the size of a finger. Three months after having opened their eggs, they began to drool [to leave secretions—TN], sticks were fixed up for them against the wall of the house, and on that bed of sticks they deposited the silk. It wasn't easy to raise silkworms. They required a lot of care. During the day or during the night, the silk was cleaned, the leavings of the worms were gotten rid of. They had to be fed well; if not, the worms didn't give enough or good enough silk.

Finally the silk was cleaned and gathered together. It was used to make belts that the men used as part of their clothing. From the wool and cotton, fabrics were made with which we dressed. Our life was invariable. We would wake up when the light of day was still far off. When the first rooster of the morning crowed, we were already sipping our *pinole* water sweetened with cane sugar to alleviate our hunger and cold. From time to time we drank tea made from lemon or orange leaves and only rarely coffee. My mother made the tortillas and embroidered. My grandmother and aunt worked at the loom. Grandfather always hired himself out as a fieldworker, the same as an uncle of ours named Emilio Cristino.

As my sister and I grew up, our tasks in the house went on growing. We took care of the chickens in the woods or gathered sticks that were used to make the fire on which the food was cooked.

I must have been eleven and my sister nine when grandfather took us to plant corn. He made little planting stakes for us, and with those stakes we opened the hole in the ground in which we clumsily deposited the kernels of corn. The whole family went to the planting. Sitting on the ground, María Ana and I dug with difficulty. I think the kernels fell on the surface of the ground in disorder, we were so little. In contrast, the adults sowed in a perfect line, leaving the kernels at the right depth. When the harvest drew near and the corn was tall, taller than María Ana and me, it made us laugh with joy.

If it wasn't the time of working in the fields, we were sent to take care of the chickens in the woods or two or three goats which were finally sold. We took advantage of this time to play with our dolls that we made ourselves. One of my dolls I called Florencia José. She was a rag doll and I made her a silk *huipil*. In the house we couldn't play because my Aunt Juanita and my grandfather were too strict. They didn't like to see us playing; everything was work, work, work.

If it was a matter of planting beans, they called us. If it was a matter of planting corn, they took us there. The same at planting as at harvest.

On ordinary days, we ate beans, if there were any, or we made do with plain tortillas splashed with hot chile sauce, but on the Days of the Dead one could eat *quelite, yerba mora,* or *guasmole.* On festival days, grandfather bought beef or goat meat that grandmother prepared in a hot stew.

The little food that grandmother served us at dawn calmed the hunger that we had held in for a long time. I think our will to live was very great, greater than the will of many men. The will to live kept us fighting from day to day to finally get some morsel that would alleviate the hunger María Ana and I felt. Aunt Juanita hid the food, and even if my mother gave us something, hunger soon bothered us again. We made efforts to hold a single mouthful in our stomachs, every evening, every morning.

Several men knew that my mother had become a widow and arrived to ask for her. They proposed to her properly: as the custom is, they arrived at dawn with *aguardiente* and chickens as a gift that they gave to my grandfather, Manuel Cosme. My mother never accepted. "My only commitment from here on will be to raise my daughters" was her reply, despite having been married only six years.

She lived with me, single, for the rest of her life.

3

Once my uncle Emilio Cristino got so sick he couldn't get up. I was a little girl of five, six, or seven. I didn't know what his sickness was. Grandmother María Estefanía, worried, went in search of a Wise Man named Juan Manuel to cure uncle.

The Wise Man Juan Manuel, who was not a very old man, arrived at our hut after nightfall. He had a bundle wrapped up in banana leaves that he treated with exaggerated care. I went up close to see what he had in the bundle, but rapidly the Wise Man Juan Manuel took it in his hands and prevented me from getting any closer, directing an authoritarian look at me. "Nobody can look at what I have here. It isn't good: a curious look could decompose what I have here," he said. Curiosity made me stay awake. I saw how the Wise Man Juan Manuel unwrapped the banana leaves. From there he took out various big fresh mushrooms the size of a hand. I was accustomed to seeing those mushrooms in the woods when I took care of the chickens and the goats. There were many of that kind of mushroom; their brown color contrasted with the green of the pastures.

The Wise Man Juan Manuel had arrived to cure uncle Emilio Cristino; for the first time I was present at a vigil with the *saint children*. I understood that later. I saw how the Wise Man Juan Manuel talked, and talked. His language was very pretty. I liked it. At times the Wise Man sang, sang, and sang. I didn't understand the words exactly, but they pleased me. It was a different language from what we speak in the daytime. It was a language that without n y comprehending it attracted me. It was a language that spoke of stars, animals, and other things unknown to me.

A long time had gone by since it had gotten dark, and still I didn': feel sleepy. Seated very quietly on my mat, I followed the vigil attentively. One thing that I did understand, yes, was that the mush- rooms had made old Juan Manuel sing. After midnight, the Wise Man lit a candle and stuck it in the ground. I saw that he danced while he said that he "saw" animals, objects, and people. No, no, I couldn't comprehend it completely. The Wise Man spoke without rest. He burned incense and rubbed "San Pedro" on the forearms of the sick person. [2]

By dawn my sick uncle, who didn't appear so sick anymore, began to sit up slowly. The Wise Man Juan Manuel animated him with his strange language. Uncle got to his feet. He hadn't done that since some days before because of his illness.

Two weeks later Uncle Emilio Cristino had recovered his health completely.

Some days after the vigil in which the Wise Man Juan Manuel cured Uncle, María Ana and I were taking care of our chickens in the woods so that they wouldn't be the victims of hawks or foxes. We were seated under a tree when suddenly I saw near me, within reach of my hand, several mushrooms. They were the same mushrooms that the Wise Man Juan Manuel had eaten. I knew them well. My hands gently tore up one mushroom, then another. I looked at them up close. "If I eat you, you, and you," I said to them, "I know that you will make me sing beautifully." I remembered that my grandparents spoke of these mushrooms with great respect. That was why I knew that they weren't bad.

Without thinking much about it, I put the mushrooms in my mouth and chewed them up. Their taste wasn't pleasant; on the contrary, they were bitter, tasting of roots, of earth. I ate them all up. My sister María Ana, watching me, did the same.

After having eaten the mushrooms, we felt dizzy, as if we were drunk, and we began to cry; but this dizziness passed and then we became very content. Later we felt good. It was like a new hope in our life. That was how I felt.

In the days that followed, when we felt hungry, we ate the mush- rooms. And not only did we feel our stomachs full, but content in spirit as well. The mushrooms made us ask God not to make us suffer so much. We told him that we were always hungry, that we felt cold. We didn't have anything: only hunger, only cold. I didn't know in reality whether the mushrooms were good or bad. Nor did I even know whether they were food or poison. But I felt that they spoke to me. After eating them I heard voices. Voices that came from another world. It was like the voice of a father who gives advice. Tears rolled down our cheeks, abundantly, as if we were crying for the poverty in which we lived.

Another day we ate the mushrooms and I had a vision: a well-dressed man appeared, he was as big as a tree. I heard the mysterious voice that said: "This is your father Crisanto Feliciano. . . ." My father. It was years since he had died, now it gave me pleasure to know him. The immense man, my father, spoke. Pointing at me he said these words: "María Sabina, kneel down. Kneel and pray. . . ." I kneeled and prayed. I spoke to God who each time I felt to be more familiar. Closer to me. I felt as if everything that surrounded me was God. Now I felt that I spoke a lot and that my words were beautiful.

María Ana and I continued to eat the mushrooms. We ate lots, many times, I don't remember how many. Sometimes grandfather and at other times my mother came to the woods and gathered us up from the ground where we were sprawled or kneeling. "What have you done?" they asked. They picked us up bodily and carried us home. In their arms we continued laughing, singing, or crying. They never scolded us nor hit us for eating mushrooms. Because they knew that it isn't good to scold a person who has eaten the *little things* because it could cause contrary emotions and it's possible that one might feel one was going crazy.

The next rainy season, when the mushrooms had returned, we ate them again.

Sometime later I knew that the mushrooms were like God. That they gave wisdom, that they cured illnesses, and that our people, since a long time ago, had eaten them. That they had power, that they were the blood of Christ.

Years later, when I became a widow for the second time, I gave myself up for always to wisdom, in order to cure the sicknesses of people and to be myself always close to God. One should respect the little mushrooms. At bottom I feel they are my family. As if they were my parents, my blood. In truth I was born with my destiny. To be a Wise Woman. To be a daughter of the *saint children.*

And I never went to school where I could have learned to read, to write or speak Castilian. My parents spoke only Mazatec. I never learned another language. What's more, I didn't know what school was, nor did I know it even existed; and if there had been a school I wouldn't have gone, because there wasn't time. In those days, people worked a lot.

4

By the end of our childhood, the work load had increased for María Ana and me. We had learned to make tortillas, to cook the meals, to wash, and to sweep.

One dawn, some people arrived who spoke a long time with my mother and grandparents. The people went and my mother told me that they had come to ask for me. They wanted me to unite myself in marriage with a young man. The people came once or twice, but I didn't see any marriageable young man among them; nonetheless, I met the one who was to be my husband the day he came for me. There wasn't any wedding. My mother, without consulting me, ordered me to gather my clothes together, saying that from that moment on I didn't belong to them anymore. "Now you belong to this young man who will be your husband. Go with him. Attend him well. You're a little woman..." were her words. That is the custom.

I was fourteen. During the first days of my new life, I felt scared because I didn't know what was happening. Later I resigned myself. With the passage of time, I loved my husband very much. His name was Serapio Martínez. He was a young man of twenty. He liked to dress in clean clothes and didn't appear to be a wastrel. I found later that he was good-hearted. He didn't drink much *aguardiente*, almost none, and he didn't like to work in the fields. With pride I can say that he knew how to read and write. He dedicated himself to the commerce of the red and black thread that is used to embroider the huipils that

1   we women wear. He also sold casseroles, plates, and cups. He travelled to Cordoba, Vera Cruz, to Tehuacán and to Puebla to buy the
merchandise that he sold in Huautla or in the nearby towns. He
travelled on foot at the beginning and transported the merchandise on
his back. It took him eight days to go to Puebla and back. With time he
succeeded in buying some pack animals on whose backs he transported what he bought there.

When I told him that I was pregnant, he took it naturally. He didn't
show any feeling, neither joy nor sorrow; he barely stammered: "Then
prepare yourself to be a mother." Upon returning from his travels he
talked to me about the conditions of the road or spoke of the new
prices of the threads or casseroles.

One time he didn't speak as usual. Upon asking him why he was
silent, he answered: "I know that in Huautla they're getting people
together to fight with arms. Some call themselves Carrancistas and
others Zapatistas. They're going around with rifles and horses. Soon
they'll come for me. They'll give me my rifle; if they see that I'm good,
they'll give me a horse."

Serapio's words were fulfilled. The men of war took him away. I
didn't put up any resistance.

He went when Catarino, my first child, was hardly ten days old.
"Don't worry, Sabi," Serapio told me. "I'll find a way to send you
some money." I watched him until I lost sight of him along the path.
He went with some men who came for him. I cried a lot. But with the
passing of the days, I comforted myself with the idea that he would
soon return. I stayed with my mother in my little hut. My grandparents had already died; uncle Emilio and aunt Juanita had died as well.

The new soldiers were quartered in Huautla for several days. Afterwards they left. Serapio was named bugler at first. A year later he was a
2   major and worked under the orders of General Adolfo Pineda, who I
know, Alvaro, was your grandfather. During the time that Serapio was
at war, money reached me that he sent irregularly. A soldier went from
house to house, leaving verbal notes, letters, and money. Serapio
didn't write me because I didn't know how to read. He sent me a note
only once. I looked for a person who knew how to read to tell me what
was written in it. He sent to say that I shouldn't worry about him, that
he was well. But on other occasions, there was neither note nor
money, only the cruel news: "Serapio has died in combat." I cried. I
cried on the little body of my recently born son, Catarino.

In that time the town lived in fear. We who had relatives in the war
were in constant dread. A man arrived and said: "Sabi, don't afflict
yourself anymore. Serapio is alive." In a little while the version
changed: "Serapio is lost, nobody knows anything about him. We're
confident he will appear soon." Later a hope: "Serapio has appeared."

And then another disillusion: "No. He's dead." In the end I accustomed myself to this life of upsets, and there were moments when it didn't matter to me if Serapio was still alive or already dead. The rumors that arrived at my door only received a cold thank you.

But I felt my heart become big with joy when, after six months, Serapio appeared before me. At first sight I didn't recognize him. He had cartridge belts, a heavy rifle, and a military cap. He spoke very little to me about his life as a soldier, only that they had chosen him for a bugler and that when his superior died in combat, he had left the trumpet to take up the rifle of the dead soldier. What's more, they saw that he was agile. To test him they once made him run next to a horse, and they saw that he had a lot of stamina. The agile had more opportunity to go up in rank. The agile and the valiant. Bravery came first. And Serapio was brave, his youth helped him.

Serapio went back to the war again and I didn't worry so much. He returned eight months later, not to go again. By that time my son Catarino was beginning to walk.

It's true that Serapio drank little *aguardiente* and that he worked a lot, but he liked women. He brought several loose women to my house. There were three of us under the same roof when that happened. The loose women left my house fifteen or thirty days after they arrived. I wasn't jealous because I felt myself to be Serapio's true wife. With him I procreated three children: Catarino, Viviana, and Apolonia. Each one of my children was born at intervals of a year and a half.

My husband's liking for women made our relations not as good as I would have liked. I loved him and it hurt me to know that he was in love with a girl in the Hot Country. He became more and more [3] distant from me because he preferred the other.

Serapio caught the *sickness of the wind* in the Hot Country and died [4] after three days of agony. His pack animals and money stayed in the hands of the other woman.

Thus my marital life ended. I had a husband for six years, the same number of years that my father lived with my mother. The same as her, I became a widow at twenty.

5

I never ate the *saint children* while I lived with Serapio, since in accordance with our beliefs the woman who takes mushrooms should not have relations with men. Those who are going to stay up shouldn't have sexual relations for four days before and four days after the vigil. Those who want to can complete five and five. I didn't take the *saint children* because I was afraid that my man wouldn't understand it. The condition should be fulfilled faithfully.

During my first years of widowhood, I felt pains from my deliveries. My waist and hips hurt me. I sent for a woman to massage me who alleviated me only a little. I also gave myself steam baths without much result. I called in a Curer and a Sucking Doctor as well but they didn't alleviate me at all. Finally I decided to take the *saint children* again. I took them alone, without recourse to any Wise One.

Those *little things* worked in my body, but I remember that the words I spoke weren't particularly good. I took them only to press my waist with my hands gently once or twice. I massaged myself in all the parts of my body where it hurt. Days went by and I got better. And I had decided to take them because I was clean. I didn't have a husband. At bottom I knew that I was a doctor woman. I knew what my destiny was. I felt it deep within me. I felt that I had a great power, a power that awakened in me in the vigils.

But in the house there was hunger. So I began to work to support my mother and my three children. Arduous constant work didn't scare me. I knew how to furrow the earth and split kindling with an axe, I knew how to plant and pick ears of corn. I worked like a strong man; sometimes I travelled to Teotitlán, where I bought pots which I resold in the market of Huautla. The raising of silkworms and the difficult work of joining wool and cotton together diminished when the merchants of Huautla began to bring cloth from the city. Since then we know muslin and colored fabrics.

In those years of my widowhood, I planted corn and beans. I also harvested coffee. On the days when I worked in the fields, I dug trenches where I deposited my little children so that they wouldn't bother me. At other times, I sold bread and candles in the ranches and the neighboring towns roundabout like San Miguel, Tenango, or Rio Santiago.

6

Some years, I don't know how many, after I became a widow for the first time, my sister María Ana got sick. She felt pains in her stomach; they were sharp stabs that made her double up and groan from pain. Each time I saw her she was worse. If she felt more or less well, she began her housework; but, without her being able to control herself, there came a moment when she fainted in the path.

Her fainting spells occurred more frequently later.

With great fear for her health, I contracted Curers to heal her, but I could see with anxiety that her illness got worse. One morning she didn't get up from her bed; she trembled and groaned. I felt preoccupied as never before. I called various Curers but it was useless; they couldn't cure my sister.

That afternoon, seeing my sister stretched out, I imagined her dead. My only sister. No, that couldn't be. She couldn't die. I knew that the *saint children* had the power. I had eaten them as a little girl and remembered that they didn't do harm. I knew that our people ate them to heal their sicknesses. So I made a decision; that same night I would take the holy mushrooms. I did it. To her I gave three pairs. I ate many in order for them to give me immense power. I can't lie: I must have eaten thirty pairs of the "landslide" variety.

When the *children* were working inside my body, I prayed and asked God to help me cure María Ana. Little by little I felt that I could speak with more and more facility. I went close to the sick woman. The *saint children* guided my hands to press her hips. Softly I massaged her where she said it hurt. I spoke and sang. I felt that I sang beautifully. I said what those *children* obliged me to say.

I went on pressing my sister, her stomach and her hips. Finally a lot of blood came out. Water and blood as if she were giving birth. I didn't get frightened because I knew that the *Little One Who Springs Forth* was curing her through me. Those *saint children* gave me advice and I carried it out. I attended my sister until the bleeding stopped. Afterward she left off groaning and slept. My mother sat down next to her to attend to her.

I couldn't sleep. The *little saints* continued working in my body. I remember that I had a vision: some people appeared who inspired me with respect. I knew they were the Principal Ones of whom my ancestors spoke. They were seated behind a table on which there were many written papers. I knew that they were important papers. There were a number of Principal Ones, six or eight of them. Some looked at me, others read the papers on the table, others appeared to be searching for something among the same papers. I knew that they weren't of flesh and bone. I knew that they weren't beings of water or tortilla. I knew that it was a revelation that the *saint children* were giving me. Right away I heard a voice. A voice that was sweet but authoritarian at the same time. Like the voice of a father who loves his children but raises them strictly. A wise voice that said: "These are the Principal Ones." I understood that the mushrooms were speaking to me. I felt an infinite happiness. On the Principal Ones' table a book appeared, an open book that went on growing until it was the size of a person. In its pages there were letters. It was a white book, so white it was resplendent.

One of the Principal Ones spoke to me and said: "María Sabina, this is the Book of Wisdom. It is the Book of Language. Everything that is written in it is for you. The Book is yours, take it so that you can work." I exclaimed with emotion: "That is for me. I receive it."

The Principal Ones disappeared and left me alone in front of the immense Book. I knew that it was the Book of Wisdom.

The Book was before me, I could see it but not touch it. I tried to caress it but my hands didn't touch anything. I limited myself to contemplating it and, at that moment, I began to speak. Then I realized that I was reading the Sacred Book of Language. My Book. The Book of the Principal Ones.

I had attained perfection. I was no longer a simple apprentice. For that, as a prize, as a nomination, the Book had been granted me. When one takes the *saint children*, one can see the Principal Ones. Otherwise not. And it's because the mushrooms are saints; they give wisdom. Wisdom is Language. Language is in the Book. The Book is granted by the Principal Ones. The Principal Ones appear through the great power of the *children.*

I learned the wisdom of the Book. Afterward, in my later visions, the Book no longer appeared because I already had its contents in my memory.

The vigil in which I cured my sister María Ana I conducted as the ancient Mazatecs did. I used candles of pure wax; flowers, white lilies and gladiolas (all kinds of flowers can be used as long as they have scent and color); copal and San Pedro as well.

In a brazier I burned the copal and with the smoke incensed the *saint children* that I held in my hands. Before eating them, I spoke to them. I asked them for favor. That they bless us, that they teach us the way, the truth, the cure. That they give us the power to follow the tracks of evil in order to be done with it. I said to the mushrooms: "I will take your blood. I will take your heart. Because my conscience is pure, it is clean like yours. Give me truth. May Saint Peter and Saint Paul be with me." When I felt dizzy, I blew out the candles. The darkness serves as a background for what is seen.

In that same vigil, after the Book disappeared, I had another vision: I saw the Supreme Lord of the Mountains, Chicon Nindó. I saw a man on horseback come toward my hut. I knew — the voice told me — that that being was an important person. His mount was beautiful: a white horse, white as foam. A beautiful horse.

The personage reined up his mount at the door of my hut. I could see him through the walls. I was inside the house but my eyes had the power to see through any obstacle. The personage waited for me to go out.

With decision I went out to meet him. I stood next to him.

Yes, it was Chicon Nindó, he who lives on Nindó Tocosho, he who is the Lord of the Mountains. He who has the power to enchant spirits. He who himself cures the sick. To whom turkeys are sacrificed, to whom the Curers give cacao in order for him to cure.

I stood next to him and went closer. I saw that he didn't have a face though he wore a white sombrero. His face, yes, his face was like a shadow.

The night was black; the clouds covered the sky but Chicon Nindó was like a being covered by a halo. I became mute.

Chicon Nindó didn't say a word. All of a sudden he set his mount into motion to continue on his way. He disappeared along the path, in the direction of his dwelling place: the enormous Mountain of the Adoration, Nindó Tocosho. He lives there, while I live on Fortress Mountain, the closest one to Nindó Tocosho. That makes us neighbors. Chicon Nindó had come because in my wise Language I had called him.

I entered the house and had another vision: I saw that something fell from the sky with a great roar, like a lightning bolt. It was a luminous object that blinded. I saw that it fell through a hole in one of the walls. The fallen object turned into a kind of vegetal being, covered by a halo like Chicon Nind6. It was like a bush with flowers of many colors; in its head it had a great radiance. Its body was covered with leaves and stalks. There it stood, in the center of the hut. I looked straight at it. Its arms and legs were like branches and it was soaked with freshness and behind it appeared a red background. The vegetal being lost itself in this red background until it disappeared completely. When the vision vanished, I was sweating, sweating. My sweat wasn't warm but cool. I realized that I was crying and that my tears were crystals that tinkled when they fell on the ground. I went on crying but I whistled and clapped, sounded and danced. I danced because I knew that I was the great Clown woman and the Lord clown woman. At dawn I slept placidly. I slept, but it wasn't a deep sleep; rather I felt that I was rocking in a revery...as if my body were swaying in a gigantic hammock, suspended from the sky, which swung between the mountains.

I woke up when the world was already in sunlight. It was morning. I touched my body and the ground to make sure that I had returned to the world of humans. I was no longer near the Principal Ones. Seeing what surrounded me, I looked for my sister María Ana. She was asleep. I didn't want to wake her. I also saw that a part of the walls of the hut had fallen down, that another was about to fall. Now I believe that while the *saint children* worked in my body, I myself knocked over the wall with the weight of my body. I suppose that when I danced I hit against the wall and toppled it over. In the following days the people who passed asked what had happened to the house. I limited myself to telling them that the rains and winds of the last few days had weakened the mud-wattled walls and finally overthrown them.

And María Ana got better. She was healed once and for all. To this day she lives in good health with her husband and her children near Santa Cruz de Juarez.

From that cure on I had faith in the *saint children*. People realized how difficult it was to cure my sister. Many people learned of it and in a few days they came in search of me. They brought their sick. They came from places far away. I cured them with the Language of the *children*. The people came from Tenango, Rio Santiago, or San Juan Coatzospan. The sick arrived looking pale, but the mushrooms told me what the remedy was. They advised me what to do to cure them. People have continued to seek me. And since I received the Book I have become one of the Principal Ones. If they appear, I sit down with them and we drink beer or *aguardiente*. I have been among them since

3

the time when, gathered together behind a table with important papers, they gave me wisdom, the perfect word: the Language of God.

Language makes the dying return to life. The sick recover their health when they hear the words taught by the *saint children*. There is no mortal who can teach this Language.

After I had cured my sister María Ana, I understood that I had found my path. The people knew it and came to me to cure their sick. In search of a cure came those who had been enchanted by elves, those who had lost their spirit from fright in the woods, at the river, or along the path. For some there was no remedy and they died. I cure with Language, the Language of the *saint children*. When they advise me to sacrifice chickens, they are placed on the parts where it hurts. The rest is Language. But my path to wisdom was soon to be cut off.

7

Twelve years after I became a widow, a man named Marcial Carrera began to woo me. Really, I didn't have any need for a man because I knew how to support myself. I knew how to work; my family, at least, didn't suffer as much as I had. There was hunger, yes, but it wasn't as burning as what María Ana and I had experienced. My work helped each one have something to eat and something to wear.

Marcial Carrera insisted. In accordance with the custom, he brought his parents to speak with my mother. My mother persuaded me to accept that man. She said that a man in the house would help to make my work less heavy. The days passed and I thought about it because my suitor didn't appear to be a worker. What's more, he had the reputation of being irresponsible and a drunk.

But in the end I gave in. I stated my conditions: if Marcial wanted a woman, he would have to come to live in my house because I wasn't going to move my mother, my children, my mat, my pots, my hoes, and my machetes to his. It seemed to me that my house was better than poor Marcial's.

Marcial accepted my conditions and he came to live in my house. With time, I found that Marcial drank a lot of *aguardiente*. He was a Curer. He used turkey eggs and macaw feathers to do sorcery.[1]

He hit me frequently and made me cry. He didn't like to work in the fields and didn't even know how to use a hoe with dexterity.

As I saw that Marcial earned little money, that it wasn't enough to cover the small expenses of the house, I was forced to return to work. I went back to retailing bread and candles.

In the thirteen years that I lived with Marcial I had six children. They died, all of them; only my daughter Aurora survived. My children died from sickness or were murdered. While I lived with Marcial I never took the *saint children*. I feared that he wouldn't understand me and would spoil my Wise Woman's bodily cleanliness.

Marcial, the same as my first husband, Serapio, liked other women. The sons of a lady with whom he had relations beat him up and wounded him with a machete. Bleeding he died sprawled in the path.

8

The fact of having become a widow for the second time made it easier, in a way, for me to decide to give myself up to my destiny. The destiny that had been fixed for me from before I was born: to be a Wise Woman. My destiny was to cure. To cure with the Language of the *saint children.* I determined to do this even though I had to go on working hard to support my family — now not as much, though, because my son Catarino was already beginning to work. He dealt in thread that he resold in the Hot Country, following in the footsteps of his deceased father.

I'm not sure, but I believe I was then more than forty years old. I didn't feel in a condition to travel to sell bread and candles in the ranches. During the time that I lived with my husband Marcial, I saved up enough to build a house seven arm-lengths long, with wooden walls and a thatched roof of sugarcane leaves. The house was alongside the path to San Miguel. In it I set up a store in which I sold *aguardiente* and cigarettes. Afterward I sold meals there to travellers.

In the days after my second widowhood, I wanted to practice curing as Marcial had done. I felt that I should cure and that I should cure with the *saint children*, but something made me hold back. As if it was fear to give oneself up to what has been given one, to what has been destined.

I tried being a Curer, yes, but it didn't satisfy me.

My feelings were that I was doing what I shouldn't do. I thought that the clean woman, the woman of Christ, the Morning Star woman, shouldn't practice being a Curer. I was destined to something superior. In curing I buried eggs as an offering to the Lords of the Mountains. I buried them at the corners of the house or inside, but I saw that worms came out where I buried them, and that caused me disgust and horror. I thought that this was not my destined path. I remembered my ancestors. My great grandfather Juan Feliciano, my grandfather Pedro Feliciano, my great aunt María Ana Jesus, and my great uncle Antonio Justo had all been Wise Ones of great prestige.

9

***

For me sorcery and curing are inferior tasks. The Sorcerers and Curers have their Language as well, but it is different from mine. They ask favors from Chicon Nindó. I ask them from God the Christ, from Saint Peter, from Magdalene and Guadalupe.

It's that in me there is no sorcery, there is no anger, there are no lies. Because I don't have garbage, I don't have dust. The sickness comes out if the sick vomit. They vomit the sickness. They vomit because the mushrooms want them to. If the sick don't vomit, I vomit. I vomit for them and in that way the malady is expelled. The mushrooms have power because they are the flesh of God. And those that believe are healed. Those that do not believe are not healed.

The people who realized that I cured María Ana brought their sick children. One, two, ten, many. I have cured many children. Sometimes I give the children a little bit of *Little-One-Who-Springs-Forth.* I vomit for the children if they don't. Before beginning the vigil I ask the name of the sick person. In that way I search for the sickness and in that way I cure. If the sick person doesn't tell me the cause of his or her malady I divine it. When the sick person sweats, that reveals that he or she is going to be healed. Sweat gets rid of the fever that comes from the sickness. My words oblige the evil to leave.

For a strong toothache seven or eight pairs are eaten, that is enough. The *children* are taken at night; the vigil is celebrated in front of images of the saints of the Church. The *saint children* cure the sores, the wounds of the spirit. The spirit is what gets sick. The Curers don't know that the visions the *children* show reveal the origin of the malady. The Curers don't know how to use them. The Sorcerers don't either. The Sorcerers are afraid of Wise Ones like me because they know that I can discover if they have caused an enchantment, if they have surreptitiously robbed the spirit of a child, of a man, or of a woman. The mushrooms give me the power of universal contemplation. I can see from the origin. I can arrive where the world is born.

The sick person gets well and the relatives come to visit me afterward to tell me that there has been an alleviation. They thank me with *aguardiente*, cigarettes, or some coins. I am not a Curer because I do not use eggs to cure. I don't ask for powers from the Lords of the Mountains. I am not a Curer because I do not give potions of strange herbs to drink. I cure with Language. Nothing else. I am a Wise Woman. Nothing else.

Men come as well to ask me to help their women give birth. I am a midwife, but that is not my work. I am the one who speaks with God and with Benito Juárez. I am wise even from within the womb of my mother. I am the woman of the winds, of the water, of the paths, because I am known in heaven, because I am a doctor woman.

I take *Little-One-Who-Springs-Forth* and I see God. I see him sprout from the earth. He grows and grows, big as a tree, as a mountain. His face is placid, beautiful, serene as in the temples. At other times, God is not like a man: he is the Book. A Book that is born from the earth, a sacred Book whose birth makes the world shake. It is the Book of God that speaks to me in order for me to speak. It counsels me, it teaches me, it tells me what I have to say to men, to the sick, to life. The Book appears and I learn new words.

I am the daughter of God and elected to be wise. On the altar that I have in my house is the image of Our Lady of Guadalupe. I have her in a niche. And I also have Saint Mark, Saint Martin Horseman, and Saint Magdalene. They help me to cure and to speak. In the vigils I clap and whistle; at that time I am transformed into God.

10

One day a couple came to my house. I was inside near the hearth, heating my tortillas. A dog barked and I went out to see what it was. I invited the visitors to come in. I interrupted my meal and attended to them.

"We're family of old Francisco García," said the man.

"The Francisco who lives in Backbone-of-a-Dog?" I asked. "What brings you here?"

"Yes. There is something, that's why we've come to see you," said the woman. "Probably you know that my father Francisco is sick."

"What caused his illness?"

"We don't know," the man went on. "We can only say that he left for his field one morning, but he soon returned before it was completely daylight. His right shinbone was hurt. He said that he was hoeing when he felt a terrible pain in the shinbone that made him fall and lose consciousness. When he came to, he returned painfully to his house. He supposes that he hit himself with the hoe. To heal him we've contracted the young doctor who has just arrived in Huautla from the city. He is a Wise-One-In-Medicine who cures bloody wounds. He's been treating old Francisco for days, but Francisco doesn't appear to be getting better. We've decided that you would really know how to heal him; you would contribute a lot together with the medicine from the young doctor. The *little things* will give strength to old Francisco and he will get well quickly....You are a woman who knows, María Sabina."

"When do you want to do the vigil?" I asked.

"As soon as possible," the man ended by saying.

The couple went. I said that that same night I would go to old Francisco García.

At nightfall I arrived at their hut. They treated me with great respect. They took me to the bed of old Francisco who lay on a mat and groaned from pain. The old man saw me and made an effort to smile. He had circles under his eyes. I examined the supposed wound in the shinbone. It looked more like a bruise without serious complications.

I began the ceremony in front of the images of the saints that the family had. I gave old Francisco six pairs of mushrooms. I took thirteen *pairs.* Other people who were present also took their pairs. I let myself be carried away. I didn't offer any resistance and I fell into a deep, interminable well. I felt a kind of vertigo. Gradually the discomfort disappeared. I had a vision: I saw a tiger about to attack one of several cattle in a corral. It was night. The animal, crouched, chest to the ground, prepared to spring and pounce on its prey, when the strong blow of a stone in its right leg stopped it. The stone had been thrown by a man in a nearby tree. The tiger fled without having accomplished its purpose, wounded and frightened.

Next a woman appeared who covered her face with her forearm so that it wouldn't be seen that she was smiling. It was a smile of satisfaction. I recognized the woman. She was the wife of Faustino Mendez, a sorceress. The voice of the mushrooms said: "She bewitched old Francisco: she turned his spirit into a tiger. It is her."

Past midnight old Francisco started to sit up little by little. By himself, without help. Finally he got completely to his feet. Erect, he stood next to the altar where the images of the saints were. He made movements as if to relax. I asked, then, that they bring him clean clothes. What he had on was contaminated. He should change because the cure was approaching, and everything dirty should be shed.

I ordered old Francisco to sit down on the chair and I asked him:

"The day that you hurt yourself, where was it? What happened? Didn't you feel that your body didn't have a spirit? That your body was empty? What places do you go to in your dreams?"

"Yes, Señora," he answered, looking at the ground as if he felt ashamed. "For some time now, my dreams are regularly the same. No sooner do I go to sleep than I dream that I'm coming to a corral where I see bulls. I want to attack the animals to eat them."

"What places have you gone to?"

"I dream that I'm in Ojitlán. It's there I want to attack the cattle."

"Don't be ashamed," I told him. "There's definitely nothing wrong

³

with that. It's not a lie. When we sleep the spirit leaves the body and wanders. It goes where it wants to go. The spirit returns if we wake up. But some people are born with their 'fate.' Their spirit turns into an opposum, into a tiger, or a buzzard. Transformed into animals they travel to distant places. If you have a 'fate' don't worry. It is not a sin nor anything to be ashamed of. There are people who are born like that; others can get to have a 'fate' by the artifices of sorcery.''   4

"Yes," he continued, "I dream that I prowl around the cattle. I hear their bellows. It happens to me every night."

The *little things* ordered me to light a candle. I took a little San Pedro with my fingers and ordered old Francisco to chew it. He did. He swallowed the San Pedro. I asked the people around me to bring a basin. They brought it. Then I asked them to press old Francisco's stomach so that he would vomit. He vomited. San Pedro made him do it. The tobacco is called San Pedro because that Saint created it.

I ordered old Francisco to change his clothes when he finished vomiting.

At dawn the sick man spoke: "I thank you for your cure, María Sabina. I feel better. I'm hungry. Very..." They served him coffee, a little bit of roasted meat, beans, and chile sauce. He ate well and abundantly.

I spoke to him once more:

"The *saint children* have revealed that a sorceress has turned your spirit into a tiger. At night, while you sleep, your 'fate' goes to attack the bulls of Ojitlán. Don't be worried anymore. The mushrooms have already cured you. You've vomited."

Although I knew that the young Wise-One-In-Medicine continued to see the patient, I was sure that the mushrooms would remedy his malady. Within a month they let me know that old Francisco was completely recovered.

The wife of Faustino Mendez, the sorceress, began to go crazy the moment Francisco vomited. That way the "fate" came out and Francisco recaptured his spirit. The sorceress, crazed, would take off all her clothes and go out into the street naked. Her husband and her children left her from shame and fear. The family fell into misfortune. Finally the lady died of insanity. Her evil turned against her.

11

The following year a daughter of old Francisco came to see me. Once inside my house she said: "All my family send you greetings. The people who visit my father ask who cured him. He tells them he has a doctor, insignificant in appearance, named María Sabina."

"Is something the matter now?" I asked.

"Señora, you know how life is. Sicknesses come and go. A child gets sick just as well as an adult. It's always happening. I've come because my nephew, Rodrigo, is sick. The young Wise-One-In-Medicine from the city has been giving him medicine, but he isn't getting any better. We're agreed that you, Señora, should cure him once and for all.

"What's the matter with him?" I asked.

1   "The priest Alfonso asked for him to be an apostle last Holy Week. Ezequiel, his father, accepted, because it pleased him that his son Rodrigo should be an apostle. In Holy Week the people and the apostles went in procession, but Rodrigo tripped at the door of the church and fell. It's been two months already that the child can't get up. The Sorcerers have gone with cacao and eggs to pay the places where the child was accustomed to play. We believe that he was enchanted by the master of some sacred place and that now there's no cure."

"Don't worry, woman," I told her. "I'll go tomorrow."

The following night I presented myself at the house of Ezequiel, taking enough *saint children* for six people.

I probed the body of the child with my fingers in the light of a candle. He didn't have any wound, but in a little while I'd know the true sickness.

The people of the house accompanied me in taking *Little-One-Who-Springs-Forth*. . . and when it was working, I had a vision: I saw Rodrigo walking in the midst of a crowd. He had a robe on. A purple robe like the one the apostles wear. The child walked solemnly. But his spirit wasn't with him, it was somewhere else; that's what the voice told me, and in that way I learned that a spirit who carried a rifle fired a shot and accidently hit the spirit of Rodrigo. At that instant the child fell at the door of the church. His spirit was wounded, but his body wasn't.

When the vision had passed I lit a taper, lifted up the little shirt of the boy and saw in his chest, around the region of the heart, a hole the size of a fist. It was a wound without blood even though it was deep. When I looked at Rodrigo's face, he looked dead. So I asked for thirteen cacao beans, ground up and mixed with water.

I asked for thirteen cacao beans because my thought ordered me to. I asked as well for a recently born chick and a cloth to use as a bandage. I sacrificed the chick and bathed its still warm body in chocolate water and put it on Rodrigo's chest. On top of it I put the bandage, wrapping it around Rodrigo's body. The child didn't take *Little-One-Who-Springs-Forth*. By dawn the effect had worn off, and I took off the bandage together with the chick in the light of day. I didn't see the wound that I had seen in the sick one's chest while the *saint children* worked inside me.

The chick was buried near the house so that it wouldn't be eaten by birds of prey or by dogs. What is used in a vigil is sacred and shouldn't be spoiled by being eaten by an animal.

I slept in the house. When I awoke, they gave me food and I started to talk with the mother of the sick child. Someone came in and announced that the young Wise-One-In-Medicine, the same one who had tried to cure old Francisco, the grandfather of Rodrigo, was waiting outside to be received and to see his patient.

I saw the Wise-One-In-Medicine enter. I was seated on the ground with my legs drawn up underneath me, leaning against the wall. He was dressed in white, clean clothes. He said the Mazatec greeting to everyone: Ni³na'ti'?nta³li² ("in the name of God good day"). We responded in the same way.

We all kept silent while he went over the sick child with his metals. Nobody told him that that same night there had been a vigil in order for me to cure the child. He spoke in Castilian with Ezequiel, the father of Rodrigo. I didn't understand anything. He gave him some little boxes and a paper. [2]

The young Wise Man had a white face and blue eyes. He took leave of everyone: Xt?a³la²nca'," he said to each one. He had learned to shake hands like the Mazatecs: he just grazed his fingers against the other person's palm like we do.

At bottom I didn't know what to think about the efficaciousness of his medicines. What I was sure of, though, was that he, with all his wisdom, ignored the true cause of the child Rodrigo's sickness.

I took leave of the sick one's parents. I told them that their child was cured...that by the end of several days the child would be completely healthy. As payment they gave me a pack of cigarettes, a little *aguardiente*, and five pesos.

A Wise One like me should not charge for her services. She should not profit from her wisdom. The one who charges is a liar. The Wise One is born to cure, not to do business with her knowledge...One receives with humility the two or three pesos that are put in one's hand. Yes...one should not make money from the *little things*.

Time went by. One day I went down to the market in Huautla. I went by to say hello to Rodrigo's father. He greeted me, smiling. Very contented.

"How is the child?" I asked Ezequiel.

"He's all better. He's already playing with his little friends again. Thank you for curing him. Because you know, you can. Thank you. Take two pesos to buy bread."

"Don't say that, Ezequiel," I answered, "because the one who has healed your son is God who is raising all of us."

From then on, old Francisco and Ezequiel, his son, had a lot of faith in me, and whenever there was someone sick in their house they called me to cure them.

12

During my vigils I speak to the saints: to Lord Santiago, to Saint Joseph, and to Mary. I say the name of each one as they appear.

I know that God is formed by all the saints. Just as we, together, form humanity, God is formed by all the saints. That is why I don't have a preference for any saint. All the saints are equal, one has the same force as the other, none has more power than another.

I know of other Wise Ones who use the *saint children* as I do. I remember Toribio García, a man of this same section, who lived along the path down below. He searched for light in the *children*, but he also sought the answer in thirteen kernels of corn that he threw on the ground. The final position of each kernel has a meaning. Like that he divined what he desired. I don't practice that type of thing: I only trust in what the *children* tell me. For me that is sufficient; my only force is my Language. Toribio was another type of Wise One. He cast kernels of corn during the vigil. At dawn he repeated the throw of chance.

During the time that I was married I didn't utilize the services of Toribio. The children of my first marriage grew up healthy.

And if I get sick now, I cure myself. The *children* cure me. I've been able to live many years...many....I don't know how many.

In my vigils I can see how our little Christ is. I contemplate him. I can have him very close to me, but I can't touch him. There are times when I want to catch what I see with my hands, but there is nothing there and on occasions that makes me laugh. I enter another world

different from the one we know in the daylight. It is a beautiful world
but an unattainable one. It is like watching the movies. I know the
movies because one day a man came and took me to the center of
Huautla to see a film in which I appear. In the movies one can see from
a distance, but if one tries one can't touch anything that one is seeing.
As in the movies, one image comes after another. Then something else
comes out and afterward still something else. I feel the effect of the
little things like that.

In that way I see the saints. One appears and I pronounce his name;
if another appears, I pronounce his name. If Benito Juárez appears, I
pronounce his name. Sometimes the Principal Ones appear, then I see
myself drinking beer with them; at other times we drink *aguardiente*. I
see animals like gigantic serpents, but I don't fear them. I don't fear
them because they are also creatures of God. Strange animals appear
such as have never been seen in this world. Nothing that the mushrooms show should be feared.

And all my Language is in the Book that was given to me. I am she
who reads, the interpreter. That is my privilege. Although the Language is not the same for different cases. If I'm curing a sick person, I
use one type of Language. If the only aim in taking the *little things* is to
encounter God, then I use another Language. Now, sober, I can
remember something of my Language:

1   *I am a woman who was born alone, says*
        I am a woman who fell out by herself, says
2   *Because your Book exists, says*
        Your Book of Wisdom, says
        Your sacred Language, says
        Your communion wafer that is given me, says
        Your communion wafer that I share, says

        In what number do you rest, beloved Father?
        Father full of life
        Father full of freshness

        I am a woman of battles
        Because I am a woman general, says
        Because I am a woman corporal, says
        I am a sergeant woman, says
        I am a commander woman, says

You Jesus Christ
You Mary
You Holy Father
Woman saint
Woman saintess
Spirit woman
I am a woman who waits, says
I am a daylight woman
I am a Moon woman, says
I am a Morning Star woman
I am a God Star woman

I am the Constellation of the Sandal woman, says
I am the Staff Constellation woman, says
Here I bring my dew
My transparent dew, says
Because I am a fresh dew woman, says
I am a moist dew woman, says
I am the woman of the dawn, says
I am the woman of the day, says
I am the saint woman, says
I am the spirit woman, says
I am the woman who works, says
I am the woman beneath the dripping tree, says
I am the woman of the twilight, says
I am the woman of the prisitine huipil, says
I am the whirlpool woman, says
I am the woman who looks into the insides of things, says
Because I can speak with Benito Juárez
Because our beautiful Virgin accompanies me
Because we can go up to heaven
I am the woman who sees Benito Juárez
Because I am the lawyer woman
Because I am the pure woman
I am the woman of goodness
Because I can go in and out of the realm of death
Because I come searching beneath the water from the opposite shore
Because I am the woman who springs forth
I am the woman who can be torn up, says
I am the doctor woman, says
I am the herb woman, says
And our beautiful Virgin Guadalupe
And our Mother Magdalene

Because I am the daughter of God
I am the daughter of Christ
I am the daughter of Mary
I am the daughter of Saint Joseph and of the Candelaria

That is part of my Language. The ignorant could never sing like the wise. The *saint children* dictate to me, I am the interpreter. The Book appears and there I begin to read. I read without stammering. The Book doesn't always appear because I've memorized what is written in it.

For the sick there is one type of Language, for those who search for God there is another. For the sick, the Language appears when I am near them. I am always next to the sick one, attentive to whether the person vomits or to whatever happens. The sick get well quickly if they chew San Pedro. If the sick chew San Pedro, I say:

I am a Saint Peter woman, says
I am a Saint Paul woman, says
I am a woman who searches beneath the water, says
I am a woman who cleans with herbs, says
I am the woman who cleans, says
I am the woman who fixes things, says
I am the woman who swims, says
I am the sacred swimmer, says
I am the Lord swimmer, says
I am the greatest swimmer, says
I am the launch woman, says
I am the Morning Star woman, says

The *little things* are the ones who speak. If I say: "I am a woman who fell out by herself, I am a woman who was born alone," the *saint children* are the ones who speak. And they say that because they spring up by themselves. Nobody plants them. They spring up because God wants them to. For that reason I say: "I am the woman who can be torn up," because the children can be torn up and taken. They should be taken just as they are picked. They shouldn't be boiled or anything. It's not necessary to do anything more to them. As they are pulled up from the ground they should be eaten, dirt and all. They should be eaten completely, because if a piece is thrown away from carelessness, the children ask when they are working: "Where are my feet? Why didn't you eat me all up?" And they order: "Look for the rest of my body and take me." The words of the *children* should be obeyed. One has to look for the bits that weren't eaten before beginning the vigil and take them.

13

Marcial, my second husband, died, and I dedicated myself to work. I sold food in my house of seven arm-lengths situated at the side of the path. I went to San Miguel or to Tenango on market days and festival days to sell candles and bread. I lived tranquilly with my children. Although already married, my daughters Viviana and Apolonia visited me frequently.

One month after Marcial died, I began to take the *little things*. As I've already said, it isn't good to use the *children* when one has a husband. When one goes to bed with a man their cleanliness is spoiled. If a man takes them and two or three days afterwards he uses a woman, his testicles rot. If a woman does the same, she goes crazy. [1]

Problems have not been lacking. One day a drunk entered my little store. He came on horseback. He entered with his horse. Inside he dismounted and asked for a beer. I served him the beer. My son Catarino, already a man, was inside the house. The drunk saw him.

"Ah, are you here, Catarino?" he asked.

"Yes, Crescencio," said my son. "I brought some merchandise for my mother to sell in her little store. I've just come from the Hot Country, from the town of Rio Sapo. I brought two ninety-two pound sacks of dried fish and some beans."

"Would you like to have a drink?" asked the drunk.

"I accept," answered Catarino. "We know how to drink."

"Serve us, Señora," the drunk ordered me. "Serve Catarino a glass of *aguardiente*."

Before I could serve, Catarino spoke:

"No, Crescencio, I won't drink *aguardiente*. If there weren't any beers, I'd drink *aguardiente*, but there are beers. I won't drink the *aguardiente* you're inviting me to. Open two beers, mama," ordered my son.

At that moment the drunk pulled a pistol out of his belt. I was afraid for my son. The drunk spoke:

"Is it true what you're saying, Catarino?" he asked, pistol in hand.

With apparent rage, he went up to my son.

"God knows whether you're a bandit or not," he added.

"Don't blaspheme, Crescencio," said my son, keeping calm. "I'm a working man. I earn my living bringing merchandise from Puebla and Mexico. It seems to me you're the bandit."

They went on talking, challenging each other.

The drunk staggered, pistol in hand. Behind him I glimpsed a crucifix; at that I got brave and interposed myself between the drunk and my son who was on my left. I went up cautiously; the drunk continued cursing. In a careless moment on the man's part, I wrested the pistol from him.

"Why have you come to fight here?" I asked. "You shouldn't do it here, because God is present here in my house."

The drunk didn't say anything more. I put the pistol in a drawer underneath the table on which I put the beers. Angry I went up to the drunk and shoved him out. But with a push he threw me to the ground and took the opportunity to run to the drawer and grab hold of the pistol. I ran and got between them to protect my son. Determined, the drunk came up to me.

"Stop, the Sacred Heart is in my hands," I shouted at him. In a moment I felt myself sprawled on the ground bleeding at the waist: two shots had hit me in the right buttock and another in the hip on the same side.

They took me on a stretcher to the center of Huautla. They took me to the young Wise-One-In-Medicine. I learned that his name was Salvador Guerra. He took out the bullets. On that occasion the doctor met me. For the first time in my life I was cured by a Wise-One-In-Medicine. I was amazed. Before operating he injected a substance in the region where I was wounded and my pains disappeared. While he cured me I didn't feel any pain; after he finished he showed me the bullets. Thankful and amazed I told him: "Doctor, you are as great as me. You make pain disappear. You took the bullets out of me and I didn't feel anything."

Three days later I returned to my house. I wanted to drink coffee, to

eat tortillas and chile sauce. I wanted to savor my own cooking. The
food that the Wise-Man-In-Medicine's helpers gave me, it was hard
for me to get down.

One afternoon, while I was in my house, a man arrived to tell me
that that same night Salvador Guerra himself was going to come with a
foreign lady who wanted to meet me. I prepared myself for a vigil.   2

At night, the young Wise Man arrived in his metal [jeep] with a
blonde lady. A translator told me that only the lady would take the
little saints. I didn't pay any attention, I prepared several pairs of *little
birds* for the Wise-Man-In Medicine. When the time came, I spoke to   3
him in Mazatec telling him to eat the *children* with me. I stretched out
my hand to give them to him. With brusque gestures he refused to
take them. So I said to him: "You gave me the medicine with which
you cure the wounded. You healed me. You took out my bullets. Now
I offer you my medicine. Take these pairs as payment for your
services." The blonde woman backed up my words. Finally the young
Wise Man took his pairs.

From then on, Salvador Guerra and I were good friends. Later our
friendship became firmer and the day he left Huautla [in 1960] the
priest, Alfonso Aragón, gave a mass to ask for a long life for all of us.
Salvador Guerra and I kneeled in front of the altar.

When the mass was over, I offered him my hand and said to him:
"Doctor!" He reciprocated by giving me his hand, saying:
"Doctoress!"

And now, when I see that drunk who wounded me cross my path, I
greet him. Poor fellow, he's fallen apart...he's a useless man. His
drunkenness has finished him off.

14

A few years before the first foreigners I met arrived in Huautla, a neighbor, Guadalupe, the wife of Cayetano García, came to my house.

"I've had an ugly dream," she said. "I want you to come to the house to see us. I don't feel well. I'm asking you as a favor. It's possible that problems are approaching for my husband because his office as *sindico* is difficult. You know, Senora, that there is violence in the town. There are envies. For nothing at all people hurt and kill each other. There are discords."

"I'll go with you right now," I told her.

Upon arriving at their house, Cayetano invited me to sit down. He took another chair. His wife did the same. In a discrete voice, the *sindico* spoke:

"I know who you are, María Sabina. That's why I've sent for you. We have faith in you. You've cured those who have been ill here in the house, but now I'm going to ask you something special. I want you to be my adviser. The town has elected me to municipal office. You know that to be one of the authorities is a big responsibility. You have to make decisions and you can make mistakes. So I ask you to advise me and guide me, because you have power; you know, you can know the truth no matter how hidden it is because the *little things* teach you. If there are any problems of litigation in the municipality, you will tell me where the guilt lies and I, as *sindico*, will say what should be done."

"Don't worry," I answered him. "We'll do what you ask. I can't say no because we're old friends and because I obey the authorities. What's more I know that you're a good man. I don't doubt it. I will be your adviser. We'll consult the *saint children* as many times as it's necessary."

Cayetano García was *síndico* for three years; in that time there were no serious problems or situations that the town government could lament.

But I should tell the incident that preceded the arrival of the first foreigners who came to me. More or less fifteen days after the drunk wounded me, Guadalupe the wife of Cayetano, some other people, and I took the *little things*. This time I saw strange beings. They appeared to be people but they weren't familiar; they didn't even appear to be fellow Mazatecs.

"I don't know what's happening. I see strange people," I told Guadalupe.

I asked her to pray because I felt a certain uneasiness at that vision. Guadalupe prayed to aid me. She prayed to God the Christ.

I received the explanation of that vision in a few days when Cayetano arrived at my house in the course of the morning. His words didn't fail to astonish me:

"María Sabina," he said, still breathing hard from the walk, "some blonde men have arrived at the Municipal Building to see me. They've come from a faraway place with the aim of finding a Wise One. They come in search of *Little-One-Who Springs-Forth*. I don't know whether it displeases you to know it, but I promised to bring them to meet you. I told them that I know a true Wise Woman. The thing is that one of them, looking very serious, put his head up close to my ear and said: 'I'm looking for ?nti¹xi³tjo³.' I couldn't believe what I was hearing. For a moment I doubted it, but the blonde man appeared to know a lot about the matter. That was the impression I got. The man seems sincere and good. Finally I promised to bring them to your house."

"If you want to, I can't say no. You are an official and we are friends,' I replied.

The following day, somebody brought three blonde men to my house. One of them was Mr. Wasson. I told the foreigners that I was sick though not precisely that a drunk had wounded me with a pistol. One of the visitors listened to my chest. He put his head on my chest to hear my heartbeat, held my temples between his hands, and put his head against my back. The man nodded while he touched me. Finally he said some words that I didn't understand; they spoke another language that wasn't Castilian. I don't even understand Castilian.

One night soon after, the foreigners were present at my vigil. Afterward I found out that Wasson had been left marvelling, and that he went so far as to say that another person in Huautla who claimed to be a Wise One was nothing but a liar. In reality he meant the sorcerer Vanegas.

When the foreigners took the *saint children* with me. I didn't feel anything bad. The vigil was fine. I had different visions than usual. I saw places I had never imagined existed. I reached the place the foreigners came from. I saw cities. Big cities. Many houses, big ones.

Wasson came other times. He brought his wife and his daughter. Different people came with him as well.

One day Wasson arrived with a group of people. With them came some fellow Mazatecs who brought a sick person wrapped up in a mat. They told me that he was an orphan, Perfecto by name, and that he had been raised by Aurelio-Path. This Aurelio was a Wise One as well, and he had tried to cure the sick boy.

But there was no remedy for the sick one. His death was near. After I saw Perfecto's appearance, I said to Aurelio: "This child is in a very grave condition. He requires a lot of care."

I took the *children* and began to work. That was how I learned that Perfecto had a frightened spirit. His sprit had been caught by a malevolent being.

I let myself be carried away by the Language that sprang from me, and though Perfecto didn't take the *little mushrooms*, my words made him rise and get to his feet and he spoke. He related, then, that while resting in the shade of some coffee trees in Canada Mamey he "felt something" in back of him.

"I had the feeling that there was something behind me," he said, "like an animal, like a donkey. I heard him lick his chops very clearly. I turned around rapidly, but I didn't see anything. That frightened me a lot and since then I've felt sick. It's true, Papa Aurelio, if you take care of me, I'll get well. María Sabina says so."

In the course of the vigil, the sick one got to his feet because the Language gave him strength. I also rubbed some San Pedro on his arms.

Weeks went by and somebody informed me that Perfecto had died. They didn't take care of him as they should have. If they had done several vigils he would certainly have gotten well. They didn't do it.

Wasson, his family and friends went and didn't come back anymore. It's been years since I've seen them; but I know that his wife died. Only Wasson returned once not many years ago. The last time I saw him he told me: "María Sabina, you and I will still live for many years."

After those first visits of Wasson, many foreign people came to ask me to do vigils for them. I asked them if they were sick, but they said no...that they had only come "to know God." They brought innumerable objects with which they took what they call photographs and recorded my voice. Later they brought papers [newspapers and magazines] in which I appeared. I've kept some papers I'm in. I keep them even though I don't know what they say about me.

It's true that Wasson and his friends were the first foreigners who came to our town in search of the *saint children* and that they didn't take them because they suffered from any illness. Their reason was that they came to find God.

Before Wasson nobody took the mushrooms only to find God. They were always taken for the sick to get well.

15

I've belonged to the sisterhoods for thirty years. Now I belong to the Sisterhood of the Sacred Heart of Jesus. The sisterhood is composed of ten women. If a society is composed of men it is called a stewardhood. Each member is also called *mother*. Our task consists of making candles and gathering money to pay for the mass that is given monthly in thanks to the Sacred Heart of Jesus. Each member gives the principal mother fifty centavos. Between all of us we get together five pesos; but if the mass is for the day of the festival of the Sacred Heart, or some other saint, then we give three pesos. We get together a total of thirty pesos. We give three pesos for the day of the Virgin of the Nativity which is the eighth of September; we also give three pesos the third Friday in March—those are our festival days. In Holy Week, when our Father is crucified, we give three pesos as well.

The curate has a list on which the name and contribution of each member is noted. The Bishop is also aware of it.

Fifteen days before the Festival of the Patron, the stewards and the members of the sisterhood go for a crucifix lent by the church. The principal steward carries the crucifix in his hand.

With flowers donated by the members of the sisterhood, an altar is decorated in the house of the principal steward; and in the path to the house, an arch of bamboo is made, adorned with flowers. The committee that went for the crucifix is received beneath the arch. Rockets are fired and flowers are strewn in the path of the crucifix. The committee of mothers and stewards is accompanied by music. The mothers go along incensing the crucifix committee with copal, and each one carries candles and flowers. At the head of the procession, a steward goes along ringing a bell.

Upon arriving at the house of the principal steward, each member of the sisterhood should hand in a pound of pure wax. Each pound of wax is melted and worked in the presence of the crucifix. The candles that are made are adorned with paper and a bow the same color as the patron Saint's clothing. After the wax has been worked, the members of the sisterhood give three pesos each to pay for the mass. This is a festival day. The musicians play and people drink *aguardiente*, smoke, and fire rockets. The candles are blessed in that way. Those candles are sacred from then on and shouldn't be lit except in religious ceremonies. They are not for giving light in the dark.

The day before the fiesta, the stewards go to neighbors' houses to ask for monetary aid. After noon the musicians arrive at the house of the principal mother. There *aguardiente* is drunk and cigarettes are passed out. A goat is killed and eaten in a stew together with bitter tamales. The stewards arrive with their wives, each of whom brings thirteen candles of a half pound each. The members of the sisterhood bring flowers of all kinds.

The musicians play the *Orange Flower*, and then the principal   1
mother dances with the principal steward. The second mother dances with the second steward, the third mother dances with the third steward.

In the evening, the mothers and stewards take the thirteen candles ɔ the church to light them at the altar of the Patron Saint, while the ⸱riest says the Rosary.

The next morning, on the festival day of the Patron, the stewards ind the mothers leave the house of the principal steward and in procession head for the church to hear the mass in which the candles are lighted again, held by the mothers in their hands. Once the mass is over, the candles are put out and the mothers take them with them. The mothers and the stewards gather again in the house of the principal steward where music is played on guitars and the plucked dulcimer. There stew is again eaten together with bitter tamales, and people smoke and dance. The stewards and some of the mothers drink *aguardiente*.

When the festival is finished, the stewards go to the Municipal Building and return the money to the authorities that they borrowed at the start for the expenses of the festival.

Every two, four, or six years, the members of the sisterhood rotate, so that each one is the principal mother once.

One never ceases to be a mother. When one dies, the sacred candles that are her property and that were not used are put in the coffin next to the corpse.

It is nearly thirty years since I learned of the sisterhoods. It came from the church, I think. From the start I participated in the sister-hoods with enthusiasm because I've always had respect for everything that has to do with God. I obey the priests. I am also obedient to the words of the municipal authorities. They are the heads. They govern us.

When the sisterhoods were begun, thirty years ago, I met Apolonio Terán in church. The two of us, as a couple, went to the houses of the neighbors to invite them to form the first sisterhood and the first stewardhood. I knew that Apolonio was a great Wise Man, that he had the power to cure. That he knew how to speak with the Lords of the Mountains. The two Wise Ones, he and I, joined together in this task without ever speaking of our own knowledge. We only spoke about questions pertaining to the sisterhoods and stewardhoods. At that time I didn't let myself be known. The wise shouldn't go around advertising what they are, because it is a delicate matter. Apolonio was an active man, he formed the sisterhoods and the stewardhoods. He gave people's names to the municipal authorities who took it upon themselves to communicate, in writing, with the elected people. The written paper was the nomination that was given to people who were asked to appear on a certain day. Once the society was formed, the authorities themselves lent money to begin the activities of the moth-ers and the stewards. The money was used to buy the wax with which the candles are made. Later the borrowed money was returned.

Apolonio and I considered the opinion of the husband, the parents, the brothers or the chidren of the person who was going to become a member of the sisterhood or the stewardhood.

16

I have suffered. And I go on suffering. Here, below the right hip, in the place where I was hit by the bullet the drunk shot at me, a tumor has come out. It has grown little by little and hurts me if it's cold. It will be five years since some people from the city came and wanted to take me there. They said that Wise-Ones-In-Medicine from those parts would cut out the tumor. Before deciding, I consulted the municipal president, Valeriano García; he opposed my going to Mexico City for them to cure me.

"You can die in the moment that they are cutting out the tumor," he said. "We could be left without María Sabina, and that would make us very sad."

Since I obey the authorities, I refused to accompany those people.

I have suffered from poverty. My hands became callous from hard work. My feet are covered with calluses as well. I've never used shoes but I know the paths. The muddy, dusty, rocky paths have made the soles of my feet hard.

Never has evil come from me, nor lies either. I have always been poor: poor I have lived and poor I will die. I have suffered. My two husbands died. Several of my children died from sickness or in tragedies. Some children died when they were very small; others were born without life. I didn't cure the little ones with my power, because at that time I had a husband; relations with men invalidate the power of the *children*.

There has been sadness in my heart. I have had to raise some of my orphaned grandchildren. One of my grandsons died recently with a swollen face. He worked as a laborer opening roads where the metal contraptions go but he drank a lot of *aguardiente*; poor thing, he was hardly twenty years old. Now I'm raising another, little one. I like children. I like to caress them and talk with them . . .It's necesary to take good care of children. They should be baptised as soon as they're born, because children who aren't baptised die if a storm occurs. The lightning bolts of the storm carry away the spirit of the children who haven't been baptised. Just last night I heard the noise produced by a lightning bolt that fell nearby here, and today I was informed that in the morning there was a baby dead in the house of a neighbor.

Catarino, Viviana and Apolonia, the children of my first husband, are alive and each of them has children.They've withdrawn from me. Family tasks keep them busy, surely. As for my second husband, only my daughter Aurora is alive.

One of my sons, the brother of Aurora, named Aurelio, was murdered. Before the tragedy happened, the *saint children* warned me of it. Those were the days when Wasson came to Huautla. It was a Thursday, during a vigil, when I had a vision: a spotted cattle skin appeared, stretched on the ground to the right of where I was kneeling. I stopped talking once I saw it, but I wasn't intimidated despite the fact that it was a purtrid animal hide. It stunk. Afterward a man appeared near the skin, dressed like a fellow Mazatec, and he shouted: "I'm the one. I'm the one. With this one it will be five. With this one it will be five I've murdered."

A neighbor named Augustín had taken the mushrooms with me to cure himself of pains he felt in the waist. I turned to him to ask:

"Did you see that man? Did you hear what he said?"

Augustín answered:

"Yes, I saw him. He's the son of Señora Dolores."

I remained very puzzled; I didn't understand the words of the man who had appeared in my vision. The following day I went on thinking about it without finding an explanation.

My son Aurelio was in Teotitlán del Camino Thursday night.

Three days after having seen the spotted skin, precisely Sunday at noon, three men arrived at my little store; one of them asked for my nineteen-year-old son Aurelio. My son had just arrived from Teotitlán and was in the next room playing the guitar that he had recently bought. One of the men was the son of the neighbor, Dolores, the same one who had appeared in my vision the Thursday before. My son Aurelio invited them in to where he was and offered them *aguardiente.*

Later the visitors and my son, under the effect of the *aguardiente*, sang, accompanying themselves with the guitar.

After they had sung several songs, there was a brief pause, and suddenly the son of Dolores insulted my son. When I looked in I saw that man lift up his shirt and take a knife out of his belt which he immediately stuck in my son's throat.

I shouted desperately, seeing Aurelio fall on all fours near the doorway to the store.

The killer, taking his knife, fled up the path in the direction of San Miguel, followed by his companions.

I threw myself, crazed from pain and anguish, onto the bloody body of my son, while another of my sons and some friends went off in pursuit of the killer whom they didn't succeed in catching.

My poor Aurelio died right there where he fell. The following day we buried him. The neighbors came to the wake. They drank *aguardiente* and played cards. I gave them coffee, bread, and cigarettes. They put money next to the corpse; with that I paid the expenses of the funeral. We buried him with music as the custom is.

As my son was being buried, I remember the horrible vision of that previous Thursday. Then I understood what the *little things* had tried to warn me about: the skin, the son of Dolores shouting: "With this one it will be five...." They were forecasts of the pain that was approaching.

The men who murdered my Aurelio are now all dead as well. They were bad people. The violence with which they acted turned against them. One by one they were murdered by people who could defend their lives in time. They must have had a reason for murdering my son. I never found out what it was. My Aurelio drank *aguardiente* but he wasn't a violent man. For several months I cried over the death of my son.

And even though I'm the "clean woman," the "principal clown woman," evil has been done to me. Once they burned my house of seven arm-lengths. It was built of wood with a thatched roof of dried sugarcane leaves. I don't know the reason why they did it. Some people thought it was because I had revealed the ancestral secret of our native medicine to foreigners.

It's true that before Wasson nobody spoke so openly about the *children*. No Mazatec revealed what he knew about this matter. I only obeyed the *sindico*; and yet I think now that if the foreigners had arrived without any recommendation whatsover, I would still have shown them my wisdom, because there is nothing bad in that. The *children* are the blood of Christ. When we Mazatecs speak of the vigils we do it in a low voice, and in order not to pronounce the name that they have in Mazatec ($?nti^1xi^3tjo^3$) we call them *little things* or *little saints*. That is what our ancestors called them.

Other people believed that the motive for burning my house was that the arsonist thought he was bewitched by me. I've already said, I'm not a Sorceress. I'm a Wise Woman. Still others said that it was the envy malevolent people felt for my power. I never found out the true motive that impelled them to do me harm. I don't even know the name of the arsonist, because I wasn't interested in consulting the *little things* about it.

Along with the house, my little store burned together with the corn, beer, *aguardiente*, the toasted seeds and cigarettes I sold, my huipils and shawls....Christ! Everything. That day I wasn't at home. The place was empty. My children and I had gone to San Miguel to the fiesta of Saint Michael to sell bread and candles. Upon returning we found nothing but ashes. Without knowing who to turn to, I went into the woods with my children. We ate wild tubers to subsist. In order not to feel so cold we made tea from lemon and orange leaves. Dona Rosaura García, a neighbor in Huautla who I met in one of the visits of Mr. Wasson, gave me a metal cup. Another person, I don't remember who, gave me a gourd bowl. That was of use to me.

Finally we went to live in the house of some relatives. And it was necessary to begin anew. I worked a lot to erect another house. This time one of adobe with a corugated tin roof. I live in it to this day.

But not all has been suffering. I become content listening to music on the plucked dulcimer. I like music. The Principal Ones like it as well...which reminds me that when they gave me the Book, there was music. The drum sounded, and the trumpet, the violin, and the dulcimer. It's because of that I sing:

> I am the drummer woman
> I am the trumpet woman
> I am the woman violinist...

I even had a dulcimer myself. I bought it and kept it in my house. I bought it because in a vigil the *children* asked me: 'Do you have a dulcimer?" and I said: "No, no, I don't have one." After I bought my dulcimer I answered them: "Yes, yes, I have a dulcimer."

Those who knew how to play the dulcimer came to my house to play it. At times I lent it, but one day suffering from lack of money, I sold it. Now I know that the dulcimer is in Santa Cruz de Juárez.

And I like to dance the Mazatec *jarabe*. I dance it in my visions with the Principal Ones. A Principal One is my partner. Afterward we drink beer and we talk. But I also dance at the festivals of the stewards. On one occasion, in the house of Doña Rosaura García, I danced the *Orange Flower*, the Mazatec *jarabe*, for Guerra, the young Wise Man, for them to see that I'm a woman who likes to have a good time. But I don't only dance, I also cook. Once I prepared edible mushrooms for the foreigners. I think that it was in the house of the teacher Herlinda Martínez. In a big pot we cooked *tjain³coa³* ("white mushrooms"), those that grow on balsa trees. We made a hot *tezmole* seasoned with onions. The foreigners ate until their stomachs were full.

17

The blonde people, men and women, arrive at my door. They call me "grandma" or "Sabinita" from outside, so I go out and invite them in. To those who would like some, I give coffee; I don't have anything more to offer them. I think that some of the blonde ones feel good in my house, as if it was theirs, because they spread their blankets or mats on the ground and rest there. At this time of year the foreigners visit me, but not all of them want vigils; they come as well in the dry season, when the *children* don't grow. The foreigners take photographs of me wherever I happen to be. They take photographs of me going along the path with my load of corn on my back or resting on a rock in the market place. I've become accustomed to all that. That reminds me that somewhere in Oaxaca City, there's an enormous photograph of me working the earth with a hoe. The people who took that picture of me bought my hoe and took it with them. I like people to give me photographs of myself.

A lot of people come to visit me. Some say they are lawyers, others say they have important posts in the city; they take my picture with their objects, standing next to me themselves, and give me some coins when they go. The people who make papers come; they bring their Mazatec interpreters and ask questions about my life. I'm sorry I don't know Castilian or how to write; otherwise, I myself would say what I know in the papers.

I know that Mr. Wasson has made records and books of my Language.

Some years ago, I was in Tehuacán for a month. Herlinda, a teacher here in Huautla, accompanied me. My stay in Tehuacán was to correct the translation that two foreign missionaries—named Florencia and George—had made of my Language. These missionaries spoke our Mazatec language well, but I couldn't know if they exactly understood my Language. If I could read what they wrote, I would know. I realized that they had some difficulty understanding me.

With the priest, Alfonso Aragón, who was in Huautla for many years, I had a great friendship. This priest had a record on which my Language was recorded; I found that out one day when he invited me to listen to it. He told me that that record was worth a lot, that it was priceless. I thanked him for his words.   I had that record myself. I ² imagine that it was Wasson himself who sent it to me so that I could listen to it. He also gave me a record player. But some people came from the city who said they were officials and took everything.

In the rainy season, when the *little saints* grow in our damp earth, more foreigners come to my house. They continue to seek me but I don't give vigils for them any longer, because I'm too old. My body gets weaker every day; I breathe with difficulty, I don't go down to the market in Huautla very often because I get very tired. There are times when my body is so weak that I fall down on the path or inside the house. I slip easily on the trails; I can't lift the axe any longer with which I used to split kindling.

Now, when I get together some money, I buy kindling and sell it to the neighbors. My biggest dream these last years has been to have a little store where I could once again sell soap, cigarettes, and soda to the passersby; but I've never had sufficient money.

More or less seven years ago, a Bishop came who wanted to take the *saint children*. I would have given them to the Bishop because I know that Bishops are great too, but it wasn't the season. It was March, and the *children* grow in June, July, August, and September, although in some cold zones they can be found during November and December, but they can only rarely be obtained in April or March. If I have a patient in the season when the mushrooms can't be found, I resort to the Leaves of the Shepherdess. Ground up and taken, they work like the *children*. Of course the Shepherdess doesn't have as much strength. Other plants exist called Seeds of the Virgin. These seeds were created by the Virgin. I don't use the seeds, although some Wise Ones do.   The Bishop advised me to initiate my children into the ³ Wisdom I have. I told him that the color of the skin or the eyes can be inherited, including the manner of crying or of smiling, but the same can't be done with wisdom. Wisdom can't be inherited. Wisdom one brings with one from birth. My wisdom can't be taught; that's why I say that nobody taught me my Language, because it is the Language the *saint children* speak upon entering my body. Whoever isn't born to be wise can't attain the Language although they do many vigils. Who could teach a Language like that? My daughter Apolonia just helps me to pray or to repeat my Language during the vigils. She speaks and says what I ask her to, but she isn't a Wise Woman; she wasn't born with that destiny. Apolonia is dedicated to raising her children and attending to her husband. She has grown children who live in Mexico City; they work there and send some money to their mother. Apolonia and Viviana, my two daughters, will never be Wise Women. They will not receive the Book from the hands of the Principal Ones. I, on the other hand, am known in Heaven, and even the holy Pope knows I exist. Important people know that I have been born. In the vigils I hear them say that I am the "little aquatic woman of the Book," that I am "the woman of the Flowing Water." It's true, that's why I'm humble, but I'm also "the woman who ascends."

4

Not anyone can be wise. I make that clear to people. One day I got angry with a school teacher. I got angry at her because she didn't want to give me some money that she should have given me. She assured me that she didn't have any money for me. I told her:

"You're a teacher and supposedly you teach children, but you want to make fun of me; you think you're superior because you know how to read and write. You should know that I don't feel insignificant before anyone. You know how to read and write thanks to the fact that your parents sent you to school to learn. You had to go to school many days to know what you know; but you should understand that I didn't have to go to any school to be wise. We Wise Ones don't need to learn what we know in a school. Wisdom comes from birth. It comes together with one when one is being born—like the placenta.

The mushrooms have revealed to me how I was in the days when I was in the womb of my mother: it's a vision in which I see myself turned into a fetus. An illuminated fetus. And I know that at the moment I was born, the Principal Ones were present. Also the heart of Christ was there.

The foreigners brought me a foreigner with a big fat body. He looked stupid. He didnt' say a word. I did a vigil because those people wanted to see if the *children* could cure the sick in the city where they live. The vigil was done in the house of Cayetano García.

The reaction of the stupid foreigner was that, past midnight, he roared like a lion. Ay! it frightened me for a moment, but the Language gave me courage. When Guadalupe, Cayetano's wife, heard the roar, she took her newborn baby away. She got it out of there so that the foreigner who roared wouldn't catch the little baby's spirit. It sometimes happens that if a persons "fate" leaves, that "fate," having become free, can enter the body of another person nearby. One gets well and the other becomes sick. The man who roared could have transferred his "fate" to the newborn. The stupid foreigner went 5 back to his country, and I don't know what's become of him since.

On a more recent occasion, a foreign couple asked me to give them the *little things* because they had a five-year- old son who was suffering from pimples on his head. The mother of the child and I both took the *children*. In the course of the vigil, the child began to cry. He cried a lot. Then it was revealed to me that the mother of the child was herself the cause of the child's sickness. Christ! It scared me to be near that lady, but I armed myself with courage and took a hold of her hair:

"Give me the spirit of the child," I told her in Mazatec. "Give it to me, give it to me," I repeated, shouting in the lady's ears while I pulled hard on her hair.

Little by little the child stopped crying as the lady gave me back his spirit. The truth was that she had a malevolent being inside her who had enchanted the spirit of her own son.

At dawn the couple took their child. They said that they were grateful for the cure. Although the pimples hadn't disappeared from the child's head, his appearance was better now than the day before the vigil. The lady said good-bye to me nicely . . . but she never knew that she herself had trapped her son's spirit, causing the pimples on his head.

18

For a time there came young people of one and the other sex, long-haired, with strange clothes. They wore shirts of many colors and used necklaces. A lot came. Some of these young people sought me out for me to stay up with the *Little-One-Who-Springs-Forth.* "We come in search of God," they said. It was difficult for me to explain to them that the vigils weren't done from the simple desire to find God, but were done with the sole purpose of curing the sicknesses that our people suffer from.

Later I found out that the young people with long hair didn't need me to eat the *little things.* Fellow Mazatecs weren't lacking who, to get a few centavos for food, sold the *saint children* to the young people. In their turn, the young people ate them wherever they liked: it was the same to them if they chewed them up seated in the shade of coffee trees or on a cliff along some trail in the woods.

These young people, blonde and dark-skinned, didn't respect our customs. Never, as far as I remember, were the *saint children* eaten with such a lack of respect. For me it is not fun to do vigils. Whoever does it simply to feel the effects can go crazy and stay that way temporarily. Our ancestors always took the *saint children* at a vigil presided over by a Wise One.

The improper use that the young people made of the *little things* was scandalous. They obliged the authorities in Oaxaca City to intervene in Huautla...though not all the foreigners are bad, it's true.

In those days, some people arrived at my house who spoke Castilian and dressed like people from the city. A Mazatec interpreter came ⁴ with them.

They entered my house without my inviting them in. Their eyes fell on some *saint children* that I had on a little table. Pointing at them, one of them asked:

"If I asked you for mushrooms would you give them to me?"

"Yes, because I believe you've come in search of God," I told him.

Another one, with an authoritarian voice, ordered me:

"You're coming with us to San Andrés Hidalgo. We're going there in search of another person who, like you, dedicates himself to making people crazy."

Meanwhile the other people who came in the group went all through my house. One of them pointd out to the rest of them a bottle that contained San Pedro. I said to them decisively:

It's ground tobacco mixed with lime and garlic. We call it San Pedro. It serves as a protection against evil spirits."

"Is it smoked?" asked one of the men in a loud voice.

"No," I replied. "It's a tobacco that's rubbed on the arms of the sick, and a little can also be placed inside the mouth.... Our ancestors used it and they called it San Pedro. San Pedro has a lot of force. It helps to get rid of sickness."

Another one of them brought the papers that spoke about me. He also showed the others the record and the record player that Wasson had given me. They all turned around to look at me, and I said to myself: "I can't talk Castilian with them, but they can see in those papers who I am." Afterwards, with a touch of gentleness, they helped me up into a truck. I obeyed without offering resistance. I sat between the man who drove and another one who sat next to the door. That second one continued leafing through the papers in which photographs of me appeared. I realized that from time to time he looked at me out of the corner of his eye.

At no time did fear seize me although I understood that these people were authorities and were trying to do me harm. We arrived at San Andres and there they arrested the Municipal Agent. Finally I found out that they accused this man and me of selling a tobacco that drove the young people crazy.

Afterward they took us to the Municipal Building. A doctor from the Instituto Indigenista spoke with the men. They talked a long while. ⁵ At the end the doctor told me:

"Don't worry, María Sabina, nothing will happen to you. We're here to defend you."

The men who arrested me also said:

"Forgive us. Go home and rest."

But they took my San Pedro tobacco, the papers, my record, and the object that made the recorded sound. They set the Municipal Agent of San Andrés at liberty too.

Genaro Terán was the municipal president of Huautla. He told me that a fellow Mazatec, whom the police were after originally, had accused me of selling the young people a tobacco that drove them crazy when they smoked it. The president revealed to me the name of my accuser.

"President," I said to Genaro Terán, "you know that our people don't use the tobacco that this unfortuante claims I sell. They accuse me of bringing gringos to my house. It's the gringos who come in search of me. They take photographs of me, they talk with me, they ask me questions (the same kind I've answered many times before), and they go after taking part in a vigil. None of these young people has gone crazy in my house. But what is this all about? What harm have I done to this man who accuses me? In all my life I've never had anything to do with him. I know him, he's the son of the late Josefina, our fellow townswoman, but I've never done any harm to this individual. This situation makes me mad. I'm ready to get into a fist fight with the man. And if he wants to fight with a knife. I have mine. And if he wants to fight with a pistol, I'll see how I can get a hold of one. If afterward the judge sentences me to several years in jail, it won't matter in the least. I'll have sated my fury. I don't like people to make fun of me."

"Don't worry," said Genaro Terán, "the case has been settled. You aren't guilty of anything. Go home, María Sabina."

It was an infamy. Just because that fellow wears pants, that doesn't make him a man. His lie hurt me. That's why I was ready to go to jail or die to prove I wasn't guilty. That man, maybe to get some money, sold the *saint children* and the tobacco that drove the young people crazy.

Finally the authorities took that man to jail because his guilt was proven.

The Huautla authorities explained to me that some foreigners were bad, that they came to spoil our customs....

Two years later, Señor Felícitos Pineda, the new municipal president, sent me an official paper in which I was asked to present myself before the public attorney in Teotitlán del Camino. It was then, Alvaro, that you took me to Mexico City. I lived in the house of some of your relatives. And you took me to a man who writes in the papers and who, like so many others, asked me questions in order to later ask
the authorities to leave me in peace. Also you took me to a very big house where there were objects made by our ancestors, stones that Indian hands carved hundreds of years ago. There were photographs of Mazatecs there. What I liked the most was to listen to my voice there, sounding incessantly. My wise Language in that place — I could

6

7

hardly believe it. I remember people came up to me to greet me. They recognized me. I also remember a picture on the wall in which I seemed to see malignant beings. Beings with black wings. I think that the demons are like that, but we Mazatecs don't have an image of the devil; for us he doesn't have face nor form.

When I returned to Huautla, Felícitos Pineda insisted that I should go before the Principal Ones in Oaxaca because they kept demanding that I appear. A few days later I presented myself in that city. I was accompanied by one of the municipal authorities of Huautla, who explained to me that he would take me to a person, one of the Principal Ones with great authority in Oaxaca. With courage, without fear of anything, I let myself be conducted to the appointed place. The moment the person saw me, he shouted my name and stood up. Smiling he came up to me. His attitude was the contrary of what I expected. He embraced me, caressed my hair, and said:

"I wanted you to come to tell you that there is nothing against you."

On taking leave of him I thanked the person for his words and right away returned to Huautla.

Now I have gone to the city on various occasions. In the first week of July, the municipal authorities of Huautla themselves take me to the *Guelaguetza* in Oaxaca. I put on my best huipil and sit there next to the Principal Ones. The nuns who are established in Huautla once took me to Mexico City, and I went with them to various churches. Among them we visited the Shrine where our Virgin Guadalupe is.

19

During the vigil, the candles of beeswax that are used in the vigils should be put out; the darkness then serves as a background for the images that one is seeing. It isn't necessary to close one's eyes, but only to look toward the infinite background of the darkness. There the Principal Ones appear seated around a table on which are all the things of this world. The table displays the clock, the eagle, and the opossum. . . .

There are different classes of *children*: those that grow in the detritus of sugar cane; those that grow in cattle excrement (called San Isidro); those that grow on rotten trees (called "birds"); and those that grow in the damp ground (called "landslide"). Those of the sugarcane and the "landslide" varieties are stronger than the "birds" and San Isidro.

The day that I did a vigil for the first time in front of foreigners, I didn't think anything bad would happen, since the order to give a vigil for the blonde ones came directly from the municipal authorities at the recommendation of the *síndico*, my friend Cayetano García. But what was the result? Well, that many people have come in search of God, people of all colors and all ages. The young people are the ones who have been the most disrespectful. They take the *children* at any time and in any place. They don't do it during the night or under the direction of the Wise Ones, and they don't use them to cure any sickness either.

But from the moment the foreigners arrived to search for God, the *saint children* lost their purity. They lost their force; the foreigners spoiled them. From now on they won't be any good. There's no remedy for it.

Before Wasson, I felt that the *saint children* elevated me. I don't feel like that anymore. The force has diminished. If Cayetano hadn't brought the foreigners...the *saint children* would have kept their power. Many years ago when I was a child, they grew everywhere. They even grew around the house; but those weren't used in the vigils, because if human eyes see them that invalidates their purity and force. It was necessary to go to distant places to search for them, where they were out of reach of human sight. The person who was going to gather them had to observe four days of sexual abstinence in preparation. During those four days the gatherer was prohibited from attending wakes in order to avoid the contaminated air of the dead.

The air that surrounds a corpse is impure; if people have wounds and get near a wake, they can get gangrene. Another recommendation to the person sent to gather the *saint children* was that, preferably, he or she should do it after taking a bath. These last few years, anyone looks at the *children*, and no care is taken in gathering them.

The corpses of animals also produce gangrene. Anything decomposed is impure.

Some foreigners say that they've come to cure themselves, and there's no lack of those who assure you that they've had operations without being cured. After they've participated in a vigil with me, they thank me and say they feel better. They say they have sugar in their blood. I don't know that sickness. I only know that the spirit is what gets sick. And the spirit is what enriches: people who have made a fortune are ones whose spirits have journeyed to the spiritual realm of wealth. This is a place where there is fortune, greatness, and happiness. The spirit arrives in this realm and robs what it can. If it succeeds in grabbing some wealth, the person will come to have money or will attain important posts. But the spirit should be careful not to be surprised by the watchmen of the realm of wealth. If a watchman surprises a spirit robbing wealth, he wounds him with a pistol. That's how spirits receive the impact of a bullet. The spirit travels and the person dreams it.

To cure people who have fever, I sacrifice a chick, opening its breast with the thumbs of my hands. I extract the heart and I give it, still beating, to the sick person to eat. The chick's corpse can be left in the highest part of a bush; that way it doesn't rot, it just dries out.

But I am old and sick. It's true, life ends. And not only do I try to cure the illnesses of some foreigners, but they have also tried to cure my afflictions. They give me medicines, or people who say they are Wise-Ones-In-Medicine from the city visit me and want to cut out my tumor. I don't pay much attention to them. There is always something that impedes me from taking the medicines or allowing them to cut out the tumor. The truth is that I don't want to take the foreigners' medicine because I have my own damp medicine. One day a doctor felt my body and left medicines for me to take, but I didn't do it because at that time many childen were dying here in my section of town. The cause of those deaths was that the elves, the masters of the places where they opened the road that goes to San Miguel and that passes near my house, charged for the profanation done to them in ruining the quietness of their places by taking many children. I didn't take the medicines because the sickness of a person who is taking medicine can get worse if at the same time she goes to a wake or there is a dead person next door. Those who know that my back hurts and that it costs me work to swallow give me a massage. First a foreign man and later a woman have given me massages. I think they were experts because afterward I felt relieved from the pains in my body. Not all the foreigners are bad. Some bring me food or fruit and I thank them. As for those who use my hearth to prepare a meal for me, I ask them to pardon me because I don't have spoons. They know that I'm poor and that I live alone except for an orphaned grandson who keeps me company.

2   The people who arrive at my door always bring me gifts. The governor of Oaxaca, Zárate Aquino, gave me two mattresses. He said that a soft bed gives more comfort to the body than the hard ground where mats are spread. To use the mattresses, I bought two wooden beds.

A young foreigner who wore multicolored clothes and sandals wanted to give me a big, pretty dog. I told him that I didn't want a dog, that I didn't have the money to maintain it. What was the animal going to eat? Shit? The young foreigner understood my situation and took his dog with him.

3   I like song birds. Two years ago I bought a chachalaca from Cañada Mamey. I bought it for eighty pesos. I knew that a storm was coming when the chachalaca began to coo; it was like a companion for me but, Jesus Christ, they robbed it from me. Now I don't have a chachalaca to distract me. . . .

20

I have never seen the demons, although to arrive where I should I pass through the dominions of death. I submerge myself and walk down below. I can search in the shadows and in the silence. Thus I arrive where the sicknesses are crouched. Very far down below. Below the roots and the water, the mud and the rocks. At other times I ascend, very high up, above the mountains and the clouds. Upon arriving where I should, I look at God and at Benito Juárez. There I look at the good people. There everything is known. About everything and everyone, because there everything is clear. I hear voices. They speak to me. It is the voice of *Little-One-Who-Springs-Forth*. The God that lives in them enters my body. I cede my body and my voice to the *saint children*. They are the ones who speak; in the vigils they work in my body and I say:

> *Because you gave me your clock*
> *Because you gave me your thought*
> *Because I am a clean woman*
> *Because I am a Cross Star woman*
> *Because I am a woman who flies*
>
> *I am the sacred eagle woman, says*
> *I am the Lord eagle woman, says*
> *I am the lady who swims, says*

Because I can swim in the immense
Because I can swim in all forms
Because I am the launch woman
Because I am the sacred opossum
Because I am the Lord opossum

I can be eagle, opossum, or woman clock. If I see them, I pronounce their names.

The *children* turn into the Principal Ones. The Principal Ones appear as well in the visions of the initiates. On their sacred table, they put clocks, papers, books, communion wafers, stars, dew, or eagles. . . . The Principal Ones ask the initiates:

"What type of Wise One do you want to be? Do you want the Lords of the Mountains, the masters of the places, to guide you, or do you want God the Christ to guide you?"

Then the initiate chooses and tells the Principal Ones what he prefers. At that moment the initiate receives a Book that contains the Language he has chosen.

I decided for God the Christ. I made it known to the Principal Ones. The realm of the Principal Ones is the realm of abundance. There there is beer and music. When I'm in that realm I ask for beers to be served to everyone. A Principal One serves the beer and then all together we give a toast. There are times when it isn't necessary to ask for beers, they're within reach of the hand. If music sounds, I dance as a partner with the Principal Ones; and I also see that words fall, they come from up above, as if they were little luminous objects falling from the sky. The Language falls on the sacred table, falls on my body. Then with my hands I catch word after word. That happens to me when I don't see the Book. . . . And I sing:

With the Virgin Magdalene
With the Virgin Guadalupe
With Lord Santiago

Because I am the water that looks, says
Because I am the woman wise in medicine, says
Because I am the woman herbalist, says
Because I am the woman of the medicine, says
Because I am the woman of the breeze, says
Because I am the woman of the dew, says

If during the vigil the mushrooms order me to suck out the sickness, I apply suction from where I am; it's not necessary for me to put my mouth against the sick part. And my Language says:

I come with my thirteen hummingbirds
Because I am the sacred hummingbird, says
Because I am the Lord hummingbird, says
Because I bring my clean sucker, says
Because I bring my healthy sucker, says
Because I bring my bamboo tube, says
My bamboo with dew, says
My fresh bamboo, says

And it's that...

I am the woman Book that is beneath the water, says
I am the woman of the populous town, says
I am the shepherdess who is beneath the water, says
I am the woman who shepherds the immense, says
I am a shepherdess and I come with my shepherd, says
Because everything has its origin
And I come going from place to place from the origin...

If I put tobacco on the arms of a sick one, then I say:

And I bring my San Pedro
Only with San Pedro
Only with San Pedro
What I work with
What I appreciate
What I work with
What I appreciate

Our Father cumulus cloud
Our Father Arosio
My Father! Father of the dew!
Father tiller
Rich Father

2

The *little saints* tell me that I am the woman of the Lord of all the Mountains. That is why I say:

I am the Woman of the Flowing Water...

They tell me that I am the woman of the oceans, that I bring wisdom in my hands. That I am the woman of Saint Peter and of Saint Paul. That I am a child-woman but that I can speak with the heroes. At times I cry but when I whistle nobody frightens me.

It's that in the middle is Language. On this shore, in the middle, and on the other shore is Language. With the mushrooms I see God, then I sing:

> *Because I am the God Star Woman*
> *The Cross Star Woman*
> *Because I can swim in the immense*
> *Because I am a well-prepared woman*
> *Because I have my healed people*
> *Because I have my healed priest*
> *And I have my healed Bishop*
> *I have my pure Bishop*
>
> *Because our people are great*
> *Because our people are excellent*
> *Holy Father*
> *Your house is big*
> *Your house is a house of authority*
> *Our Bishop*
> *People of our heart*
> *Good and clean priest*
> *Good and clean Bishop*
> *Good and clean candle*
> *Good and clean nun*
> *Because your Book exists*
> *Your Book that I bring*

Then...

> *I am the woman of the sacred Sun Stone, says*
> *I am the woman of the Lord Sun Stone, says*
> *I am the shooting star woman, says*
> *I am the shooting star woman beneath the water, says*
> *I am the lady doll, says*
> *I am the sacred clown, says*
> *I am the Lord clown, says*
> *Because I can swim*
> *Because I can fly*
> *Because I can follow tracks...*

The *saint children* cure; they cure fever, chills, yellow skin, or toothache. They drive the evil spirits out of the body or rescue the spirit trapped by an enchantment from the masters of the springs or mountains. They heal those who have a "fate" because of sorcery.

They are taken and later one vomits the malignant spirit.

If I see papers on the rich table of the Principal Ones, I say:

I am the woman who writes...

Language belongs to the *saint children*. They speak and I have the power to translate. If I say that I am the little woman of the Book, that means that a *Little-One-Who-Springs-Forth* is a woman and that she is the little woman of the Book. In that way, during the vigil, I turn into a mushroom — little woman — of the book...

If I am on the aquatic shore, I say:

I am a woman who is standing in the sand...

Because wisdom comes from the place where the sand is born.

21

I like to smoke cigarettes and to drink a little *aguardiente*, but I never get drunk. I'm already old. I get tired quickly. My back hurts me and my chest when I swallow my food. I don't talk much because my mouth has lost some teeth. I'm ashamed of being toothless, and it makes it difficult for me to eat tough meat. I prefer to drink liquids.

It's a long time that I've lived alone. My children have gone their separate ways: each one of them is dedicated to his or her family. I've remained alone. My children hardly visit me. The foreigners who come to see me distract me and I feel myself kept company by their presence.

My mother, María Concepción, died less than ten years ago. She was ancient. She got sick and I tried to cure her. I did three vigils to give her strength, but she herself realized that her end was near and that there was no remedy.

A little before dying, she said to me:

"Resign yourself, Bi," — that's what she called me — "I thank you for what you're doing for me, but it's time for me to die. I don't have anything to reproach you for. On the contrary, I'm content with the attentions that you've given me in life. But I feel bad to leave you. What will become of you after my death? I have confidence that God will know how to take care of you..."

And I'm old too. That's why I ask God to bless me. I always ask for grace each day...I ask grace for the world and for myself.

I know that soon I'm going to die. But I'm resigned. I will die at the moment God wants. Meanwhile let life follow its course; let us go on living our time in this world that is Christ's. This world of Christians where there is also evil and discord. This world where people fight for anything.

I know the realm of death because I've been there. It is a place where there is no noise, because noise, no matter how slight, is bothersome. In the peace of that realm, I see Benito Juárez.

The day that I die, what our custom dictates will be done. They will twist the neck of a rooster that should die next to my corpse. The spirit of the rooster will accompany my spirit. The rooster will crow four days after I have been buried; then my spirit will wake up and will go forever to the realm of death. During the wake, my family will place jars of water next to my lifeless head. It will be the water that I will have to take with me so that I'm not overcome by thirst while I journey to the realm of death. Inside my coffin, they will put seven gourd seeds, greens, and some balls of the dead,[1] all tied up together in a cloth bag. It will be the food that I will take so that hunger doesn't bother me on the way.

The women who go to my wake will make *tezmole* with the meat of the sacrificed rooster. The *tezmole* will be eaten only by the reciter of prayers and people who are going to dig my grave. If I have sacred candles left over from my activities as a member of the sisterhood, they will put them next to my corpse. They will dress me in a clean huipil and my best shawl. Between my hands will be placed a palm cross that has been blessed.

We Mazatecs respect the dead. On the Days of the Faithful Dead, in the first days of November, we make offerings of *cempasúchil* flowers entwined in arcs of bamboo set up over the family altar, and on the table we put fruit and food for the dead. Tamales with pork, coffee and bread.

A group of people form a band of masqueraders. Each one is called a *Bulging Navel*. They disguise themselves with masks and the clothing of men or women, and go around to the music of violins, guitars, and a loud drum. They visit the houses of the neighbors, singing:

> *Bulging Navel*
> *Lime fruit*
> *I ask you for a favor*
> *Just a single favor*
> *Give me a little lemonade*

In each house they dance in couples and eat tamales, drink coffee or *aguardiente.*

What the *Bulging Navels* represent are the souls who, it is said, return to eat and to satiate their thirst for the food of this world.

For many years now, the people who want to disguise themselves as *Bulging Navels* have come to my house. Here they transform themselves. I lend them the hats with their brims an arm's length wide, woven from vines, that my grandchildren make for them. The rest of the year I keep these big hats hanging from the roof of my house.

September 1975–August 1976

THE CHANTS

THE CHANTS

Folkways Session *recorded the night of July 21-22 1956, by V.P. and R. Gordon Wasson in the home of Cayetano García of Huautla de Jiménez, Oaxaca* (Mushroom Ceremony of The Mazatec Indians of Mexico, Folkways Records and Service *Corporation, NYC, U.S.A., FR 8975). Translation from Mazatec into Spanish by Alvaro Estrada and Eloina Estrada de González. English verson by Henry Munn.*

I am a woman who shouts, says
I am a woman who whistles, says
I am a woman who thunders, says
I am a woman who plays music, says
I am a spirit woman, says
I am a woman who shouts, says
Ah, our Jesus Christ, says
Ah, our Jesus, says
Our Saint Peter woman, says
Our Saint Peter woman, says
Our *Ustandi* woman, says
Our shooting star woman, says
Our shooting star woman, says
Our whirling woman of colors, says

Our undergrowth woman, says
Ah, our Jesus Christ, says
Our saint woman, says
Our saint woman, says
Our woman saintess, says
Our woman of light, says
Our saint woman, says
Our spirit woman, says
Ah, our Jesus Christ, says
Our spirit woman, says
Our woman of light, says
I am a spirit woman, says
I am a woman of light, says
I am a woman of the day, says
I am a clean woman, says
I am a lord eagle woman, says
Ah, our Jesus Christ, says
Our admirable woman, says
Our radiant woman, says
Our woman of light, says
Our spirit woman, says
Ah, our Jesus Christ, says
Our woman who flies, says
Ah, our Jesus Christ, says
Our diviner woman, says
Our woman bowed down to the ground, says
Ah, our Jesus Christ, says
Our whirling woman of colors, says
Our Jesus Christ, says
She is a clock woman, says
She is a clean woman, says
Ah, Jesus Christ, says
She is a clean woman, says
She is a well-prepared woman, says
She is a clean soul, says
She is a well-prepared soul, says
She is a well-prepared soul, says
She is a well-prepared soul, says
She is a well-prepared soul, says
Ah, Jesus Christ, says
Ah, Jesus, says
Ah, Jesus Christ, says
Ah, Jesus, says
You holy Father, says
You are the saint, says

You are the saintess, says
Ah, it is certain and true

[*THE EXPRESSION IS HUMMED RATHER THAN SPOKEN OUT LOUD*]

You are the saint, says
You are the saintess, says
Those that are saints, saints, those that are saintesses, those that
are saints, saintess, saint, saintess, they are the ones that are
called saint and saintess, says
Saints they are called, says
Saintesses they are called, says

I am a woman born
I am a woman fallen into the world
I am a law woman
I am a woman of thought
I am a woman who gives life
I am a woman who reanimates
I have the heart of Christ, says
I have the heart of the Virgin
I have the heart of Christ
I have the heart of the Father
I have the heart of the old Old One
It's that I have the same soul, the same heart as the saint,
as the saintess, says
You, my Mother Shepherdess, says
You, my Father, says
Living Mother, Mother who sways back and forth, says
Mother of sap, Mother of the dew, says
Mother who gave birth to us, Mother who is present, says
Mother of sap, Mother of breasts, says
You, Mother of sap, Mother of breasts, says
Green Mother, Mother of clarity, says
Budding Mother, Mother of offshoots, says
Green Mother, Mother of clarity, says
Ah, Jesus Christ, says
Ah, Jesus, says
Our Green Father, says
Our Father of clarity, says
Budding Mother, Mother of offshoots, says
Green Mother, Mother of clarity, says
Ah, Jesus Christ, says
Our saint woman, says
Our woman saintess, says
Our spirit woman, says
Our woman of light, says

She is a woman of the day, says
Our woman of light, says
She is a woman of the day, says
She is a woman of light, says
She is a spirit woman, says
Ah, Jesus, says
She is a woman of the light, says
She is a woman of the day, says
She is a woman who flies, says
I am a woman who looks into the insides of things, says
I am a woman who investigates, says
I am a woman who shouts, says
I am a woman who whistles, says
I am a woman who resounds, says
I am a woman torn up out of the ground, says
I am a woman torn up out of the ground, says
I am a woman wise in medicine, says
I am a woman wise in herbs, says
Ah, Jesus Christ, says
She is a woman of labor, says
I am a woman wise in medicine, says
I am a woman wise in words, says
I am a woman wise in problems, says
I am a hummingbird woman, says
I am a hummingbird woman, says
I am a woman with vibrant wings, says
I am a woman with vibrant wings, says
Ah, Jesus Christ, says
I am a clean woman, says
I am a well-prepared woman, says
I am a Saint Peter woman, says
I am a Saint Peter woman, says
I am an *Ustandi* woman, says
I am an *Ustandi* woman, says
I am a shooting star woman, says
I am a shooting star woman, says
Cayetano
[*HE REPLIES: "YES. WORK, WORK."*]
I am a clean woman, says
I am a well-prepared woman, says
I am a woman who looks into the insides of things, says
I am a woman who looks into the insides of things, says
I am a woman who looks into the insides of things, says
I am a woman who looks into the insides of things, says

I am a woman of light, says
I am a woman of light, says
I am a woman of light, says
I am a woman of the day, says
I am a woman who resounds, says
I am a woman wise in medicine, says
I am a woman wise in words, says
I am a Christ woman, says
Ah, Jesus Christ, says
I am a Morning Star woman, says
I am the God Star woman, says
I am the Cross Star woman, says
I am the Moon woman, says
I am a woman laborer, says
Father Jesus Christ, says
I am a woman of heaven, says
I am a woman of heaven, says
Ah, Jesus Christ, says
I am the woman of the great expanse of the waters, says
I am the woman of the expanse of the divine sea, says
Because I can go up to heaven, says
Because I can go over the great expanse of the waters, says
Because I can go over the expanse of the divine sea, says
Calmly, says
Without mishap, says
With sap, says
With dew, says

Saint, saint, saint, saint, saint, saint, saint, saint, saint, saint, saint,
saint, saint, saint, saint, saint, saint, ma ma ma ma ma mama
who are in the house of heaven
Christ
You Father, you Christ
Ki so so so so so so si
You my Father, you my Father
You old One
Mother Shepherdess
Mother Conception
Mother Patroness
Mother Mary of Mercy
You my Mary Conception
You my Mary Patroness
My Mother
All the saints, all the saints that exist

Mother of Mazatlan
Mother of the Sanctuary
You my Mother of Mazatlan
You my Father of the Sanctuary
My Mother of Izcatlán
Our Virgin of Baby Water
All the Virgins
All the Fathers

Father Jesus, Jesus, Jesus, Jesus
You Mother, Mother, my Mother who art in the house of heaven
You Mother who art in the house of heaven
In your beautiful world, says
In your fresh world, says
In your world of clarity, says
I am going there, says
I am arriving there, says
Because there is the path of the tracks of the palms of my hands
Because I have a tongue, because I have a mouth, says
Because I have my palms, says
Because I have my hands, says
Because I have my tongue, says
Because I am speaking poorly and humbly, says
I speak to you, you are the only one, my Mother,
    to whom I can speak with humility, you my Mother
    who art in the house of heaven, says
My Father who art in the house of heaven, says
I am going there, says
I am arriving there, says
I go there showing my Book, says
I go there demonstrating my tongue and my mouth, says
I go there pointing to the tracks of the palms of my hands, says
I am a Saint Peter woman, says
I am a Saint Peter woman, says
I am an *Ustandi* woman, says
I am a shooting star woman, says

He is the Father, says
He is the saint, says
She is the saintess, says
He is the saint
She is the saintess
It is certain, says
It is true, says
I look into the insides of things, says

I investigate, says
My clean Book, says
My well-prepared Book, says
My clean quill, says
My well-prepared quill, says
My clean staff, says
My well-prepared staff, says
It is true, says
Father, says
Cayetano García
They are important people, says
A father and a mother
Jesus, says
They are important people, great people
Respectable people, admirable people
He also lightnings forth, says
He shouts, says
Cayetano García, says
It is certain, says
It is true, says

Saint
Jesus, Jesus, Jesus
You Mother, you Mother, you Mother Shepherdess, says
Our Mother Conception
Our Mother Patroness
Our Mother Magdalene
You, doll Mother of the Rosary, says
And you, Father of the Sanctuary
Our Father
Green Father
Father of clarity
You my Mother of Mazatlan
Jesus Christ
Mother of Cuicatlan
Mother Patroness
Jesus Christ
Mother Conception
You doll Mother Guadalupe of Mexico and Oaxaca
Jesus Christ
Because it is the paper of the judge
It is the Book of the law
It is the Book of government
I know how to speak with the judge
The judge knows me

The government knows me
The law knows me
God knows me
So it is in reality
I am a justice woman
I am a law woman
It is not anything salted, it is not a lie
Jesus Christ

Ah, Jesu Kri
I am a woman who shouts
I am a woman who whistles
I am a woman who lightnings, says
Ah, Jesu Kri
Ah, Jesusi
Ah, Jesusi
Cayetano García   [*SHE CALLS HIS NAME TO GET HIS ATTENTION.*
                         "YES," HE RESPONDS, "WORK, WORK."]

Ah, Jesusi
Woman saintess, says
Ah Jesusi
      [*HERE SHE BEGINS HUMMING AND CLAPPING AND UTTERING THE*
      MEANINGLESS SYLLABLES "SO" AND "SI." THROUGHOUT THE
      ENTIRE PASSAGE THAT FOLLOWS SHE GOES ON CLAPPING
      RHYTHMICALLY IN TIME TO HER WORDS.]
hmm hmm hmm
hmm hmm hmm
hmm hmm hmm
hmm hmm hmm
hmm hmm hmm
so so so si
hmm hmm hmm
hmm hmm hmm
Woman who resounds
Woman torn up out of the ground
Woman who resounds
Woman torn up out of the ground
Woman of the principal medicinal berries
Woman of the sacred medicinal berries
Ah Jesusi
Woman who searches, says
Woman who examines by touch, says
ha ha ha
hmm hmm hmm
hmm hmm hmm

She is of one word, of one face, of one spirit, of one light, of one day
hmm hmm hmm
Cayetano García   [HE ANSWERS, "YES...."
     SHE SAYS: "ISN'T THAT HOW?" HE RESPONDS, "YES, THAT'S IT." SHE
                              SAYS: "ISN'T THAT IT? LIKE THIS. LISTEN."]
Woman who resounds
Woman torn up out of the ground
Ah Jesusi
Ah Jesusi
[IN THE BACKGROUND THE MAN LAUGHS WITH PLEASURE.]
Ah Jesusi
Ah Jesusi
Ah Jesusi
hmm hmm hmm
so so so
Justice woman
hmm hmm hmm   ["THANK YOU," SAYS THE MAN.]
Saint Peter woman
Saint Paul woman
Ah Jesusi
Book woman
Book woman
Morning Star woman
Cross Star woman
God Star woman
Ah Jesusi
Moon woman
Moon woman
Moon woman
hmm hmm hmm
hmm hmm hmm
Sap woman
Dew woman
[THE MAN URGES HER ON. "WORK, WORK," HE SAYS.]
She is a Book woman
Ah Jesusi
hmm hmm hmm
hmm hmm hmm
so so so
Lord clown woman
Clown woman beneath the sea
Clown woman   [THE OTHER WORD IS UNINTELLIGIBLE.]
Ah Jesusi
hmm hmm hmm
hmm hmm hmm

so so so
Woman who resounds
Woman torn up out of the ground
hmm hmm hmm
Because she is a Christ woman
Because she is a Christ woman
ha ha ha
so so so
so so so
so so so
Whirling woman of colors
Whirling woman of colors
Woman of the networks of light
Woman of the networks of light
Lord eagle woman
Lord eagle woman
Clock woman
Clock woman
ha ha ha
so so so
so so so
so so so
[*"THAT'S IT. WORK, WORK," EXCLAIMS THE MAN.*]
hmm hmm hmm
hmm hmm hmm
so so so
hmm hmm hmm
so so so
so so so
si si si
si si si
si si si
so sa sa
si si si
so sa sa sa
hmm hmm hmm
hmm hmm hmm
hmm hmm hmm
si so soooooooooiiiiii   *THE END OF "SO" IS DRAWN OUT INTO*
     A LONG TONE. SHE CALLS, "CAYETANO GARCÍA." "WORK, WORK,"
     HE REPLIES. SHE GOES ON HUMMING, CLAPPING FASTER AND
     FASTER. "CAYETANO GARCÍA," SHE CALLS AGAIN, IN BETWEEN
     HER HUMMING, ALMOST AS IF SHE WERE BRINGING HIM TO LIFE
     WITH HER CLAPPING. "WORK, WORK," HE SAYS, "DON'T WORRY."
     AND THE PASSAGE ENDS ON A LONG EXPIRING "SIIIIII."

You my Father
You Christ
You Christ
Along the path of the tracks of your hands, along the path of the
   tracks of your feet
Where you triumphed, Christ
Where your saliva is, where your sweat is, Christ
That is why I am searching for the path of your hands, that is why I
   am searching for the path of your feet
Where you stopped, Christ
Where you stopped, Father
Where you stopped, Old One
You are a respectable Father, a radiant Father
You are a respectable Mother, a radiant Mother
You are a green Father, a Father of clarity
You are a green Mother, a Mother of clarity
You are a budding Mother, a Mother of offshoots
You are a green Mother, a Mother of clarity

Father Jesus Christ
We go to you speaking poorly and humbly, holding out our hands to
   you in supplication
With all of the saints
With all of the saintesses
Because there are saints, because there are saintesses
Because there are saints, because there are saintesses
All the clean spirits
All the good souls
It is a clean soul
It is a well-prepared soul
It is a respectable soul
It is a radiant soul
Greenness and sap
Flower of the dew
Flower in bud
Translucent flower
Flowering flower
Respected flower
Ah Jesus Christ
It is a flower of fresh water
A flower of clear water
Fresh flower
Translucent flower
Because there are clean flowers where I am going
Because there is clean water where I am going

Clean flower, clean water
Fresh flower
Growing flower
Mine that is increasing
Green mine
Budding mine
There is no wind, there is no spit, there is no garbage, there is no
    dust
There is no whirlwind, there is no weakness in the air
That is the work of my saints, that is the work of my saintesses
Ah Jesus Christ
Ah Jesusi
Ah Jesusi
Ah Jesus Christ
He is the saint
Ah, she is the saintess
Ah, he is the saint
Ah, she is the saintess
Ah, he is spirit
Ah, he is spirit
Ah, it is light
Ah, it is dew
Ah, it is sap
Ah, it is sap
Ah, it is greenness
Jesus Christ
Jesus
Jesus Christ
There is no complaint, there is no evil, there is no disgust, there is no
    anger
It is not a matter of hexing anyone, it is not a matter of lies
It is a matter of life and well-being, of lifting up, of restoring
["THANK YOU," SAYS THE MAN.]

[HERE BEGINS THE SECOND SIDE OF THE RECORD.]

You are a man of business, a man of recompense, a man born and
    fallen into the world, a man of cacao now, you are a man of
    money, a man with a green staff, a staff of clarity, a respectable
    man, an admirable man
All the saints
All the saintesses
Lord Saint Peter
Lord Saint Paul

Pedro Mara
Pedro Martinez
With all of the saints, with all of the saintesses
As many saints as there are
Cayetano Garcia
As many saintesses as there are
I mention them all
The path of the tracks of your hands, the path of the tracks of your feet
Path of sap
Path of dew
Holy Father
In the name of the Son and the Holy Spirit

> [*"HAVE THE PEOPLE GONE TO SLEEP?" SHE ASKS CAYETANO,
> MEANING WASSON AND HIS COMPANIONS. "WHAT?" HE SAYS.
> "HAVE THE PEOPLE GONE TO SLEEP?" "NO, THEY'RE STILL
> AWAKE." "AH, THEY'RE AWAKE." SHE THEN RESUMES SINGING. IN
> THE BACKGROUND, CAYETANO ASKS THE VISITORS IN SPANISH:
> "YOU PEOPLE ARE STILL AWAKE AREN'T YOU?" "YES, OF COURSE,"
> SOMEONE ANSWERS. "AND THE OTHER ONE?" ASKS CAYETANO.*]

With all the saints, with all the saintesses, says
I will prepare as many saints and saintesses as there are
I will prepare thirteen lord eagles
I will prepare thirteen lord opossums
I will prepare thirteen   [*THE WORD IS UNINTELLIGIBLE,
                                  SHE IS SPEAKING SO FAST.*]

I will prepare thirteen Saint Peters and Saint Pauls
Pedro Mara
Pedro Martinez, says
As the Holy Trinity did and disposed
The path you God the Father followed, the path you God the son
    followed, the path the Holy Spirit followed
Thus is the path he formed and traced with his clean thought, his
    clean heart
Mountains were formed, ridges were formed
So did he think it out, he examined it, gazing into the heavens and
    into the earth, says
We are looking for the path of the tracks of your palms, the path of
    the tracks of your hands, Christ, says
You my Father
With everything in the world
Virgin Mother Shepherdess
Mother of the harvest

Rich Mother
Mother who gives well-being
Green Mother
Powerful Mother
Mother Patroness
Mother Concepción
Mother Patroness, says
Jesus
Our doll Virgin Water of the Marketplace
Our doll Virgin who holds up the earth
Designated woman, designated woman
Charcoal stencil woman, charcoal stencil woman, says
Where the Mother was born
Where the Nun was born
Where the good and clean Archbishop was born
Where the good, clean Father was born
Where the clean sea is
Holy Father
There we are arriving
If there is any evil dream or nightmare, we are going to get rid of it
In the name of the Son and the Holy Spirit
May this sickness of weakness be gotten rid of
Whether it's whirlwind, whether it's wind, whether it's whirlwind,
    whether it's wind

Holy Father, says
May the saint come, says
May the saintess come, says
May Lord Saint Peter come, says
May Lord Saint Paul come, says
May there come thirteen lord eagles, says
May there come thirteen sacred eagles, says
May there come thirteen lord whirlwinds of colors, thirteen sacred
    whirlwinds of colors, says
May there come thirteen lord networks of light, thirteen sacred
    networks of light, says
Because I have my thirteen women who dive beneath the great waters
Because I have my thirteen women who dive into the divine sea
I have my thirteen children scattered beneath the divine sea
Holy Father
With all the saints, with all the saintesses, says
As the saint wise in medicine did, says
As the saint wise in herbs did, says
Holy Father, says
You turned into medicine, says

You turned into herbs, says
You are the medic, says
When we are sick you cure us, says
You treat us with herbs, says
There is no problem, says
There is no difficulty, says
There is no resentment, there is no rancor, says
The path of struggle, says
The path of recompense, says
The path of work, says
With all the saints, as many saints and saintesses as there are
As the Father of the harvest did
Rich Father, says
Rich Father, says
I supplicated him, I begged him, searching for the medicinal flower,
    searching for the medicinal herb

so so so so so so sooo
so so so so so so sooo
ki so so so
ma ma ma mai
ma ma mai
ki ki ki ki ki ko kai
ko ka ko ko ko ko ka ki ki ki ki Kristo
siempre siempre   [ALWAYS, ALWAYS]
sien sien sien sien sien siempre
sien sien sien sien siempre
sien sien sien sien sien siempre
ai ai ai
ma ma mai
ki ki ki
ma ma mai
ma ma mai
ki so so soi
I am asking for blessing, for the blessing of life and well-being
What I am asking about is the root, the offshoots, the buds
Is all the babies and the children
It is for them that I ask blessing
Receive my words, my Mother who art in the house of heaven
Mother Shepherdess
What I ask for is goodness, Mother Shepherdess
You my Mother Shepherdess
Mother of sap
Mother of the dew
Mother of sap

Mother of breasts
Mother of the Harvest
Rich Mother
Mother who gives well-being
Mother who is present
Christ
You, Father Christ
Jesus Christ
Let us go with freshness and clarity
Let us go with light and in the light of day
I think one can live poorly, that one can live humbly, I think one can
    speak, I think one can speak, I think one can dress poorly

Mother of good palms
Mother of good hands
Your words are medicine
Your breath is remedial
That is the work of our flower with sap, our flower of the dew
Our budding children, our sprouting children
Holy Father
You my Father
And you Mother who art in the house of heaven
You, Christ, you my Father
We are going to cure, we are going to cure with herbs
That is what our budding children, our sprouting children are for,
    that is the work of our flower with sap, our flower of the dew
That is the work of the lordly one with the vibrant wings, the sacred
    one with the vibrant wings
That is what our hummingbird children are for
That is what our hummingbird is for
That is what the lordly one with the vibrant wings is for
That is what the sacred one with the vibrant wings is for
It is the same as the Mountain of Medicine, the Mountain of Herbs
Fresh herbs
Herbs of clarity
Medicinal herbs
Sacred herbs
I bring with me thirteen doctors beneath the water
I bring with me thirteen doctors beneath the sea
They are children who resound, children torn up out of the ground
Holy Father
You Saint
You Saintess
Ah Jesus Christ
You Saint   ["MASSAGE HER," SHE TELLS CAYETANO.]

Dew woman, says
Fresh woman
Woman of clarity, says
Woman who prays to heaven
Moon woman
Woman of the day, says
With all the saints, says
With all the saintesses, says
Holy Father, says
Mother Shepherdess, says
Mother Conception, says
Now that you are in your place and present
Woman of sap, woman of the dew, says
Our doll Mother of the Rosary, says
With all the saints, says
Lord of the Sanctuary, syas
Our doll Virgin of Cuicatlan, says
Our doll Virgin of Mazatlan, says
With all the saints
Lord Saint Matthew, says
You who hold the paper in your hands, you who at this moment hold the
    Book in your hands, says
With as many saints, with as many saintesses as there are saints

With as many saints, as many saintesses as there are
Now we bow ourselves down before you, speaking with humility
    beneath your shadow, speaking with clarity, says
We speak with tenderness, we speak with clarity, says
We speak with humility, we speak with offshoots, says
We speak with freshness, we speak with clarity, says
Fresh are our words, fresh our breath, fresh our saliva
Words are medicine
Medicine is the breath
Clean saliva, well-prepared saliva
Illumination of life
Illumination from on high, says
Illumination of the sap
Illumination of the dew
Holy Father
God the Father
God the Holy Spirit
Lord Saint Peter
Lord Saint Paul

Pedro Mara
Pedro Martinez, says

[*"ISN'T IT SO?" SHE ASKS CAYETANO. "IT IS," HE SAYS.*]

Our doll, our Virgin
My Father
Christ
It is your fresh flower, your flower of clarity, my Father
It is your flower of light, your flower of the day, my Father
Your poor flower, your humble flower, my Father
Why are you so poor and humble?
It is not in vain that you bowed down and inclined yourself
We, too, will go on being poor and humble
You my Father
You, Christ
You, Lord Saint Peter
Our *Ustandi* beneath the water
Our *Ustandi* beneath the sea
Our Saint Peter
Our Saint Paul
I will go on being poor, my Father
I will go on being humble, Christ
It is your blood that I want you to give me, my Father, your heart is
    what I want you to give me, give me your words, Christ, your
    saliva, my Father who art in the house of heaven
I will follow the path of your hands, I will follow the path of your
    feet, my Father
Where you stopped, my Father
Where you stopped, Christ
There I am going to leave my Saint Peter woman, my Saint Peter man
Accompany me Lord Saint Peter, Lord Saint Paul

Mother Patroness
You Heart of Jesus
Jesus Christ
I have your staff of support, your staff of the dew
I have your good and clean Bishop
I have paper
I have my Book
I am known in the house of heaven
You know me, my Mother
God, my Father, knows me
Jesus Christ you will always, always reign in the house of heaven

Jesus
Heavenly Mother
I bring your medicinal herbs in my hands, I always have your sacred herbs
    in my hands
There is no problem, there is nothing bad in what I have in my hands
It is freshness and clarity
Life and well-being
That is what I ask for, for buds and offshoots, Jesus Christ
Days of life are what I ask you for, my Father

["THANK YOU," SAYS THE MAN.]

Mother Patroness
Jesus
My Mother Mary
Jesus
I go along the path of the tracks of your palms, I go along the path of
    the tracks of your hands
I am going there, I am arriving there
If it is a matter of evil, if it is a matter of anything salted, if it is a
    matter of resentment and rancor
If it is a matter of garbage, if it is a matter of dust, if it is a matter of
    whirlwind, if it is a matter of wind
That is the work of the saint, saint, saint, saint, saint, saint, saintess
That is the work of the saint, saintess, saint, saintess, saint, saintess,
    saint, saint, saintess, saint, saintess

Ah, Maria
Ah, Jesus
Jesus, Jesus
Father
Ma ma ma Mother Mary
Jesus
Jesus Christ, Christ, Mother Mary, Jesus
You, Mother Mary
Saint, saint, saint, saint, saint
I am going to receive the bewitched spirit in the traced path, I am
    going to receive its soul, I am going to receive its destiny, I am
    going to receive the tracks of the path of its feet
Jesus
Saint, saint, saint, saint
Lord Saint Peter
Lord Saint Paul
Saint, saint, saint, saint
Christ

Mother Shepherdess
Mother Conception
Mother Patroness
Jesus Christ
You Mother Patroness
You Mother Shepherdess
Mother of the harvest
Rich Mother
Green Mother
Mother of clarity
Christ
Mother Conception
Mother Patroness
You, Jesus Christ
Mother Shepherdess
Mother Conception
Mother Patroness
Only you, Mother
Saint
You, Christ
You, Saint Child of Atocha
You, Saint Isidro
Father of the harvest
Rich Father
He is a green Father
He is a Father of clarity
Saint, saint, saint
All the saints, all the saintesses
Christ
You, Mother Conception
Mother Patroness
Our Mother Mary of Mercy
Our Mother Mary of Mercy
Saint Child of Atocha
You are the Moon
You are the Morning Star woman, the Cross Star woman, the God
   Star woman
You are the Moon
You are the Morning Star woman, the Comet Star woman, the Cross
   Star woman
All the saints
You my Father
You, Old One
You come here, you come to arrange things, my Father Christ

As you took breath, my Father
As you rested, my Father
So we are going to rest, to take breath
With freshness, with clarity, with the light of day
Christ
Mother Guadalupe
Mother Conception
Mother Patroness
Mother Nativity
Mother Conception
I am a diviner woman, says
I am a woman who searches, says
Ah, Jesus Christ
I am a lord eagle woman, says
I am an opossum woman, says
I am a woman who sees, says
Ah, Jesus Christ
I am a clean woman, says
She is a woman who resounds, says
She is a woman torn up out of the ground, says
I am an *Ustandi* woman beneath the water, says
I am an *Ustandi* woman beneath the sea, says
I am a shooting star woman, says
I am a woman laborer, says
> ["YOU SEE?" SHE SAYS TO CAYETANO. "YES," HE ANSWERS. "ISN'T
> THAT HOW?" "YES, IT IS." THEN AFTER A PAUSE SHE SAYS:
> "WHAT'S SO DIFFICULT ABOUT DOING THAT?"]

Session given by María Sabina and her niece, María Aurora, in July 1970 in the house of Celerino Cerqueda and his wife Julia of Huautla de Jiménez, Oaxaca. No foreigners were present. The chants were recorded by the host and translated from Mazatec into Spanish by Eloína Estrada de González. English version and notes by Henry Munn.

———————

She begins by reciting the Lord's Prayer in pidgin Spanish. Then:

Father Jesus Christ
God the Son and God the Holy Spirit
Lord Saint Peter
Lord Saint Paul
Saint, saint, saint
Holy saint Father, says
Father Jesus Christ, says
God and Son, says
God the Holy Spirit, says
Saint Peter
Saint Paul
Saint, saint
You are the saint, says
You are the saintess, says

Holy Father, says
Father Jesus Christ, says
God and Son, says
God the Holy Spirit, says
Saint Peter, says
Saint Paul, says
Holy Father, says
Father Jesus Christ, God and Son, says
You are the saint, saint Christ
You Father Jesus Christ, beneath your eyes, in your presence, you
    who are watching, Father
Beneath your eyes and your lips, Old One
From where you look, beneath your gaze, beneath your lips, saint Father
You are the saint and you are the saintess
Holy Father

[*THERE IS A BREAK, AN INTERVAL OF SILENCE. "WHY'S THAT?" SHE
ASKS HERSELF, SEEING SOMETHING. "WHY DOES IT SAY THAT?"
AFTER A MOMENT THE CHANT RESUMES LIKE PLAINSONG,
UNDERNEATH THE SOUND OF THE RAIN ON THE ROOF.*]

You saint Christ
Holy Father
You are the saint
You are the saintess
Holy Father
Because she is a saint woman
Because she is a woman saintess
Because she is a saint woman
Because she is a woman saintess
Holy Father
She is a saint woman
She is the little woman of the expanse of the waters
She is the woman of the expanse of the waters
She is a saint woman
She is a spirit woman
A woman of good words, of good words, good breath, and good
    saliva
She is a spirit woman
One and only Father
Father of sap
Father of the dew
He is with Saint Peter
He is with Saint Paul

You are the saint and you are the saintess
I am the woman of the great expanse of the waters
I am the woman of the expanse of the divine sea
She is the Woman of the Flowing Water
She is the Woman of the Flowing Water
She is a woman whose palms are like spoons
She is a woman with hands of measure
Holy Father
She is a woman whose palms are like spoons
She is a woman with hands of measure
Because she is the child of Christ, because she is the child of Mary
My Father
Father of sap, Father of the dew
Fresh Father, Father of clarity
Because she is a saint woman
She is a spirit woman
She is a woman of good words, of good words, good breath, good
   saliva
She is a saint woman
She is a woman saintess
She is a spirit woman
She is a Saint Peter woman
She is a Saint Paul woman
Holy Father
She is the daughter of Christ, she is the daughter of Mary
She is a saint woman
She is a woman saintess
Holy Father
Father Jesus Christ
It's that I'm a saint woman
It's that I'm a spirit woman
It's that I'm a woman of light
She is a woman of the day
She is a clean woman
She is a well-prepared woman
She is a woman of light
She is a woman of the day
Because I am a woman who lightnings
I am a woman who thunders
I am a woman who shouts
I am a woman who whistles
I am a woman who looks into the insides of things
A woman of good words, of good words, good breath, good saliva
Holy Father

She is a saint woman
She is a spirit woman
She is a woman of good words
She is an opossum woman
She is an opossum woman
She is a woman who sees
Holy Father
Saint woman
I am a spirit woman
A woman of good words, of good words, good breath, good saliva
I am the little woman of the great expanse of the waters
I am the little woman of the expanse of the divine sea
Holy Father
She is an opossum woman
She is an opossum woman
She is a woman who sees
She is a woman who sees
She is the child of Christ
That is your work, says
That is your clock, says
Father of sap
Father of the dew
That is your clock
That is your book
Holy Father
She is a little woman wise in medicine
She is a little woman wise in medicine
She is a woman wise in medicine
She is a doctor
She is the woman of the great expanse of the waters
She is the woman of the great expanse of the waters
She is the woman of the expanse of the divine sea
She is a saint woman
She is a spirit woman
She is a woman of good words
She is a woman of good words
She is a woman of good breath, good saliva
Ah, Jesus Christ
She is a saint woman
She is a spirit woman
She is the daughter of Mary, she is the daughter of Saint Joseph
She is a saint woman
She is a spirit woman
Holy Father

She is the Morning Star woman
She is the Morning Star woman
She is the Cross Star woman
Holy Father
Father Jesus Christ
I am the woman of the expanse of the waters
I am the woman of the expanse of the divine sea
Holy Father
I am a saint woman
I am a spirit woman
Father Jesus Christ
She is a saint woman
I am a woman who looks into the insides of things, a woman who
    investigates
Holy Father
I am a woman born
I am a child born
I am a woman fallen into the world
Holy Mary
Holy Father
Benito Juárez
It's true, says
It's certain, says
He's Benito Juárez, says
I am the Morning Star woman, says
I am the Cross Star woman, says
She is the Constellation of the Sandal woman, says
She is the Hook Constellation woman, says
That is your clock, says
That is your Book, says
I am the little woman of the great expanse of the waters, says
I am the woman of the expanse of the divine sea, says
Holy Father, says
She is a woman of good words, says
Of good words, good breath and good saliva, says
Father Jesus Christ
She is a saint woman, says
She is a spirit woman, says
Holy Father, says
She is a hummingbird woman, says
She is a hummingbird woman, says
She is a woman with vibrant wings, says
Holy Mary
I am a mother woman, says

She is a woman of good words, says
Of good words, good breath, good saliva, says
Holy Mary, says
She is the Morning Star woman, says
She is the Cross Star woman, says
She is a saint woman, says
Holy Father, says
Father Jesus Christ, says
God and Son, says
God the Spirit, says
Holy Father, says
Holy Father, says
She is a saint woman, says
Holy Mary, says
Holy Father, Father Jesus Christ, God and Son, God the Holy Spirit
Lord Saint Peter
Lord Saint Paul
Saint, saint, saintess
Holy Father
Saint, saintess
She is the Morning Star woman, says
She is the Cross Star woman, says
Holy Father, says
Holy Mother

[*SHE CLAPS SOFTLY IN THE BACKGROUND AS SHE SINGS.*]

She is a music woman, says
She is a trumpet woman, says
She is a woman violinist, says
It's certain, says
It's true, says
I am a woman who looks into the inside of things, says
I am a woman who investigates, says
She is a music woman, says
She is a drum woman, says
She is a woman of good words, says
Of good words, good breath, says
I am a little woman born, says
I am a little woman fallen into the world, says
Holy Father, says
I am the child of Christ, says
I am the child of Mary, says
Holy Father, says

I am a little woman who resounds, says
I am a little woman torn up out of the ground, says
It's certain, says
It's true, says
I am a woman who looks into the insides of things, says
I am a woman who investigates, says
I am a little music woman, says
I am a little drum woman, says
Holy Father, says
She is a saint woman, says
She is a spirit woman, says
Spirit Woman
Woman of words
Saint woman
Saint woman
Holy Father
Father Jesus Christ, God and Son, the Holy Spirit
Clean woman
Well-prepared woman
Holy Father
Spirit woman
Woman of good words
Holy Father
Saint woman
Woman saintess
Saint woman
Woman who looks into the insides of things
I am the daughter of Mary
I am the child of Saint Joseph
I am a woman of good words
A woman of good words
A woman of good words
Holy Father
I am the child of Christ
I am the child of Mary
Holy Father
It's certain, says
It's true, says
Holy Mary
Because we are the children of Mary
Because we are the children of Saint Joseph
Holy Father
Father Jesus Christ
Saint woman

Spirit woman
Holy Father

> [ASIDE TO HER NIECE: "HOW DO YOU FEEL? ARE YOU SEEING
> WELL?" HER NIECE REPLIES: "YES, I'M SEEING FINE.'
> MARIA SABINA: "SHALL WE GO ON LIKE THIS?" NIECE: "WHY
> NOT?" MARIA SABINA: "THAT'S WHAT I'M ASKING YOU. SHALL
> WE CONTINUE LIKE THIS?" NIECE: "YES IN THE SAME WAY."]

The path of your business, says
The path of your goods, says
Holy Father, says
Father Jesus Christ, says
I am the little woman of the great expanse of the waters, says
I am the little woman of the great expanse of the waters, says
I am a little opossum woman, says
Holy Father
I am the child of Christ, the child of Mary, the child of Saint Joseph
Morning Star woman, says
Cross Star woman, says
Father, says
Woman of the great Sun Stone, says
Saint, says
Saint woman, says
Woman saintess, says
Holy Father, says
Father Jesus Christ, says
God and Son, says
God the Spirit, says
Because he is the saint, says
Thus did I come forth important
Thus did I come forth sacred
I came forth with sap
I came forth with the dew
Your Book, my Father, says
Your Book, my Father, says
Clown woman beneath the water, says
Clown woman beneath the sea, says
Because I am the child of Christ, says
Because I am the child of Mary, says
Because I am the child of Saint Joseph, says
Father, says
She is a woman of good words, says
She is a woman of good breath, says

Good are her words, good is her breath, says
The path of your feet, the path of your hands, says
Holy Father, says
Good are her words and breath, says
Child of Mary
Child of Saint Joseph
Holy Father
Child of Christ, says
Child of Mary, says
Woman of the Flowing Water, says
Woman of the great Sun Stone, says
Woman of important origin, says
It's true, says
We are going to see what's certain, what's true
Holy Father
Because I am the child of Mary, says
The child of Saint Joseph, says
I am the Morning Star woman, says
Cross Star woman, says
Constellation of the Sandal Woman
Hook Constellation woman
Clean woman, says
Well-prepared woman, says
That is your paper, says
That is your Book, says
One and only true Father, says
Reasonable Father, says
Father of the dew, says
Father of freshness, says
Father of clarity, says
Respectable Father, says
Father of good days, says
Holy Father
Spirit woman
I am a woman of good words, says
My words are good, says
I am a good person, says
I love my children, says
I love my people, says
Clean Christians, says
And my clients, says
It's true, says
It's certain, says
Benito Juarez, says

Our Mother Guadalupe, says
Our beautiful Mother Guadalupe, says
Mother Magdalene, says
Child of Christ, says
Child of Mary, says
Child of Saint Joseph, says
It's true, says
Moon woman, says
Star woman, says
Constellation of the Sandal Woman, says
Hook Constellation woman, says
Holy Father
Child of Christ
Child of Mary
I am a saint woman, says
I am a music woman, says
I am a drum woman, says
I am a woman born, says
I am a woman fallen into the world, says
That is your Book, says
That is your Book, says
Book of sap, says
Book of dew, says
Fresh Book, says
Book of clarity, says
Woman of sap, says
Lord of good will, says
Father of the dew, says
Father of the harvest, says
Rich Father, says
Green Father, says
All powerful Father, says
God the Son and Holy Spirit
There is no problem
Her children are crying, her babies are crying, says
I am a woman who looks into the insides of things and investigates,
    says
I am a woman of sap, says
I am a woman of the dew, says
I am a green woman, says
I am a woman of clarity, says
There is nobody who frightens us, says
There is nobody hovering around, says
I am a woman who cleans, says

That is your Book, says
That is your paper and your Book, says
One and only Father, says
Reasonable Father, says
Father of the dew, says
Fresh Father, says
Father of clarity, says
Holy Father
Beneath the gaze of our Father, says
Beneath the gaze of the person with the staff and the baton of
   authority, says
Yes it's certain, says
It's true, says
I am a woman who looks into the insides of things and investigates,
   says
The tracks of his hands and his feet, says
The path of sap and dew
The path of freshness and clarity
The path of goodness and the day
I am the one who examines the tracks of the feet and the hands, says
Holy Father, says
It is nothing bad, says
It is with good will, says
It is only in order to enliven and renew life
These are my children, says
These are my babies, says
They are my offshoots, says
My buds, says
I am only asking, examining, says
About his business as well
I begin in the depths of the water
I begin where the primordial sounds forth, where the sacred sounds
   forth
I feel very good, says
Healthy
My race is very good, says
What is of value is the ceremony, what is of value is gold, says
Father, says
Saint, says
Saintess, says
Saintess, says
I am a woman who looks into the insides of things and investigates,
   says
The tracks of the feet, says

The path of sap and dew, says
In this way it is taught to the children, says
In this way it is taught to our people, says
Where their enjoyment is, their well-being, says
It is health and life, says
We don't want anyone to break our bond and our root, says
Root of sap and of dew, says
Root of greeness and clarity, says

María Aurora:
    I am the woman of the shade, says
    Man, Lord of the door and the dooryard, says
    Man, Lord of the door and the dooryard, says
    Man of life and health, says
    She is a great woman of the shade, says
    A woman of the house
    A woman of the kitchen
    There is no resentment nor rancor, says
    There is no garbage, says
    There is no whirlwind, says
    There is no bad air, says
    Woman of the shade, woman of the doors, says
    Woman of the dooryard, says
    He is a man, Lord of the doors, says
    A good man, the Lord of the dooryard, says
    Woman of the house, says
    Woman of the shade, says
    Woman who dances, says
    Woman who shakes things up, says
    Bless her, says
    Against evil whirlwinds and bad air, says
    You are her voice and her breath, says
    Around her hearth is where she plays music and resounds, says
    Shouts and whistles, says
    She is the mistress of the household, says
    The mistress of the shade, says
    Her voice and her breath are good, says
    There is no problem nor any difficulty, says
    There is no garbage, there is no dust, says
    Around her fire and the three stones of her hearth
    Lady mistress of the shade and of the house, says
    Man of a good house and of good shade, says
    The water and the tortillas he provides are good, says

María Sabina:
    Yes, he is a good man, says

María Aurora:
    Good life and good food, says
    He is a man of laughter and good words, says
    She is a good woman, a woman of words, says
    There are no problems, says
    Her words and her breath are good, says
    She supports poverty, says
    The path of life and of well-being, says
    Their babies and their children, too, says

María Sabina:
    Their babies and their children, too, says

María Aurora:
    Their root and their offspring, too, says
    The path of business and well-being, says
    It is of sap and dew, says
    It is of freshness and clarity, says
    Here are herbs with berries, good herbs, fresh herbs, says
    Whether it be a whirlwind of garbage or dust, says
    Goddess of the shade, says
    Goddess of the fire and the house, says,
    If it is a whirlwind, if it is wind in the path, says
    If it is garbage in the path, says
    If it is the garbage of envy, says
    She is the one who plays music, the one who resounds, says
    God of the shade, says
    God of the house, says
    God of the dooryard, says
    The path of stations, says
    The path of well-being, says
    It is what I am looking into and investigating, says
    Whether there is any garbage
    There is neither garbage nor dust, says
    There is no sickness, no despair, says
    Their babies and their children also, says
    Those are my roots and offspring, says
    They are offspring
    They are life and well-being, says
    They are freshness and tenderness, says
    Here are potions of medicinal herbs, says

Woman wise in medicine, woman wise in herbs, says
Doctor woman of potions, doctor woman of importance, says
We're going to see if it's true, says
I am the woman who examines the tracks of their feet and their
    hands, says
The path of their feet and their nails, says
And also their children and babies, says
Their roots and their offspring, says
Life and well-being, says
There are no problems nor any difficulties, says
The tracks of their steps, of their life
How did the trees, the mountains, and the rocks come to be?
The rocks and the gullies?
We are going to look into it and ask about it
He just had patience and hope

María Sabina:
He just waited and looked into it
Woman who sees
Whirling woman of colors
Woman of clarity
Woman who goes through the waters
Father of well-being and richness, says
Father of freshness and sap, says
Holy Father
I am the Morning Star woman
I am the Cross Star woman, says
That is your paper, says
That is your Book, says
There is only one true God the Father
Father of sap and dew, says
Father of freshness and tenderness, says
Holy Father, says
Woman of the great ravine
Waterfall woman
Morning Star woman, says
Cross Star woman, says
Holy Father, says
Saint woman, says
Woman saintess, says
Spirit woman, says
Holy Father, says
Spirit woman, says
Woman of the shade, says

Woman of the day, says
Woman who goes through the water
Woman who travels on the heights
Woman who sounds forth with grandiloquence
Woman who sounds forth with divinity
Woman of superior reason, says
That is your paper
That is your Book
There is only one true God
We're going to see whether it's true, says
Whirling woman of colors, says
Woman on the sea, says
Good is her voice, her breath, her words, says
Holy Father
I am the Cross Star woman, says
The Constellation of the Sandal woman, says
The Hook Constellation woman, says
That is your work, says
That is your clock, says
That is your radiance, says
Woman of the expanse of the waters says
Angel woman, says
Holy Father, says
Woman of music, says
Holy Father
Brilliant Star woman, says
Cross Star woman, says
Clean woman, says
Well-prepared woman, says
We are going to demonstrate our courage, our character, says
The Judge knows me, the Government knows me, says
God knows me, says
Benito Juárez, says
Mother Guadalupe, says
Mother Magdalene, says
I am a saint woman, says
I am a spirit woman, says
Saint woman, says
Spirit woman, says
Woman of truth, says
Woman of the day, says
Ah, Jesus
It's true what I say
We're going to pay with gold, says

With a mass, says
It's true, we're going to make sure, says
I am a woman of letters, says
I am a Book woman, says
Nobody can close my Book, says
Nobody can take my Book away from me, says
My Book encountered beneath the water, says
My Book of prayers
Big star woman, says
Cross Star woman, says
I am a woman of goodwill, says
I am a woman with a good heart, says
That is your saliva, Holy Father, says
Spirit woman, says
Woman of the day, says
Holy Father, says
We're going to see whether it's true, says
I am the one who looks into the insides of things, who plays
    music and sounds forth, says
I am she who shouts and whistles, says
We're going to see the truth
I am the Morning Star woman
I am the woman of words, of good words, good breath, and
    good saliva, says
Because I am the child of Mary, says
The child of Saint Joseph, says
We are going to look into things in order to know the truth,
    says
Holy Mary, says
Saint woman, says
Spirit woman, says
Woman of good words, of good breath, says
Child of Mary, says
Child of Saint Joseph, says
Yes it's true, says
Woman of the big stars, says
Cross Star woman, says
Launch woman, says
Shooting star woman, says
Moon woman, says
Star woman, says
Yes it's true, says

María Aurora:
>   Let us go calmly, without mishap, says
>   According to the law of God, says
>   Like our Father came, says
>   Like our Mother came, says

María Sabina:
>   When they were united

María Aurora:
>   They were created, they were formed with wisdom

María Sabina:
>   There is no resentment nor any rancor

María Aurora:
>   There is no resentment nor any rancor, says
>   As he came forth important, as he came forth sacred, says
>   From out of the night and the darkness, says
>   Then the trees grew; the mountains and their ridges were
>   formed, says
>   He only thought about it and looked into it to the bottom, says
>   Then the plains and the hollows hardened, says
>   That is what we are going to do, too, says
>   And that is what our children have to do, says
>   That is how our offspring should do, our buds, says
>   As the mountains and ridges were formed, says
>   As the trees grew, as the plains hardened, says
>   It's certain, says
>   It's true, says
>   There is goodness, says
>   There is well-being, says

[HERE AND THROUGHOUT THIS PASSAGE, MARIA SABINA BEGINS TO
SAY THE NAME OF HER NEICE AT INTERVALS AS IF SHE WERE CALLING
HER SPIRIT: "MARIA AURORA, MARIA AURORA."]
>   It is life and well-being, says

María Sabina:
>   María Aurora

María Aurora:
>   It is dew and sap, says
>   There is no resentment, says
>   There is no rancor, says

María Sabina:
> María Aurora

María Aurora:
> It is recompense, says

María Sabina
> María Aurora

María Aurora:
> It is well-being, says
> She is the woman of the house, the woman of the shade, says
> She is the woman of the doorway, the woman of the dooryard,
>   says
> There is no resentment, says
> There is no rancor, says
> We have medicine water here, says
> We have herb water here, says
> We have health here, says
> We have well-being, says
> He only thought about it and looked into it to the bottom, says
> A new year, a new day
> As the night came, as the darkness came, says
> Trees were born, rocks were born, says
> If anyone is coming behind us, if anyone is pursuing us, says
[MARIA SABINA ASSENTS, "YES," IN THE BACKGROUND.]
> If anyone is criticizing us, says
> If anyone is watching us, says
> We're not trying to do harm to anybody, says
> We're not doing anything evil, says
> There is no resentment, says
> There is no rancor, says
> It is a matter of goodness, says
> It is a matter of well-being, says

María Sabina:
> María Aurora

María Aurora:
> With sap, says
> With dew, says
> If anybody thinks what we're doing is evil, says
> If anybody thinks it has to do with enmity, says
> It's only a matter of understanding, says

It's a matter of well-being, says
It's life and well-being, says

María Sabina:
    The path of the tracks of your hands and the path of the tracks
        of your feet, says

María Aurora:
    It's sap and dew, says
    If anyone is pursuing us, says
    If anyone is in back of us, says
    If anyone is critizing us, says
    If anyone is spying on us, says
    It's certain, says
    It's true, says
    It's certain, says
    It's true, says
    We're going to play music, says
    We're going to thunder, says
    That is the work of Saint Peter beneath the water, says
    Saint Peter beneath the sea, says
    We're going to shout, says
    We're going to whistle, says
    Along the path of your hands, along the path of your wrists, says
    Along the path of life, the path of well-being, says
    There is no problem, says
    There is no difficulty, says

María Sabina:
    We're not trying to do harm to anybody

María Aurora:
    Clean Christian, says
    Well-prepared Christian, says

María Sabina:
    María Aurora

María Aurora:
    There is no resentment, says
    There is no difficulty, says
    It's a matter of life and well-being, says
    With sap and dew, says

María Sabina:

> The path of the tracks of the hands, the path of the tracks of the
> heels, the path of the tracks of the hands, the path of the tracks
> of the feet

María Aurora:

> If anybody wants to hex us, says
> If anybody wants to tell lies, says
> It will become garbage, it will becoame dust, says
> It will become whirlwind, it will become wind, says
> It's certain, says
> It's true, says
> It's not a matter of evil, says
> It's not a matter of doing harm, says
> It's only a matter of well-being and life, says
> With sap, with dew, says

María Sabina:

> I am a sap woman, a dew woman, says
> I am a fresh woman, a woman of clarity, says
> I am a woman of light, a woman of the day, says
> I am a woman who looks into the insides of things, says
> I am a woman who investigates, says
> Holy Father, says
> Holy Father, says
> I am a Saint Peter woman, says
> I am a Saint Paul woman, says
> I am a saint woman, says
> I am a spirit woman, says
> A woman of good words, of good words, good breath and good
>   saliva, says
> It's certain, says
> It's true, says
> That is your clock, says
> That is your communion wafer, says
> That is your number, says
> One and only Father
> Father of sap, Father of the dew, says
> Father of freshness, Father of clarity, says
> Holy Father, says
> I am the child of Mary, the child of Saint Joseph, says
> I am the child of the Candelaria, says
> It is certain, says
> It is true, says

I look into the insides of things, says
I investigate, says
Holy Father, says
Holy Father, says
I am the woman of the great expanse of the waters, says
I am the woman of the expanse of the divine sea, says
I am a launch woman, says
I am the Cross Star woman, says
I am the Constellation of the Sandal woman, the Hook
    Constellation woman, says

Holy Mother, says
Flower of sap, flower of the dew, says
I am the little lordly one with the vibrant wings, says
I am the little sacred one with the vibrant wings, says
I only look into the interior of my Christian and investigate, says
Clean Christian, says
Well-prepared Christian, says
Holy Father, says
I am a mother woman, says
She is a mother woman beneath the water, says
She is a woman of good words, says
She is a music woman, says
She is a woman violinist, says
I am the child of Christ, says
I am the child of Mary, says
Holy Father, says
Father Jesus Christ, says
She is a saint woman, says
She is a spirit woman, says
Holy Father, says
I am a mother woman, says
I am a woman wise in medicine, says
I am a mother woman, says
I am a woman wise in medicine, says
I am a woman wise in words beneath the water, says
I am a woman wise in words beneath the sea, says
Holy Mother, says
I am the child of Mary, says
I am the child of Saint Joseph, says
I am the child of the Candelaria, says
You my Father
Awesome Father, Father of clarity, says
Father who grew, Father who rose up, says

Father of sap, Father of dew, says
Holy Mother, says
[ASIDE TO HER NIECE: "DO WE STILL HAVE A LONG WAYS TO GO?"]

María Aurora:
    As he presented himself with clarity and rectitutde beneath the eyes
      of our Father, beneath the eyes of our Mother

María Sabina:
    Isn't that how it is?

María Aurora:
    As he came forth Lord, as he came forth sacred
    Like Saint Peter and Saint Paul
    They are the ones who have powerful eyes, powerful is their will,
      powerful their faces, powerful their day

The two women together:
    As he made it, as he designed it, as he found it
    As he made it, as he designed it

María Aurora:
    Saint Peter, Saint Paul
    As he appeared in the night, in the darkness, above the great
      expanse of the waters, above the expanse of the divine sea; He
      came forth Lord, he came forth sacred
    Saint Peter, he is the one with powerful eyes, powerful is his
      will, powerful his face, powerful his day
    He is the one whose will shines, he is the one who thunders, he
      is the one who sounds forth
    Saint Peter, Saint Paul
    Woman of principal medicinal berries, woman of sacred
      medicinal berries
    Woman of principal medicinal berries, woman of sacred
      medicinal berries
    There are fifty-three, fifty-three clean and well-prepared saints
    Spirit woman
    Woman who looks into the insides of things, who investigates
    Woman who thunders, woman who sounds forth
    Calmly and without mishap
    Calmly and without mishap
    With sap, with dew
    Spirit woman beneath the water, spirit woman beneath the sea
    We have life and well-being

There are herbs with berries, sacred herbs
With Saint Peter, says
With Saint Paul, says
He is the one who arranges things and points out the path of the
    palms, the path of the hands, the path of the heels, the path of
    the feet, says
As he did in the night, as he did in the darkness
Saint Peter, Saint Paul
He is the one whose gaze is powerful, powerful in his will,
    powerful his face, powerful his day
Father Lord Saint Michael
Father Lord Santiago

María Sabina:
Who can frighten him?

María Aurora:
Father Lord Saint Michael
Father Lord Santiago
They are the ones who have powerful eyes powerful wills,
    powerful faces, powerful days
He is the one whose gaze is powerful, powerful is his will
He is the one who thunders, he is the one who sounds forth, he
    is the one who shouts, he is the one who whistles
With the God of the house, with the God of the shade, with the God
    of the door, with the God of the dooryard
Father Lord Saint Michael
Father Lord Santiago
They are the ones whose presences are powerful, powerful is
    their day
They are the ones who appeared and brought the keys and brought
    everything
They bring with them *Gustalinia* beneath the water, *Gustalinia*
    beneath the sea
They are the ones who shouted and whistled
They formed thunder, they formed storms
They are the ones whose eyes shine, their will shines, their faces
    shine, they day shines
Saint Peter, Saint Paul
With the God of the house, with the God of the shade, with the
    God of the door, with the God of the dooryard

María Sabina:
    Lord Saint Peter
    Lord Saint Paul
    I am a spirit woman, says
    I am a woman of light, says
    I am a woman of the day, says
    My father, says
    I am an *Ustandi* woman beneath the water, says
    I am an *Ustandi* woman beneath the sea, says
    I am a little Saint Peter woman, says
    I am a little Saint Paul woman, says
    I am the child of Christ, says
    I am the child of Mary, says
    I am a little Lord eagle woman, says
    I am a little opossum woman, says
    I am a little woman who sees, says
    That is your clock, my Father, says
    That is your work, says
    That is your paper, says
    I am the little woman of the great expanse of the waters, says
    I am the little woman of the expanse of the divine sea, says
    Holy Father, says

    I am the child of Christ, says
    I am the child of Mary, says
    The child of Saint Joseph, says
    Our Father of sap, our Father of dew, says
    Our fresh Father, our Father of clarity, says
    I am a little launch woman, says
    I am a little shooting star woman,says
    I am the Morning Star woman, says
    I am a comet woman, says
    I am a woman who goes through the water, says
    I am a woman who goes through the sea, says
    I am the great Woman of the Flowing Water, says
    I am the sacred Woman of the Flowing Water, says
    Where our people are, our Principal Ones, our high class people,
        says
    Our people of reason, says
    Holy Father, says
    Our Archbishop of Clean Water, says
    Our Nun of Clean Water, says
    Our Member of the Sisterhood of Clean Water, says
    Where you were strewn, Sainted Pope, says

All powerful, one and only Father, says
Father of sap and dew, says
I'm seeing you, here I have your paper, says
I have your number, says
Valuable number, says
Pound of value, says
I bring with me my Lord opossum, my sacred opossum, says
I bring with me my Lord eagle, my sacred eagle, says
I bring with me my Lord hawk, says
Ah Jesus Christ, says
Lord Patron Saint John, says
It's true, says
He is Lord Santiago, says
Yes, Jesus Christ, says
He is Lord Saint Andrew, says
Ah Jesus Christ, says
I am a woman who looks into the insides of things, says
A woman who investigates, says
Our Father scribe, says
He who art in the house of heaven, says
Beneath the eyes of glory, says
I am the little woman of the great expanse of the waters, says
I am the little woman of the expanse of the divine sea, says
Our Benito Juárez, says
Mother Guadalupe, says
Mother Magdalene, says
Heart of Jesus, says
Yes, it's certain, says
It's true, says
I am a little woman who goes through the water, says
I am a little woman who goes through the water, says
I am a little woman who goes through the sea, says
I am a little woman who sounds forth with grandiloquence, says
I am a little woman who sounds forth with divinity, says
It's certain, says
It's true, says
I am a little Saint Peter woman, says
I am a little Saint Paul woman, says
I am the *Ustandi* woman of sap, says
I am the *Ustandi* woman of dew, says
She is an *Ustandi* woman beneath the sea, says
I am a shooting star woman, says
I am a music woman, says
I am a drum woman, says

I am a woman violinist, says
Because I am a woman of letters, says
Because I am a Book woman, says
That is your Book, says
Where our Principal Ones are, says
Our people of reason, says
Beer of value, says
Beer, says
My one and only Father, says
Beer that my friends drink, says
Beer that the Archbishop drinks, says
And my Nun also, says
My member of the Sisterhood, says
Archbishop of Clean Water, says
The sainted Pope, says
There I am, says
That is your paper, says
That is your Book, says
Because we are the children of God, says
We are the children of Christ, says
It's certain, says
It's true, says
One and only Father, says
Dear Old One, says
We are not going to pay any attention to ailments of weakness,
      says
With my Lord eagle, says
With my opossum, says
I only look into the insides of my Christians and examine them,
      says
I bring my light, says
Ah, Jesus Christ, says
With my shooting stars, says
With my whirlwinds of colors, says
Holy Father, says
From where the Father came, from where the Mother came
Where the clean Book is, the good Book
I'm going to show you where the Moon comes out, where the
Morning Star comes out, where our God the Father comes out

Father Christ, Holy Trinity, Saint Peter and Saint Paul
I am a spirit woman, says
A woman of good words, says
My words are good, my breath is good, says

In your hands is your work, one and only Father, says
That is your clock, says
That is your lord eagle, says
That is your lord hawk, says
Lord Patron Saint John, says
Lord Saint Michael Archangel, says
Lord Santiago, says
You go mounted on your horse, says
Holy Father, says
You go mounted on your horse, Lord Santiago, says
My heart is very content, says

[SHE CLAPS WITH HAPPINESS.]

Our doll Mother Magdalene, says
Our Mother Patroness, says
Our doll Mother Mary Conception, says
It's certain, says
It's true, says
I am a woman who divines what exists, says
I am a Saint Peter woman, says
Because I am a woman of good words, says
Of good words and good breath, says
I am the woman of the great expanse of the waters, says
Because I am a launch woman, says
Because I am a launch woman, says
I am the Morning Star woman, says
Where the Morning Star came out, says
Where the Comet appeared, says
Holy Father, says
Our fresh Father, our Father of clarity, says
Our Father of sap, our Father of the day, says
Holy Father, says
I am going to lightning, says
I am going to shout, says
I am going to whistle, says
I am going to look into the insides of things says
I am going to examine, says
My clean Christian, says
My well-prepared Christian, says
I am a woman wise in words beneath the water, says
I am a woman wise in words beneath the sea, says
Holy Father, says
Our good and clean Archbishops are present, says
Our members of the Sisterhood, says
Our good and clean Nuns, says

The sainted Pope is here, says
All of the Principal Ones are here, says
Our people of reason, says
I drink beer, says
Holy Father, says
What is of value is the head, says
What is of value is gold, says
Our head, says
Holy Father, says
It's certain, says
I am the woman of the great rain, says
I am the woman of the sacred rain, says
I am the Woman of the Flowing Water, says
I am the little whirling woman of colors beneath the water, says
I am the little whirling woman of colors beneath the sea, says
It's certain, says
I am a woman who goes through the water, says
Holy Father, says
I am a woman who goes through the water, says
I am a woman of good words, says
Good are my words, good my breath, good my saliva, says
Holy Mother, says
I am a mother woman, says
I am a mother woman beneath the water, says
I am a woman general, says
I am a woman corporal, says
Holy Father, says
I am a woman corporal, says
I am a lawyer woman, says
A woman of transactions, says
I'm not afraid, says
I'm going to demonstrate my courage, says
Benito Juárez, says
Our Mother Guadalupe, says
Our Mother Magdalene, says
Our Holy Father, says
I am a woman general, says
I am a sergeant woman, says
I am a corporal woman, says
I am a woman commander, says
I am a lawyer woman, says
I am a woman of transactions, says
It comes from the great expanse of the waters, from the expanse of
    the divine sea, says

I go up to heaven, says
Beneath the gaze of your glory, says
There is your paper and your Book, says
That is the best quill, says
that is the best Book, says
I am the little woman of the great expanse of the waters, says
I am the little woman of the expanse of the divine sea, says
[. . .]
Ah Jesus Christ, says
I am a woman who goes through the water, says
I am a woman who sounds forth with grandiloquence, says
I am a woman who sounds forth with divinity, says
Where the shooting stars are showering, where the flocks of Lord
   eagles are, the sacred eagles, says
I am an opossum woman, says
That is your opossum, says
One and only Father, says
It is your Book, says
There is no resentement nor rancor, says
It is what is and has been made, says
It's marvellous what one sees, says
We are going to demonstrate our courage, says
Holy Father, says
Holy Mother, says
I come with my Mother, says
I come with my Mother, says
I come with my doctor, says
I am a woman wise in words beneath the water, says
I am a woman who goes through the water, says
She is the little mistress of the cumulus clouds, says
She is the little woman of the cumulus clouds, says
[. . .]
Holy Father, says
She is a woman beside the water, says
Lord of the cumulous clouds, says
Father of the dew, says
Our Father of the harvest and of richness, says
Our Father of greenness and clarity, says
Holy Father, says
My words reach there, says
My breath and my saliva reach there, says
I am recognized there as a woman of God, says
I am the child of Christ, says
I am the child of Mary, says

I am the child of Saint Joseph, says
Holy Father, says
I am the Morning Star woman, says
I am the Cross Star woman, says
Because she is the Constellation of the Sandal woman, says
Because she is the Hook Constellation woman, says
Because I am the Moon woman, says
I am a Saint Anthony of Atocha woman, says
Holy Father, says
We are going to greet our Lord Tocosho, says
It's certain, says
It's true, says

I am a womanwise in words beneath the water, says
I am the child of Christ, says
I am an opposum woman, says
I am a woman who sees, says
I am a whirling woman of colors, says
Holy Father, says
Our children who go through the water, says
Our children who go through the sea, says
Our clean children, says
Our well-prepared children, says
I am a little woman of the networks of light, says
I am a little woman of the networks of light, says
I am a little whirling woman of colors, says
I am a little Lord eagle woman, says
I am a little opossum woman, says
Holy Father, says
We are demonstrating our courage
Benito Juárez, says
Mother Guadalupe, says
Mother Magdalene, says
Holy Father, says
I am the child of Christ, says
I am the child of Mary, says
I am the child of Saint Joseph, says
Heart of Jesus, says
May he live! says
Mother Patroness, says
Doll Virgin Patroness, says
Here I have your staff, says
Here I have your baton of authority, says
Holy Father, says

I am a woman of offshoots, a woman of buds, says
I am seeing God, says
I am seeing the saints, says
Holy Mother, says
Woman of good words, says
Good are my words, good my breath, says
Holy Father, says
Nobody is sick, says
There is nothing sad, says
It's necessary to help the poor and humble on their way, says
I receive them, says; I make the sign of the cross over them, says;
    and I pray, says
Inform me about them, I ask truth for the helpless and the poor
Holy Father, says
I'm not envious, I have no rancor, says
I don't speak bad words, I ask you for the truth, one and only
    Father, says
There is no resentment, says
There is no rancor, says
Because I don't have bad words, says
Because I'm asking you truly, one and only Father, says
I ask you for your communion wafer, one and only Father, says
I ask you for your number, you who place and arrange every-
    thing, one and only Father, says
As you rested and took breath, I took rest and take breath, one
    and only Father
Here I am asking you for your communion wafer
[SHE FALLS SILENT WITH A SIGH.]

María Aurora:
    Let us go with sap, with dew, says
    Let us go with freshness, with clarity, says
    As Mary did, says
    As Saint Joseph did, says
    As our Magdalene did, says
    Like her who appeared humble and poor, says
    I speak with freshnes and clarity,says
    We have well-being says
    We have recompense, says
    I am going to speak with humility, I am going to speak with
        simplicity, says
    I will speak through space in the light of day, says
    She received the benediction, says
    She was blessed, says

she is a saint woman, says
She is a woman saintess, says
It's certain, says
It's true, says
She implored in supplication, she implored publicly, says
She implored with humility, she implored with simplicity, says
Kneeling on her knees, with knees for hands, with knees for feet, says
Knees of life, knees of well-being, says
Knees of sap, knees of dew, says
It's certain, says
I only look into the insides of things and investigate, says
Garbage came, says
Wind and whirlwind came, that is what befell his body, says
We can turn it into dust, we can destroy it, says
We also can shout and whistle, says
We are going to make dust out of it and destroy it, says
It is whirlwind and wind, says
It is sickness of weakness, of collapse? says

María Sabina:
     What is it, garbage or dust?

María Aurora:
     What befell his body? says
     It's the house and the shade, says
     It's the door, it's the dooryard, says

     The path of struggle, the path of recompense, says
     Garbage came, says
     Whirlwind came, says
     Wind came, says
     Is it garbage of the path? says
     Is it garbage of witchcraft? says
     I'm going to shout, says
     I'm going to whistle, says
     He's going to be cured, he's going to be cured with herbs, says
     There are herbs with berries, there are sacred herbs, says
     He's going to get well, says
     He's going to be cured with herbal treatment, says
     Our babies and children also, says
     Our offshoots and buds, says
     I only look into the insides of things and investigate, says
     I only feel with my hands the pulse of the wrists, says
     There is medicine water, says

There is herb water, says
Herbs with berries, sacred herbs, says
Now we will see the truth, says
Now I am going to thunder, says
I am going to play music, says
Along the path of the pulse of the wrists, along the path of the
    palms of the hands, says
Along the path of the pulse of the ankles, says
We are going to thunder, says
We are going to play music, says
My children also, says
My babies also, says
My offshoots, says
My buds, says
God of our house, says
God of our shade, says
God of our door, says
God of our dooryard, says
It's true, says
If there is anybody who is criticizing us, says
If there is anybody who is watching us, says
I'm going to turn it into dust, says
I'm going to destroy it, says
I shout and I whistle, says
Goddess of the house, says
Goddess of our shade, says
Goddess of our door, says
Goddess of our dooryard, says
Who is watching us?
Who is criticizing us? says
There is no rancor, says
There is no resentment, says
Beneath your gaze, says
In your presence, says
Father in glory, says
I will go on living humbly, says
I will go on living poorly, says
Where did the whirlwind come from? says
Where did the wind come from? says
It is that that befell him, says
That that befell our house, our shade, our door, our dooryard, says
I'm going to shout, says
I'm going to whistle, says
I'm going to thunder, says

I'm going to play music, says
He is a man of good words, says
He is a man of good breath, good saliva, says
There isn't any resentment, says
There isn't any rancor, says
He is a man of good breath and good saliva, says
A man of the house, a man of the shade, says
A man of the door, a man of the dooryard, says
He is a man who thunders and plays music, says
He is a man of good words and good breath, says
It is the path of business, it is the path of recompense, says

María Sabina:
Good words, woman! Good words!

María Aurora:
It is the path of life, it is the path of well-being, says
It is the path of the sun, it is the path of the household, says
Goddess of our house, says
Goddess of our shade, says
Our tortillas and our water are good, says
Our fire and our hearth are good, says
There is no whirlwind, says
There is no dust, says
There is no whirlwind nor evil wind, says
Our babies also, says
Our children also, says
It's certain, says
It's true, says
Our tortillas and water are good, says
We have good food and good drink, says
It is life and well-being, says

María Sabina:
They're good people.

María Aurora:
With sap and with dew, says
With freshness and with clarity, says
It is only whirlwind, garbage and dust, says
It is only whirlwind and wind, says
That is why she thunders, says
Why she plays music, says
That is why she shouts, says
That is why she whistles, says

María Sabina:
> Woman of the great expanse of the waters, woman of the
> expanse of the divine sea

María Aurora
> It's certain, says
> It's true, says
> I am the woman of the principal medicinal berries, says
> I am the woman of the sacred medicinal berries, says
> I am a woman wise in words beneath the water, says
> I am a woman wise in words beneath the sea, says
> I will look into the insides of things and investigate, says
> I will play music and thunder, says

María Sabina:
> María Aurora

María Aurora:
> With the God of our house, says
> With the God of our shade, says

María Sabina:
> María Aurora

María Aurora:
> With the God of our door, says
> With the God of our dooryard, says

María Sabina:
> María Aurora

María Aurora:
> I will shout and whistle, says
> I will thunder and play music, says
> The path of business, the path of recompense, says
> The path of life, the path of well-being, says

María Sabina:
> María Aurora

María Aurora:
> Year of life, year of well-being, says
> Year of sap, year of dew, says

María Sabina:
[*IN THE BACKGROUND*]
> The path of the hands, the path of the heels,
> The path of the hands, the path of the feet

María Aurora:
> It is life and well-being, says
> It is sap, it is dew, says

María Sabina:
IN THE BACKGROUND
> The path of the tracks of the hands, the path of the tracks of the
>   feet

María Aurora:
> It's certain, says
> It's true, says
> We are going to continue, says
> We will continue calmly, we will continue without mishap, says
> With sincerity, with dew, says
> Where did the garbage come from? says
> Where did the dust come from? says

María Sabina:
> There is no resentment, there is no rancor

María Aurora:
> We are going to play music, says
> We are going to thunder, says
> We are going to clean our babies and our children, says
> Our offshoots and our buds, says

María Sabina:
> With your wife and your family

María Aurora:
> Around our fire and the three stones of our hearth, says
> Lady mistress of our house, says
> Lady mistress of our shade, says
> Lady mistress of our door, says
> Lady mistress of our dooryard, says
> Our clean sacrament, says
> Well-prepared sacrament, says
> She is a woman of life and well-being, says

María Sabina:
>   Receive her, your wife, who is your sacrament

María Aurora:
>   Who is a woman received at the door of the church, says
>   A woman of the church and of the mass, says
>   We have medicine water, says

María Sabina:
[IN THE BACKGROUND]
>   Calmly and without mishap
>   The path of the hands, the path of the heels, the path of the
>   hands, the path of the feet

María Aurora:
>   We have herb water, says
>   It's certain, says
>   It's true, says
>   The sacrament is what is of value, says
>   The appropriate sacrament, says
>   She is the woman of the principal medicinal berries, says
>   She is the woman of the sacred medicinal berries, says
>   Our woman of the fire, says
>   Our woman of the three stones of the hearth, says
>   Our man of the fire, says
>   Our man of the three stones of the hearth, says
>   Our little woman of the principal medicinal berries, says
>   Our woman of the sacred medicinal berries, says
>   Our man of the principal medicinal berries, says
>   Our man of the sacred medicinal berries, says
>   We have recompense, says
>   We have well-being, says
>   We have life and well-being, says
>   With sap and with dew, says
>   There is nothing salted, says
>   There are no lies, says
>   Beneath your gaze, beneath your lips, beneath your glory, says
>   Beneath your gaze, beneath your lips, Eternal Father, says
>   It is there that I ask and implore you, says
>   It is there that I speak with humility and simplicity, says
>   As my tongue can, says
>   As my mouth can, says
>   I ask and inquire of you, you who know and understand, says
>   Whether there is any guilt? says

Is it air of resentment? says
Is it air of rancor? says
Is it garbage of resentment? says
Is it garbage of rancor? says
God of the house, says
God of the shade, says
God of the door, God of the dooryard, says
It's true, says
It is the path of business,the path of recompense,says
It is the path of life, the path of well-being, says
He is a man who thunders, says
He is a man who plays music, says
She is a woman who shouts, says
She is a woman who whistles, says

María Sabina:
The path of the tracks of the hands, the path of the tracks of the
    heels, the path of the tracks of the hands, the path of the tracks
    of the feet
With sap, with dew

María Aurora:
Calmly, says
Without mishap, says
With sap, says
With dew, says
The path of business, the path of recompense, says
The path of life, the path of well-being, says

María Sabina:
The path of the hands, the path of the heels, the path of the
    hands, the path of the feet

María Aurora:
We don't want garbage, says
We don't want dust, says
We don't want whirlwind, says
We don't want bad air, says
She thunders, says
She plays music, says
She comes with her Saint Peter, says
She comes with her Saint Paul, says
She is *Ustandi* beneath the water, says
She is *Ustandi* beneath the sea, says

She shouts and whistles, says
He brings his network of light, says
His great whirlwind of colors, his sacred whirlwind of colors, says

María Sabina:
Who can frighten him?

María Aurora:
He brings his race, says
He brings his canon, says
He is the one who thunders, says
He is the one who plays music, says

María Sabina:
With his wife and his family

María Aurora:
The path of his palms, the path of his hands, says
The path of life and well-being, says
The path of business and recompense, says
Around his fire, around the three stones of his hearth, says
There is no garbage, says
There is no dust, says
There is no sickness, says
There is no faintness, says
He is the one who thunders, says
He is the one who plays music, says
With the God of his house, says
With the God of his shade, says
He is a man of good words, says
He is a man of good breath, good saliva, says
She is a woman of good words, says
She is a woman of good breath, good saliva, says
She is a spirit woman, says
She is a woman of good breath, says

María Sabina:
Receive her anew because there is no problem nor any difficulty

María Aurora:
There is no problem nor any difficulty, says
The sacrament is what is of value, says
The appropriate sacrament,says
It's certain, says

It's true, says
We look into the insides of things and investigate, says
The path of the tracks of the hands, the path of the tracks of the feet
The path of life, the path of well-being, says
We have life, says
We have well-being, says
We have herbs with berries, sacred herbs, says
Beneath your eyes, beneath your lips, you my mother, Virgin
    Guadalupe who art at the door of heaven, says
In your hands are the medicinal herbs
Herbs with berries, sacred herbs, says

María Sabina:
Medicinal herbs and sacred herbs of Christ
Medicinal herbs and sacred herbs of Christ

María Aurora:
There is a cure for the baby, says
There is a cure for this person, says
There is a cure for your Christian, says
Your well-prepared Christian, says
Your clean Christian, says
Your well-prepared Christian, says
We don't want garbage, says
We don't want dust, say
We don't want whirlwind of resentment, says
We don't want whirlwind of rancor, says
It is a matter of life and well-being, says
It is sap and dew, says
It is a matter of greenness and clarity, says
It's true, says
I am she who shouts, says
I am she who whistles, says
I am she who thunders, says
I am she who plays music, says
He is a man of good words, says
He is a man of good breath, of good saliva, says
He is a man who was raised well, says
He is a man of business and recompense, says
His breath is good, says
His saliva is good, says
Good is his breath and his saliva, says
It is the path of his business, the path of his recompense, says
It is the path of life, the path of well-being, says

María Sabina:
> With his wife, his family and his children

María Aurora:
> It's certain, says
> It's true, says
> It is the life and well-being, says
> It is sap and dew, says
> People are envious of his work,says
> They are envious of his effort, says
> That is what I am asking about, says
> There is medicine, says
> There are herbs, says
> For the babies, says
> For the children, says
> I look into the insides of things and investigate, says
> I will thunder and play music, says
> I am the one who thunders, says
> I am the one who plays music, says
> We have medicine water, says
> We have herb water, says
> We have herbs with berries, sacred herbs, says
> That is my business and my recompense, says
> There are herbs with berries, says
> There are sacred herbs, says
> There is a cure, says
> There are herbs, says
> For our baby and our child, says
> For our offshoot and bud, says
> He will get better, says
> It will be gotten rid of, says
> The garbage and dust that befell his body, says
> The sickness of weakness, the sickness of faintness will be gotten rid
>   of, says
> God of his house, says
> God of his shade, says
> The path of business and recompense, says
> The path of life and well-being, says
> With sap, with dew, says
> There is no resentment, says
> There is no rancor, says
> His words are good, says
> His breath and his saliva are good, says
> There is nothing salted, says

There is no lie, says
They are certain words, says
They are true words, says
It is the path of clean work, says

María Sabina:
I am the woman of the great expanse of the waters, says
I am the woman of the expanse of the divine sea, says
I jump into my launch, says
I am a little launch woman, says
I am the little Morning Star woman, says
I am the little Cross Star woman, says
I am a clean woman, says
I am a well-prepared woman, says
My words are good, says
My breath is good, says
I am a Saint Peter woman, says
I am a Saint Paul woman, says
I am an *Ustandi* woman beneath the water, says
I am a shooting star woman, says
I am the little elder vibrant-winged one, says
I am the little woman with vibrant wings, says
I am a little fresh flower woman, says
I am a little sacred flower woman, says
I offer my flower, says
My flower beneath the water, says
My little hummingbirds, says
There are thirteen of them, says
Beneath the water, beneath the sea, says
I am a little woman of Rome, says
Ah Jesus Christ, says
I am a clean woman, says
I am a well-prepared woman, says
We are demonstrating our courage, says
Benito Juárez, says
Mother Guadalupe, says
Mother Magdalene, says
I am a saint woman, says
I am a spirit woman, says
Holy Father, says
That is your book, says
That is your book, my Father, one and only Father, says
That is your clock, says
Holy Father, says

Father Jesus Christ, says
We are demonstrating our courage, says
I am the little woman of the great expanse of the waters, says
I am the little Woman of the Flowing Water, says
I am the little woman of the great rain says
Where our most respected and important people are, say
Our people of reason, says
What is of value is the head, says
Holy Father says
My beer, says
Ah Jesus Christ, says
They are drinking my beer, says
My Principal Ones, says
Ah Jesus Christ, says
I am a woman who looks into the insides of things, says
I am a woman who investigates, says
I am a little woman born, says
I am a little woman fallen into the world, says
My Mother Conception, says
My one and only Father, says
And my own father, says
Saint Feliciano, says
My father, says
My mother, says
My mother, says
I who came from inside the stomach of my mother, says
You who gave birth to me, says
Ah Jesus Christ, says
I who came from inside the stomach of my mother Maria
   Conception, says
My saint Feliciano, says
My father, says
Jesus Christ, says
My father Feliciano, says
My Peter, says
I came forth a singer, says
Because my father was a singer, says
My old man, says
So did we come forth important and sacred, says
Holy Father, says
I am the Moon woman, I am a star woman, says
I am the Constellation of the Sandal woman, the Hook
   Constellation woman, says
I am the Morning Star woman, says

I am the Morning Star woman, says
That is your horse, Lord Santiago, says
Lord Patron Saint John, says
That is your Lord eagle, says
Your Lord hawk, says
Your opossum, says
It is your saint that I bring, my Father, says
There I am asking you for your communion wafer, says
I ask you for your number, says
At the hour when you rest, says
I ask you for your saliva, says
At the hour when you take breath, says
That is why I am the child of God, says
I am the child of Christ, says
Heart of Jesus, says
Long life! says
Benito Juárez, says
Mother Guadalupe, says
Mother Magdalene, says,
It's certain, says
It's true, says
Now is when it is recognized whether one is the child of God,
    says
·I arrive in heaven beneath the gaze of Glory, says
Where the principal broom is, the sacred broom, says
Your clean herb, says
Your well-prepared herb
I am a woman who goes through the water, says
I am the woman of the great expanse of the waters, says
I am the Woman of the Flowing Water, says
I am a saint woman, I am a star, I am the moon, says
I am a comet, too, says
I am a music woman, says
I am a drum woman, says
Holy Father, says
I am a woman general beneath the water, says
I am a woman general beneath the sea, says
I am a woman fire, says
Holy Father, says
Father Jesus Christ, says
I am a saint woman, says
I am a spirit woman, says
A woman of good words, says
Of good words, good breath, good saliva, says

I step on them and grind them into dust, says
Father Jesus Crhist, says
I turn anyone who wants to follow the tracks of my feet into garbage
    and dust, says
Anyone who wants to get in my way or follow me, says
From whatever side, says
I have your book, says
I am the little woman of the great expanse of the waters, says
I am the little woman of the expanse of the divine sea, says
Holy Father, says
It's true, says
Our Father is rich, says
He is a singer, says
Holy Father, says
I am the child of Christ, says
I am the child of Mary, says
I am the Morning Star woman, says
I am the Cross Star woman, says
I am the Moon woman, says
I go up to heaven, says
I am the woman of the great expanse of the waters, says
I am the woman of the expanse of the divine sea, says
There I am asking you for your principal herb, your sacred herb, says
Your clean herb, your well-prepared herb, says
I am going there, says
On my knees for hands, on my knees for feet, says
On my knees of tortillas, on my knees of water, says
Holy Father, says
I am arriving prostrating myself beneath the gaze of God the Father,
    Christ, says
Holy Father, says
Where the blood of the saint Pope was sprinkled, says
My member of the Sisterhood, says
My Nun, says
My good and clean Archbishop, says
My priest, says
My people of reason, says
It's certain, says
It's true, says
I am a lawyer woman, says
I am a woman of transactions, says
I go up to heaven, says
Holy Father, says
I am known to God, says

I am known to the saints, says
It's true, says
It's certain, says
I am a woman of good words, says
I am a Saint Peter woman, says
I am a Saint Paul woman, says
I am an *Ustandi* woman, says
I am a shooting star woman, says
I am a music woman, says
I am a drum woman, says
Holy Father, says
It's certain, says
It's true, says
Our Lord of the cumulus clouds, says
Our Father Arosio, says
It's certain, says
It's true, says
Father of the harvest, Father of richness, says
Lord Chicon Tocosho, says
It's certain, says
Father Jesus Christ, says
I am a woman who sounds forth with grandiloquence, says
I am a woman who sounds forth with divinity, says
I am the woman of the great Sun Stone, says
I am an opossum woman, says
Holy Mother, says
Lord Santiago goes along mounted on his horse, says
It's certain, says
He is our patron, says
It's certain, says
It's true, says
I am a woman of good words, says
Good are my words and my breath, says
Good is my saliva, says
It is beer, says
Valuable beer, says
It's certain, says

María Aurora:
    Let us go with sap, let us go with dew, says
    Let us go with tenderness, let us go with clarity, says
    We are the ones who are going to thunder, says
    We are the ones who are going to play music, says
    The path of the hands, the path of the feet, says

The path of life, the path of well-being, says
If anyone is critizing us, says
If anyone is spying on us, says
If anyone is envious, says
If anyone is annoyed, says
I am the one who is going to thunder, says
I am the one who is going to play music, says
There is no resentment, says
There is no rancor, says
It is life and well-being, says
It is sap and dew, says
It is tenderness and clarity, says
It is the path of business, says
It is the path of recompense, says
It is the path of life, the path of well-being, says
It is the path of sap, the path of dew, says
I examine, says
I examine one's appearance in the light of day, says
I examine in the daylight, says
It's certain, says
It's true, says
If there is anyone who is criticizing us, says
If there is anyone who is watching us, says
It is the path of business, the path of recompense, says
It is the path of life, the path of well-being, says

María Sabina:
        With his wife, his family, and his children

María Aurora:
        It's certain, says
        It's true says
        In the house, in the shade, says
        Around the fire, around the three stones of the hearth, says
        It is well-being, says
        It is good will, says
        It is life and well-being, says
        It is sap and dew, says
        If there is anyone who is envious, says
        If there is anyone with bad will, says
        If there is anyone who wants to get in the way, says
        Anyone who wants to get into a fight with us can't touch us,
            says
        They can't do anything to us, says

What if it's a matter of something salted? says
What if it's a matter of lies? says
It's certain, says
It's true, says
She is the woman of the principal medicinal berries, says
She is the woman of the sacred medicinal berries, says
She is the little woman of the Flowing Water, says
He is the Man of the Flowing Water, says
She is a woman whose palms are like spoons, says
She is a woman with hands of measure, says
I am the woman of the mine that is growing, says
I am the woman of the mine that is augmenting, says
It's certain, says
It's true, says
I am the little Woman of the Flowing Water says
I am the little woman of the great expanse of the waters, says
I am the woman of the expanse of the divine sea, says
I am a woman who looks into the insides of things, says
I am a woman who investigates, says
I am an elder master of the mountains woman, says
I am a sacred master of the mountains woman, says
I am the one who thunders, says
And plays music, says
I am the little woman of the principal medicinal berries, says
I am the woman of the sacred medicinal berries, says
She is the little Woman of the Flowing Water, says
She is the Woman of the Flowing Water, says
He is the Man of the Flowing Water, says
He is the Man of the Flowing Water, says
She is a woman whose palms are like spoons, says
She is a woman with hands of measure, says
There is health, says

María Sabina:
> Father of the cumulus clouds

María Aurora:
> There is life and well-being, says
> Mine that is growing, says
> Mine that is augmenting, says
> I just look into the insides of things and investigate, says
> I only thunder, I only play music, says
> I only shout, I only whistle, says

It is true
Little woman of the mine that is growing, says
Little woman of the mine that is augmenting says
Man of the mine that is growing, says
Man of the mine that is augmenting, says
He is a man who thunders, says
He is a man who plays music, says
He is a man of the great expanse of the waters says
He is a man of the expanse of the divine sea, says
She is a woman of the great expanse of the waters, says
She is a woman of the expanse of the divine sea, says
It's certain, says
It's true, says
Let us go, says
Approaching, looking, says
Because there I'm going, says
Where the finest liquor is being distilled, says
Valuable beer, says
Measured beer, says
Where the mine is that is growing, says
Where the mine is that is augmenting, says
Where the woman is whose palms are like spoons, says
The woman with hands of measure, says
The man whose palms are like spoons, says
The man with hands of measure, says
Only the mine that is growing, says
[THE FIRST ROOSTER OF THE MORNING CROWS AND GOES ON CROWING,
FROM TIME TO TIME, THROUGH WHAT FOLLOWS.]
Only the mine that is augmenting, says
Only harvest and wealth, says
Only life and well-being, says
Only tenderness and clarity, says
Health is coming, says
Well-being is,coming, says
The mine is coming that is growing, says
The mine that is augmenting, says
The woman whose palms are like spoons, says
The woman with hands of measure, says
We are only going to shout and whistle, says
We are only going to thunder and play music, says
For our children, for our babies, says
For our offshoots, for our buds, says
Nothing can befall them, says
Nothing can touch them, says

Neither garbage, says
Nor dust, says
Nor whirlwind along the path, says
Nor whirlwind in the path of witchcraft, says
He is the one who thunders, says
He is the one who plays music, says
The path of his business, the path of his recompense, says
May he have many years of harvest, says
May he have wealth, says
If there is anyone who is criticizing us, says
If there is anyone who is watching us, says
Anyone who has a hot tongue, says
Whose breath is hot, whose saliva is hot, says
I'm going to thunder, says
I'm going to play music, says
I'm going to shout, says
I'm going to whistle, says
It is the path of business, the path of recompense, says
It is the path of life, the path of well-being, says
It is a matter of sap, a matter of dew, says
It is a matter of tenderness, a matter of clarity, says
There is no resentment, says
There is no rancor, says
There is no argument, says
There is no anger, says
It is done with, says
There is no argument, says
There is no resentment, says
There is no rancor, says
It is life and well-being, says
It is sap and dew, says
It is tenderness and clarity, says
That is what I'm asking for, says
That is what I want to know, says
I don't want whirlwind, says
I don't want wind, says
I don't want garbage, says
I don't want sickness, says
I don't want weakness, says
Weakness of space, says
Weakness brought by the day, says
His father is here, says
His mother is here, says
We're going to keep it over there, says

María Sabina:
> Over there behind the mountain

María Aurora:
> We're going to hide it, says
> Seven to the left, says
> Seven to the right, says
> True words, says
> Straight words, says

María Sabina:
> With words we live, with words we grow

María Aurora:
> We'll see what's certain, says
> We'll see what's true, says
> It is a matter of sap, says
> It is a matter of dew, says
> That is what I am asking about, says
> That is what I want to know, says
> There is no resentment, says
> There is no rancor, says
> If there is anyone who wants to shut us up, says
> If there is anyone who wants to get in our way, says
> They can't do it because nobody can touch us, says
> There is no resentment, says
> There is no rancor, says
> There is nothing salted, says
> It isn't a lie, says
> It's certain, says
> If there is anyone with hot breath, says
> If there is anyone with hot spit, says
> They can't do anything to me, says
> They can't touch me, says
> Let it fall back on them, says
> If anyone is criticizing me, says
> If anyone is watching me, says
> If anyone has hot breath, hot spit, says
> It's certain, says
> Let it fall back on them, around their hearth, around the three stones
>   of their fire, if that's what they drink, says
> If that's what they eat, says
> I don't want evil, says
> Nor resentment, says

Nor rancor
I am the child of Mary, says
I am the child of Saint Joseph, says
I am the child of Christ, says
I don't want whirlwind, says
I don't want rancor, says
If there is anyone who is hot and plain, says
If there is anyone who is hot and salted, if there is anyone whose
 words are salted, says
If there is anyone who has hot breath, hot spit, says
They can't do anything to me, says
They can't touch me, says
I am the child of Mary, says
I am the child of Saint Joseph, says
I am the child of Christ, says
I am the child of God, says
If anyone knows anything of resentment, says
If anyone knows anything of rancor, says
It's certain, says
It's true, says
I am the little Woman of the Flowing Water, says
I am the little Woman of the Flowing Water, says
I am the little woman of the great expanse of the waters, says
I am the litttle woman of the expanse of the divine sea, says
I come with my *Ustandi* beneath the water
I come with my *Ustandi* beneath the sea
I am the little woman of the principal medicinal berries,
I am the little woman of the sacred medicinal berries,
I am the woman of the great expanse of the waters, says
I am the little woman of the mine that is growing, says
I am the woman of the mine that is augmenting, says
I am a woman whose palms are like spoons, says
I am a woman with hands of measure, says
It is neither resentment nor rancor
It is neither resentment nor rancor
Your Christian, you whose world it is, says
It is sap and dew, says
It is life and well-being, says
It is sap and dew, says
That is what the herb with berries is for, the sacred herb, says
Bring your medicine water, says
Bring your herb water, says
Make the precious dew fall, says
The measured dew, says

Water the admirable flower, the admirable flower standing in the
    midst of the world, in the midst of the earth and the water, says
World of abundance, big world, says
Water it, says
Make the precious dew fall, says
Make the measured dew fall, says
They are going to grow and fill out, says
They are going to shoot up and become tall, says
Because they are the babies and the children, says
The offshoots, the buds, says
It is life and well-being, says
It is sap and dew, says
It is greenness and clarity, says
That is what I am asking about, says
That is what I want to know, says
Nobody can touch us, says
If there is anyone who is criticizing us, says
If there is anyone who is watching us, says
If there is anyone who can salt things, says
If there is anyone who can tell lies, says
If anyone has a long tongue, says
If anyone has a big mouth, says
If anyone has hot breath, hot spit, says
It's certain, says
It's true, says
Saliva is what is of value, says
Saliva is what is measured, says
Because there is medicine water, says
Because there is herb water, says
It is sap and dew, says
It is life and well-being, says
It's certain, says
It's true, says
Let us go, says
Along the path of our palms, along the path of our hands says
The path of our life, the path of our well-being, says
It is harvest and wealth, says
It is life and well-being, says
It is sap and dew, says
That is what the mine is for that is growing, says
The mine that is augmenting, says
She is a woman whose palms are like spoons, says
She is a woman with hands of measure, says
That is what I am asking about, says

That is what I want to know, says
That is what I am asking for with humility, says
That is what I am asking for with simplicity, says
It's certain
That is what I am asking for with humility, says
Where the woman of the mine that is growing is, says
The woman mine that is augmenting, says
I speak humbly, I speak with simplicity, says
My palms are empty, my hands are empty, says
I will go on speaking with humility, I will go on speaking with
    simplicity, says
With the light of day, says
May we be blessed, says
May we receive benediction, says
We will have many years of life, says
We will have many days, says
We will have life for many years and much time of harvest, says
It comes with sap, says
It comes with dew, says
Life and well-being, says
Tenderness and clarity, says
Our years are increasing, says
Our harvest is increasing, says
We are going to have buds and sprouts, says
We are going to have sap and dew, says
We are going to grow and develop, says
We are going to grow tall and put on weight, says
We are going to have many years of life, says
We are going to have many years of harvest, says
Many years of life, says
Many years of harvest, says
Many days, says
That is what I am asking and praying for, says
It has nothing to do with resentment, says
It has nothing to do with rancor, says
God would punish us if what we are doing were a matter of
    resentmet or rancor
It is the path of God

[THERE FOLLOWS A FEW MOMENTS OF TALK. MARIA SABINA SAYS:
"IT'S A LONG TIME THAT I'VE BEEN WORKING IN THIS. SOME
RECOGNIZE MY SERVICES AND GIVE ME SOME MONEY, OTHERS DON'T.
IT DOESN'T MATTER. I DON'T SHOW OFF WHAT I EARN, I DON'T LIVE IN
LUXURY, LOOK AT MY HOUSE FILLED WITH DUST, THE LITTLE I HAVE I

GIVE IN CHARITY TO MY FRIENDS AND IN THE END I DON'T HAVE
ANYTHING. FROM THE WAY I'M LIVING IN MY POOR HOUSE FILLED
WITH DUST, THERE'S NO SIGN THAT I'M EARNING ANY MONEY." THEN
MARIA AURORA RESUMES SINGING.]

Valuable Book, says
Measured Book, says
It's certain, says
It's true, says
Admirable Book, says
Immense Book, says
It came forth Lord, it came forth sacred, says
Many years ago, says
Many days ago, says
Admirable Book, immense Book, says
Whoever is able to see it, says
Whoever is able to touch it, says
It's true, says
Can't estimate its value, says
Can't take its measure, says
Valuable Book, says
Measured Book, says
They are true words, says
Straight words, says
Little woman who resounds, says
Little woman torn up out of the ground, says
He is a man who resounds, says
He is a man torn up out of the ground says
Little woman who gathers up the primordial, says
Little woman who gathers up the sacred, says
I am a little woman who looks into the insides of things, says
I am a woman who investigates, says
Because I was born, says
Because I slid out, says
Because I fell out, says
That is your work, says
It is your clean saint, says
It is your well-prepared saint, says
Valuable saliva, says
True saliva, says
They are true words, says
They are straight words, says
Because it is clean saliva, says
Because it is well-prepared saliva, says

It is life and well-being, says
I thunder, says
I play music, says
I shout, says
I whistle, says
Our *Ustandi* beneath the water, says
Our *Ustandi* beneath the sea, says
She is a clean little saint woman, says
She is a well-prepared saint woman, says
Saint of value, says
Measured saint, says
Nobody can attain it, says
Nobody can touch it, says
Our admirable Book, says
Our immense Book, says
It is beneath the water, says
It is beneath the sea, says
I bring it, says
I leaf through it, says
Our admirable Book, says
Our immense Book, says
It is beneath the great expanse of the waters, says
It is beneath the expanse of the divine sea, says
From Jerusualem to Rome, says
Where our great ones are, says
The important ones, says
Nun of Clean Water, says
Archbishop of Clean Water, says
Member of the Sisterhood of Clean Water, says
It's true, says
Nobody can attain it, says
Nobody can touch it, says
My clean Book, says
My well-prepared Book, says
It's true saliva, says
It's honest saliva, says
They are true words, says
Words of God, says
Words of Mary, says
Words of Saint Jospeh says
Words of Christ, says
If anyone wants to frighten us, says
By means of the rope of our personality, the rope of our destiny
    says,

The rope of our life, the rope of our well-being, says
If anyone wants to cut the rope of our personality, says
The rope of our destiny, says
His eyes will become crossed, says
His personality and his destiny will double up, says
In the midst of the path, says
In the midst of his witchcraft, says
He will get frightened, says
He will look away, says
Anyone who criticizes us, says
Anyone who spies on us, says
Along the path of our business, the path of our recompense, says
The path of our life, the path of our well-being, says
If anyone casts an evil eye on us, says
If anyone turns their mouth of foul words on us, says
Their foul breath, their foul spit, says
If anyone has hot breath, hot spit, says
I am the one who thunders, says
I am the one who plays music, says
In the midst of the path, says
In the midst of withcraft, says
I shout and whistle, says
I thunder and play music, says
Little music woman, says
Little drum woman, says
Little woman violinist, says
It's true, says
Little elder master of the mountains woman, says
Little woman of the whirlpool in the lake, says
Little woman whose palms are like spoons, says
Woman with hands of measure, says
Little woman of the mine that is growing
Woman of the mine that is augmenting
There is recompense, says
There is goodness, says
There is harvest and wealth says
It is life and well-being, says
If there is anyone behind our back, says
If there is anyone pursuing us, says
I'm going to teach them, says
I'm going to show them the path of rectitude, says
If it's only a matter of their salt, says
If it's only a matter of their lies, says
Whoever criticizes me and judges me, says

I'm going to show the path of rectitude, says
We're going to set them on the way, says
We're going to make them leave the path of withchcraft, says
They have to be lifted up, says
They have to be raised, says
Onto the path of rectitude, says
The path of truth, says
The path of life, the path of well-being, says
With that their bodies are going to grow tall and get fat, says
They are going to grow and put on wieght, says
Their babies, says
Their children, says
Their offshoots, says
Their buds, says
It is the path of life, says
It is the path of well-being, says
If one knows how to bow down, says
If one knows how to go, says
There is the honest path, says
There is the path of rectitude, says
Honest words, says
Straight words, says
We can't cast evil glances at each other nor criticize each other, says
Because the eyes and mouth of our Father Christ are everywhere, says

He is of one heart, says
He is raising us, he is giving us life, says
His clean Christian, says
His well-prepared Christian, says
So was sown the seed of our admirable flower, our immense flower,
    in this wide world, in this immense world, says
Because the world is all one, the big world, says
From there may there come medicine water, herb water, says
Herbs with berries, sacred herbs, says
The dew of the shade is coming, the dew of clarity, says
She is going to be cured, says
She is going to be cured with herbs, says
With berries, with holiness, says
Clean Christian, says
Well-prepared Christian, says
There is no resentment, says
There is no rancor, says
It's certain, says

It's true, says
There are herbs of the precious dew, says
The measured dew, says
She brings her medicine water, says
She brings her herb water, says
She is the Morning Star woman, says
She is the Cross Star woman, says
She is the Constellation of the Sandal woman, says
She is the Hook Constellation woman, says
She found shade, a house, says
She found a door, a dooryard, says
She is the Cross Star woman, says
She as the Morning Star woman, says
She can resolve everything, says
She can get rid of everything, says
She is a respected little woman, a great woman, says
She is a Constellation of the Sandal Woman
She is a Hook Constellation woman
She is a Morning Star woman
She is a Cross Star woman
She is a Comet woman
She turned into a saint,
She turned into a saintess,
She was purified, says
It's true, says
She found a door and a dooryard, says
It's true, says
They became one, says
They identified with each other, says
She found a house, shade, says
A door, a dooryard, says
She is a Cross Star woman, says
She is a Morning Star woman, says
He is a Cross Star man, says
He is a Morning Star man, says
It is one word, says
It is one breath, one saliva, says
it is clean saliva, says
It is good saliva, says
She is the Cross Star woman, says
She is the Morning Star woman, says
She is the Comet woman, says
It's true, says
She is a woman who sounds forth with grandiloquence, says

> She is a woman who sounds forth with divinity, says
> She is a woman of the great expanse of the waters, says
> She is a woman of the expanse of the divine sea, says
> It's true, says

María Sabina:
> God exists. His place is very cool. Look at how it is
>   where God is

María Aurora:
> Our little woman sacred vibrant-winged one, says
> Our clean little hummingbird woman, says
> Our well-prepared little hummingbird woman, says
> Our little woman great vibrant-winged one, says
> Our little woman sacred vibrant-winged one, says
> Our clean woman, says
> Our well-prepared woman, says
> Our little woman great vibrant-winged one, says
> Our little woman sacred vibrant-winged one, says
> Our clean hummingbird woman, says
> It's certain, says
> It's true, says
> She looks into the insides of things and investigates, says
> Our woman shepherdess beneath the water, says
> Our woman shepherdess beneath the sea, says
> Our woman shepherdess beneath the water, says
> Our woman shepherdess beneath the sea, says
> Our Vigin Mother Shepherdess, says
> There is the harvest, the wealth, says
> There are her animals, her goats, says
> Our little woman shepherdess, says
> There is the recompense, the goodness, says
> As she did, says
> When she was a shepherdess, says
> As she herded together, says
> Her animals, her goats, says
> So we are going to do ourselves, says
> We are going to herd together, says
> We are going to protect, says
> Our babies, says
> Our children, says
> There is recompense, says
> It is a path of rectitude, says
> I am going to teach the path of rectitude, says
> It's certain, says

It's true, says
Our little woman shepherdess beneath the water, says
Our woman shepherdess beneath the sea, says
Our little clean hummingbird woman, says
Our well-prepared hummingbird woman, says
Our little woman of great vibrant wings, says
Our woman of sacred vibrant wings, says
Our clean number woman, says
Our well-prepared number woman, says
That is your clock, says
That is your lord eagle, says
That is your whirlwind of colors, says
That is your network of light, says
It's true, says
We are going to arrive there, says
We are going to prostrate ourselves, says
Where there is recompense, says
Where there is goodness, says
We are going to arrive there, says
We are going to prostrate ourselves, says
It's true, says
I will only look into the insides of things and investigate, says
We are going to arrive there, says
We are going to prostrate ourselves, says
Our woman great vibrant-winged one, says
Our woman sacred vibrant-winged one, says
Our clean hummingbird woman, says
Our well-prepared hummingbird woman, says
Valuable number woman, says
Measured number, says
Our little music woman, says
Our drum woman, says
Our little woman of the networks of light, says
Our little mistress of the mountains woman, says
Our little number woman beneath the water, says
Our number beneath the sea, says
Valuable book, says
Measured book, says
From there I am going to begin, says
From where it sounds forth with grandiloquence, says
From where it sounds forth with divinity, says
There recompense is, says
There goodness is, says
There the harvest and the wealth are, says

There greenness and clarity are, says
She is a little woman who sounds forth with grandiloquence, says
He is a little man who sounds forth with divinity, says
He is a clean little man, says
She is a well-prepared woman, says
Woman of true words, says
Measured words, says
Words of life, says
words of well-being, says

María Sabina:
She is a saint woman, says
She is a saint woman, says
She is a spirit woman, says
She is a woman of light, says
She is a woman of the day, says
Holy Father, says
She is a mother woman, says
She is a saint woman, says
She is a spirit woman, says
She is a Mother Saint Peter woman, says
She is a Saint Paul woman, says
She is an *Ustandi* woman beneath the water, says
Holy Father, says
She is a clean woman, says
She is a well-prepared woman, says
She is a woman of light, says
She is a woman of the day, says
She is a spider woman, says
She is a hummingbord woman, says
She is a little woman great vibrant-winged one, says
She is a little woman sacred vibrant-winged one, says
Holy Father, says
She is the woman of the principal medicinal berries, says
She is the woman of the sacred medicinal berries, says
She is the woman of the whirlpool in the lake, says
[. . .]
Holy Father, says
I am a mother woman, says
I am a saint woman, says
She is a woman wise in medicine, says
Holy Father, says
Holy Mother, says
She is the Morning Star woman, says

She is the Cross Star woman, says
She is the Comet Star woman, says
Holy Father, says
She is a launch woman, says
She is a shooting star woman, says
She is a shooting star woman, says
She is a shooting star woman, says
She is a launch woman, says
She is a launch woman, says
Holy Father, says
She is a woman who is growing, says
She is a woman who is augmenting, says
Holy Father, says
She is the Moon woman, she is the star woman, says
She is the Moon woman, she is the star woman, says
She is the Morning Star woman, says
She is the Cross Star woman, says
She is a woman of good words, says
Of good words, good breath, good saliva, says
Holy Mother, says
I am the woman of the great expanse of the waters, says
I am the woman of the expanse of the divine sea, says
I am a spirit woman, says
Our Archbishop of Clean Water, says
Our Nun of Clean Water, says
Our Sainted Pope, says
Holy Father, says
Our people of reason, says
Our Principal Ones, our great ones, says
Holy Father, says
I am the lady of the great expanse of the waters, says
I am the lady of the great Sun Stone, says
I am the little woman of the great Sun Stone, says
She is a woman of good words, says
Of good words, good breath, good saliva, says
Holy Mother, says
I am a woman who makes things resound, says
I am a woman who looks into the insides of things, says
I am a music woman, says
I am a woman violinst, says
I am a drum woman, says
Holy Father, says
I am the woman of the great expanse of the waters, says
I go up to heaven, says

Where your principal herb is, your sacred herb, says
Beneath your eyes, beneath your glory, says
Holy Father, says
Our Benito Juarez, says
Mother Guadalupe, says
Mother Magdalene, says
I just lightning, says
I just shout, says
I just whistle, says
I am a lawyer woman, says
I am a woman of transactions, says
Holy Father, says
That is his clock, says
That is his lord eagle, says
That is his opossum, says
That is his lord hawk, says
Holy Father, says
Mother, says
I am a mother woman beneath the water, says
I am a woman wise in medicine, says
Holy Father, says
I am a saint woman, says
I am a spirit woman, says
She is a woman of light, says
She is a woman of the day, says
Holy Father, says
[ASIDE SHE ASKS, TIRED OUT, "IS THERE MUCH MORE TO GO?" SINGING
UNTIL THE TAPE RUNS OUT.]
I am a shooting star woman, says
I am a shooting star woman, says
I am a whirling woman of colors, says
I am a whirling woman of colors, says
I am a clean woman, says
I am a clean woman, says
I am a woman who whistles, says
I am a woman who looks into the insides of things, says
I am a woman who investigates, says
I am a woman wise in medicine, says
I am a mother woman, says
Holy Father, says
I am a woman wise in medicine, says
I bring my lord eagle, says
I bring my opossum, says
I bring my whirlwind of colors, says

Father in heaven, says
Saint Christ, says
Father scribe, says
I am a spirit woman, says
I am a woman of light, says
I am a woman of the day, says
I am a Book woman, says
Holy Father, says
I am a saint woman, says
I am a spirit woman, says
I am a woman who looks into the insides of things, says
I am a whirling woman of colors, says
Holy Father, says
With the saint, says
With the saintess, says
Holy Mother, says
I am a spirit woman, says
I am a saint woman, says
I am a Lord eagle woman, says

NOTES AND
COMMENTARIES

NOTES AND COMMENTARIES

Mazatec is an unwritten language. The orthography used here follows the method of transcribing Mazatec that was developed by Eunice V. Pike, Kenneth L. Pike, and George and Florence Cowan—linguists associated with the Summer Institute of Linguistics. Mazatec is a tonal language in which the meaning of a word is determined by its intonation as well as by its phonetic features. The numbers indicate the four tone levels or registers of the langauage: "1" is the highest tone, "4" the lowest. Two or three numbers together on a syllable indicate a glide. A sign like a question mark without a dot at the bottom signifies a glottal stop. A hyphen indicates an enclitic after a stress: a syllable appended to the stem of the word. In the Mazatec language the "x" has a pronunciation somewhat like "sh," though the correct pronunciation is still stronger, like a combination of "s," "j," "y," and "h," and the "nt" sound is close to the English "d." Thus the sacred mountain Ni^3nto^3 $To^4co^2xo^4$ is pronounced "Nindo Tocosho."

The reader is referred to George M. Cowan's excellent, comprehensive essay, "The Mazatec Language," in R. Gordon Wasson, *María Sabina and Her Mazatec Mushroom Velada* (New York: Harcourt Brace Jovanovich, 1974). For a more techical study of Mazatec see Eunice V. Pike, "Huautla de Jiménez Mazatec," in the *Handbook of Middle American Indians*, vol. 5 (Austin, Texas: University of Texas Press, 1967).

NOTES TO THE LIFE

Notes added by the translator for the convenience of the American reader are marked [TN.]; otherwise all notes are the author's.

CHAPTER 1

1. [TN.] *Agencias* are outlying towns and hamlets (ranches) under the jurisdiction of the municipal government of Huautla. Each of them is governed by an agent who acts as a representative of the municipal president.

2. Baptism Certificate of María Sabina (reproduced in the text) issued by the parish priest, Arturo García, August 25, 1976, based on the original facts recorded in the archive of the Huautla church. One can see that the names of the baptismal godfathers registered in the document don't coincide with those given by María Sabina. Nevertheless, it should be pointed out that even today it is difficult to know the exact name of some Mazatecs because of their deficient pronunciation of Spanish names. An example will illustrate this: In the course of an interview, María Sabina told us she had a great uncle named N'dosto. She conceded that she didn't know the words "in Castilian," but Evaristo G. Estrada tells me that the name corresponds to that of Antonio Justo. "It is probable," another informant told me, "that those who wrote this type of document at the beginning of the century invented the names of people because the people themselves didn't know what their names were [in Spanish]!" Note furthermore that none of the individuals has a last name, because "they weren't used before." In the present document, there is also the obvious noncoincidence of the birth date reported by María Concepción to her daughter, María Sabina, as "the day of the Virgin Magdalene" (July 22). With respect to the names of the parents, the only one that differs is the the first name of Crisanto Feliciano, given as such by María Sabina, but appearing as Lauriano in the Baptism Certificate.

3. [TN.] *Pinole* is toasted corn powder.

4. This is a term which is used freqently in the text. It is the name that is given to the Mazatec shaman. The native words are *cho⁴ta⁴ chji⁴ne⁴* ("wise person"). Among the Mazatecs are found three categories of curers. On the lowest level is the Sorcerer (*tji³ʔe³*), who is said to be able to transform himself into an animal (*nagual*) at night. He has a great capacity for doing evil and for turning other people into *naguales*. On the intermediate level is the Curer (*cho⁴ta⁴xi³vʔe'nta³*) properly speaking, who uses massage, potions, and devices such as his own language in which he invokes the Lords of different places, mountains, and springs. These two categories are well known in rural Mexico, but in Huautla there is a third and still superior one: that of Wise One and doctor (*cho⁴ta⁴ chji⁴ne⁴*), who doesn't do evil nor use potions to cure. His therapy involves the ingestion of the mushroom, through which he acquires the power to diagnose and

The notes to The Life are largely Alvaro Estrada, while those to The Chants are largely Henry Munn.

cure the sick person, whom he also gives several pairs of mushrooms to eat. See chap. 10, notes 3 and 4, p. 199, on *pairs* and *nagual*, respectively.

5. *?Nti¹xti³santo* ("saint children"), *?nti¹xi³tjo³* ("little one who springs forth," the name of the mushrooms), *?nti'sa²nto⁴* ("little saints"), and *?nti'tso³jmi²* ("little things") are four euphemistic terms given to the mushrooms in Mazatec. María Sabina calls them *saint children* or simply *children*. The traditional respect that the Mazatecs accord the magic mushrooms makes them differentiate them from the edible mushrooms known as *tjain³'coa³* ("white mushroom," *nanacate* in Nahuatl) or *tjain³ni²* ("red mushroom"), two varieties distinguished by their color and highly appreciated for their taste, which is "like that of chicken cooked in *tezmole*." *Tezmole* is a soup thickened with cornmeal and spiced with hot chiles. The poisonous mushrooms are designated *tjain³sca¹* ("crazy mushroom"). There is no question that the Mazatecs have a complete knowledge of the different types of mushrooms.

6. The Sucking Doctors are a variety of Curer. Aguirre Beltrán treats the subject with a great deal of discernment: "Suction takes place by applying the mouth directly to the region that is presumed sick, or by placing a hollow bamboo in between. In all cases, the doctor-diviner extracts the sickness—that is, the spirit of the sickness—materialized in a diversity of small objects that, depending on the region and the ethnic group, may be flint knives, bits of paper, bugs, etc." (Gonzalo Aguirre Beltrán, *Medicina y magia* [Mexico: Instituto Nacional Indigenista, 1963], p. 52.)

7. *Chi³con³ Ni³nto³* (Man of the Mountain). A being of Mazatec myth. It is said that he is Lord and Master of the Mountains, that he is white, and that he has the power to enchant spirits and to exorcise evil influences or spirits that cause illness. Some identify him with Quetzalcóatl. (For more information about him see above, chap. 6, and below, chap. 2, note 1, on p. 197; chap. 17, note 4, on p. 204.)

8. [TN.] The Mazatecs pay the Lords of the Mountains and the spirits of the different places for their benificence with cacao beans, which represent money. In pre-Hispanic Mexico these beans were widely used as a medium of exchange. They now have no value in commercial exchanges, but retain a symbolic value in transactions with the spirits.

9. From the versions that I've found in Huautla, given by old people, the procedure of the Sorcerers in this rite is as follows:
When the corn begins to come out in ears at the beginning of July, the farmers wait, at dawn, to hear the tjin-tjin of a turkey from the eastern horizon. It is as if an enormous turkey were gobbling from the domain of the Lord of Thunder. It is said that this powerful Lord sends the turkey to advise the farmers that the moment has arrived to perform the rite in which the planted field is offered to him. The farmers are neighbors who help each other sow the corn without any

payment in money. They are volunteers who donate their services to individual members of the community. Thus the family who owns the field invites the farmers to participate in the ritual of fertility and protection of the cultivated field as soon as they have heard the call of the sacred turkey. The farmers then gather at dawn around an expert Sorcerer, powerful as well because of his knowledge, who begins the ritual by sending the farmers to the planted area to bring back thirteen corn plants pulled up completely, "roots and all." Upon their return to the hut, the Sorcerer receives the corn plants, pulls off the green ears, and puts them in the ashes of the ceremonial hearth. Then he chooses a turkey, the biggest if the family has several, or he makes do with the only one there is. The families fatten the turkeys in the course of the year "between one corn planting and another."

The Sorcerer takes the chosen turkey and sacrifices it, cutting off its head with a slash of the machete. He empties the blood into a bowl in which he also mixes thirteen ground cacao beans. When the mixture is ready, the Sorcerer sprinkles the hoes, the planting stakes, the tumplines, the machetes, the bags, and all the farming implements that have served to make the planting possible. The Sorcerer invokes the powerful Lord of Thunder, asking him to protect the cornfield to which the ceremony has been dedicated. He asks that a curse fall on whoever ruins or robs an ear of corn: that pimples break out on his neck; that nothing be able to heal him; that there be no cure on earth for whoever dares to damage the cultivated field. The sorcerer and the farmers go to the planted field and walk along its borders, sprinkling the turkey blood mixed with chocolate. They go to the corners of the field, to the bends in the boundary line, to the places where they think robbers might get in. The sprinkling finished, the committee returns to the house of the owner, where the Sorcerer extracts the thirteen ears of young corn from the ceremonial ashes. The roasted young corn together with the corn plants is later buried by the farmers at the center of the sown land.

Meanwhile the turkey meat is prepared in *tezmole* (see note 5 above) for the farmers to eat. Bitter tamales are prepared as well in the form of a ball made from fermented dough. The farmers gather and get down to eating. The Sorcerer presides over the table and tells them: "Each of you should remember that it is not good to throw away even a crumb of what you are going to eat, because it is a sacred repast that not even dogs should touch. If that should occur, the ceremony that we have performed would be invalidated. You should not forget that starting from this moment you are obliged to fast sexually for fifty-two days. In those days of abstinence, there should be no anger or bad feelings between the participants. If in the course of our meal some unexpected visitor should come, we should not invite him to anything, because all the food in this house at this moment is sacred. The water, the *tezmole*, the tamales, the coffee, belong to the Lord of Thunder. And no one alien to our ritual should be invited, because such a visitor could profane our ceremony by using some woman. The sexual act eliminates the purity of every ceremony. But whoever profanes our ceremony in that way will be punished. His testicles will rot."

The farmers and the family of the owner of the cultivated field then eat with utmost care, each one holding a deep plate underneath his chin in order not to drop a crumb of tamale or a drop of *tezmole* until the plates are completely clean.

The *tezmole* should be consumed completely; in that way those who fast leave no trace of what their food was. What's more, no one feels that he has eaten. They have the sensation of an empty stomach "because he who has really eaten is the Lord of Thunder."

It is added, furthermore, that if a farmer or an inopportune visitor who has been invited to the meal invalidates the ceremony of fertility and protection of the crop, the turkeys that have been fattened for the next corn harvest grow thin and are hardly worth being used ritually.

The owner of the cornfield places crosses made from the leaves of the plant at conspicuous points of the cultivated field. The cultivated field can also be one of sugarcane or beans.

CHAPTER 2

1. Ni^3nto^3 *(mountain)* $To^4co^2xo^4$ ("a type of red berries") is the mountain situated in front of Huautla. It is known in Spanish as the Mountain of the Adoration. According to legend, Chi^3con^3 Ni^3nto^3, more properly called Chi^3con^3 $To^4co^2xo^4$, lives there. (See chap. 1, note 7, p. 195.)

2. He was originally from the Sierra of Ixtlán, Oaxaca, and a contemporary of Benito Juárez.

3. [TN.] *Quelite* and *mora* are greens like spinach that are gathered wild. *Guasmole* is a semitropical fruit that is cooked in *tezmole*. It is abundant only in autumn.

4. *Aguardiente* is a clear, very strong alcohol distilled from sugarcane, common in the states of Oaxaca, Chiapas, and Veracruz.

CHAPTER 3

1. I asked María Sabina what the mushroom session is called, a ceremony or a mass? "No," she said, "it's only said "*vi yo choan* stay awake." It is customary to say "*ca vi yochoan jin*," ("that night we stayed awake"). It is understood that mushrooms were eaten. The Mazatec expression corroborates the name used by R. Gordon Wasson, who writes: "We call the session a *velada*, a 'night vigil,' which is how those Mazatecs who speak Spanish refer to it."

2. San Pedro is the name given to a ground-up tobacco (*nicotiana rustica*) mixed with lime and sometimes with garlic as well. Its use is ceremonial, and it is considered to have power against the evil influences of sorcery. It can be carried in a little cloth bag like a scapular medal. This tobacco is identified as *piciete* or *Piziate*, and the word is an obvious deformation of the ancient Mexican Nahuatl expression, *picietl*.

CHAPTER 4

1. The use of the huipil, a regional dress worn by Indian women, goes back to pre-hispanic times. The Mazatec huipil is a kind of rectangular sack with an opening for the head and three-quarter-length sleeves. It is decorated with bright ribbons which go down it and around it at the bottom, and has hand-embroidered birds, peacocks, and flowers on the breast and back. It is worn in combination with an undergarment that is wrapped around the waist and held up with a sash, whose lower part, which falls beneath the top dress to the ankles, is decorated with figures of horses or simply blue and white stripes.

2. Adolfo Pineda, of Mazatec origin, was one of the leaders of the Carrancista movement in Huautla during the Mexican Revolution.

3. The Mazatec Hot Country comprises the low zone of the region, with mostly waterside towns—situated in the shores or islands of the Miguel Alemán reservoir—whose inhabitants work as fishermen, coffee cultivators or collectors of barbasco. In these towns dialects of mazatec are spoken.
[TN.] At the time María Sabina is speaking of, this area was covered with tropical vegetation and crossed by numerous rivers situated at the foot of the Sierra Mazateca near the border of the state of Veracruz. It had not yet been flooded to create the reservoir which supplies hydroelectric power to towns in Veracruz.
Barbasco is a root that provides the major ingredient in contraceptive pills. Formerly it was used by the Indians as a fish poison.

4. *Ch?in³ntjao⁴* ("bronchial penumonia"). "This sickness is brought by hurricane winds. If the clouds of an approaching storm are dark, they bring *ch?in³ntjao⁴*." So I was told by Ricardo García Enríquez, a medicine man who lives near Huautla in the outlying *agencia* of Xochitenalco.

CHAPTER 5

1. [TN.] Teotitlán del Camino, Oaxaca, today Teotitlán de Flores Magón, is a town at the foot of the Sierra Mazateca in the great valley that runs from Puebla and Tehuacan in the north to Oaxaca in the south. Before the road was built to Huautla in 1958, it took people eight to ten hours to walk there out of the mountains.

CHAPTER 6

1. A variety of psychoactive mushroom, *Psilocybe caerulescens Murril var. Mazatecorum Heim.* (See chap. 19, p. 90.)

2. According to the explanations that old people in Huautla have given me, the Principal Ones are persons who head a municipal office or else it is the title that is

given to persons who have important posts. In Mazatec they are called *cho⁴ta⁴ti'tjon²*. With respect to the visions of María Sabina, the Principal Ones are the personification of the mushrooms she has eaten. The mushrooms turn into "people who handle important papers." Another person in Huautla has told me that the Principal Ones are like shadows or people that are "seen" during the trance dressed like fellow Mazatecs, but with brilliant, multicolored clothing.

3. San Juan Coatzospan is a Mixtec-speaking town in the midst of the Mazatec region.

CHAPTER 7

1. The objects used in sorcery (a subject that is not treated with the thoroughness due it in this volume) include macaw feathers, cacao beans, turkey eggs ("because they have more power than those of a hen"), wax candles, copal, a brazier, and tobacco (San Pedro). In a subsequent volume I will present the rituals of sorcery and curing, as well as the plants used in Mazatec medicine.

CHAPTER 10

1. To this day the sections of Huautla are named for some outstanding feature of the landscape: the form of a neighboring hilltop, the name of a nearby picturesque tree, or some local oddity. The oldest person or the one with the most influence in the section is given as a last name the word which designates the place. For example: there are names such as *Ntsio²ya'lo²xa⁴*, which means literally, "Fidencio Orange Tree," or *Chajva² ya' ma²nco⁴*, which means "Juan Mango Tree," because in the house of Mr. Fidencio (García) there is an orange tree, or in the house of Mr. Juan there is a mango tree. The person—now deceased—to whom María Sabina refers was known by the name of *Sco²yats?in⁴-le⁴nia'*, that is, "Francisco Backbone-of-a-Dog," because he lived near the section Backbone-of-a-Dog, whose name comes from a nearby summit that looks like the vertebra of a gaunt dog.

2. In Huautla doctors are called *chiji⁴ne⁴xqui³* ("wise in medicine"). In this case, María Sabina is referring to Doctor Salvador Guerra, who was born in Jalapa, Veracruz in 1925 and who stayed in Huautla seven years, from 1951-1960. Today Salvador Guerra is a cardiologist in one of the best hospitals in Mexico City.

3. The mushrooms, according to tradition, are taken in pairs; it is said that they are "married" or a couple. One is a man, the other is a woman.

4. María Sabina, using her own word, calls *soerte* (a deformation of the Spanish word *suerte*, "luck") what students of pre-Hispanic and colonial Mexico call *nagual* (or a phenomenon related to *nagualism*: the *tona.*). Apparently the word used by María Sabina comes from the popular Mexican saying that "Each is born

with his *suerte*," an expression which means that the fate connected with the day sign of one's birth will determine the life of each person. If one obtains well-being and happiness or on the contrary lives in misery and constant unhappiness because of the dire events in one's life, it is because "fate" has predetermined it.

For María Sabina the *soerte* is the spirit of a person, capable of leaving the human body to turn itself into an animal, usually a tiger. "The transformation of the *nagual* into a beast almost alway has as its aim the provocation of harm," writes Aguirre Beltran. "The *nagual* only has the power of metamorphosis during the night. If it is captured in the form of an animal and kept in such a situation until dawn, it dies." Of the related concept of *tonalism*, the same authority says: "In certain indigenous ethnic groups, among them the Mazatecs, Zapotecs, and Mayas, there existed—and in some communities there still exists—an idea that mystically links a person with an animal. The mystical link is of such a nature that the fate which the individual or animal incurs has repercussions on both: if death overtakes one, they both die. This animal, guardian and protector, receives the name of *tona*...."

Among the Mazatecs it is said that the person whose spirit enters the body of an animal, dreams that he or she goes to distant places. Na⁴ntsia²nc?a′ (Florencia-the-tall), an old lady of Huautla, told me that in her youth she dreamed every night that she came to a path where there were many stones. A relative of hers named Calixto said at that time: "She-goat! Your spirit turns into a buzzard at night. The place you go to is on the way to Tenango."

Aguirre Beltrán adds: "The priest in *nagualism* transforms, transfigures or metamorphosizes himself into another being, losing his human form and acquiring an animal form; in *tonalism* the animal and the individual coexist separately— they lead parallel lives—and are only united by a common destiny." ("Nagualism and Related Complexes," in *Medicina y magia*, pp. 101.)

CHAPTER 11

1. The priest, don Alfonso Aragón Robles, of Sola de Vega, Oaxaca, arrived in Huautla around 1943 to take charge of the parish. A magnificent orator, intense but with a certain sense of humor, he stimulated Catholicism in the region. He returned to his birthplace at the end of 1960, and his recent death has made it impossible to know his opinion of the Indian Wise Ones. Still, from what I do know, he created no conflict between the church and the native doctors; on the contrary he maintained a degree of contact with them.

2. Doctor Guerra tells me: "I treated so many people that I don't remember what sickness Francisco García or his newphew Rodrigo suffered from. Those were times when the city doctors who established themselves in Huautla did so for only a short time. I knew that Mazatec families with a sick person in the house held vigils at the same time that they contracted my services to treat the sick. What can I say about María Sabina 'seeing' the cause of sicknesses in the trance induced by the mushrooms? I too could see the interior of bodies. With my x-ray apparatus."

CHAPTER 12

1. The word "says" is added because "the one who speaks is the mushroom." It is an impersonal language, according to the shaman.

2. She uses the Spanish word *Libro*.

3. The Mazatecs have formed their own constellations from the stars. The best known are the so-called Horse, Sandal, Staff, and Cross.

CHAPTER 13

1. My mother, Maximina Pineda, age sixty-five, says: "Women who have sexual relations in the woods are punished, because the places in the woods have their masters. A slope, a ravine, or a spring has its master. Each master is an elf or a group of elves. It's for that reason that the places in the woods are sacred. The late Aniceta, from the nearby town of Mazatlan, copulated with various men in the woods. At last, as a consequence of her audacity, Aniceta got an inflamed stomach as if she were pregnant. One day she took the mushrooms to cure herself, but under their effect, the lady felt that she was gushing mud from her vagina and later that she was giving birth to rats. She saw and felt how mud and rats came out of her vagina. Women who don't respect the sexual fast before and after taking the mushrooms are punished in the same way. Only by taking the mushrooms did Aniceta get over her illness."

2. María Sabina is referring to the painter, Lady Abdy, who arrived in Huautla in 1958, recommended by the writer, Gutierre Tibón. I remember that the painter had a big blue umbrella. Various Mazatecs went up to her to say: "Señora, sell me your umbrella." Adds Salvador Guerra: "We went to María Sabina's around nine at night. The vigil finished, we returned at five in the morning. I don't know how I got to my house after leaving the painter at her hotel. When I got out of the jeep I saw that the big trees in the nearby park were swaying like fragile palms in a hurricane. That night I had visions that were linked so closely to my private life that for the moment I prefer not to talk about them."

3. *Pajaritos*, a variety of psychoactive mushroom; *Psilocybe mexicana Heim.* (See chap. 19, p. 90.)

CHAPTER 14

1. Cayetano García was *síndico* from 1953 to 1955, during which time Erasto Pineda served as municipal president. Cayetano recalls: "Wasson asked us for a Wise One, and I agreed to take him to María Sabina. Afterward it was necessary to go to Rio Santiago to get good mushrooms, since they were scarce right then in Huautla, in order for the foreign visitors to know our customs."

[TN]. In Mexican town government, the *síndico* is the representative of the

District Attorney (Ministerio Publico) wherever, as in Huautla, there is no District Attorney's Office. Whereas the municipal president is the administrative representative of the town, the *síndico* is the social representative. In Huautla he takes care of the public thoroughfares and the graveyards. He handles infractions of the law and also intervenes in property disputes. In the absence of the president he takes his place.

2. María Sabina calls Robert Gordon Wasson, "Bason."

3. The reference is to Aurelio Carrera, who died at the age of approximately ninety. The people of Huautla called this Wise One Lio²ntia⁴² ("Aurelio-Path") because his house was located at the side of one of the main footpaths.

4. María Sabina says frequently that the foreigners take the mushrooms with the sole aim of "looking for and finding God": Ni³na' va³sje²³, in Mazatec.

CHAPTER 15

1. *Orange Flower (Na³xo¹ lo²xa⁴)*. A Mazatec song danced on festive occasions. It is composed of verses that allude to the happiness of dancing on orange flowers.
[TN.] The men and women face each other in two lines and stamp with their feet, changing places with each other at specified times throughout the melody. It is especially danced at weddings.

2. Apropos, here is an interview that I conducted in August 1970 with the parish priest of Huautla, Antonio Reyes Hernández:
"I have lived for twenty years in the Sierra Mazateca," he said. "For twenty years, I was in Chiquihuitlán. Now I have been in Huautla for a year. There are baptism books in the parish file that date from 1866. The bells were cast in 1863 in the town itself. The church was constructed by the Dominicans in 1777. It worries me to know that people who live on the other side of that curtain of mountains have the idea that Huautla is a center of vice. The truth is that not even a house of prostitution has been established here, and the inhabitants devote themselves to the work of harvesting coffee in order to subsist."
I asked him whether the ecclesiastical authorities didn't oppose the "pagan" ceremonies that are commonly practiced by Sorcerers, Curers, and Wise Men in the Mazatec zone as a pre-Hispanic inheritance.
"The church," responded the priest, "is not against these pagan rites—if they can be called that—but, on the contrary, takes the word of God to all ears and convinces the few who still mix local beliefs with the Catholic religion of the truth of Christianity. There is not much of that; María Sabina herself is a member of the Association of the Apostles of Prayer and comes to mass the first Friday of every month. She uses her scapular medal. She is a humble person, as I can see myself, and doesn't do harm to anyone. On the other hand, the scandalous publicity she is given hurts her and gets her into trouble with the authorities. They should leave her in peace. The reporters—who calls them? What do they come for? I tell you

this, Alvaro, even through I know that to speak to people who write in the newspapers is dangerous. It's dangerous to talk with reporters."

I asked: "What about the Wise Ones and Curers?"

"The Wise Ones and Curers don't compete with our religion; not even the Sorcerers do. All of them are very religious and come to mass. They don't proselytize; therefore they aren't considered heretics, and it's not likely that anathemas will be hurled at them. Aie yi yi, we wouldn't think of it."

CHAPTER 16

1. "If the baby dies because the storm has taken it away," according to Fortunata García of Huautla, "it turns purple. I saw a death like that in a community near Rio Santiago."

Without claiming to be an authority in medical matters, I would suggest that in this case the Mazatecs are referring to what is known as "fulminating bronchitis." The fact that the corpse is left purple and that the attack occurs when there is a storm, i.e., at times of extreme humidity, makes me suppose that that is the cause of death for infants not treated with the necessary precautions. My father, Evaristo G. Estrada, adds the following about unbaptised babies: "If there is a storm one makes the sign of the cross with water mixed with lime on their forehead or places a cross there made from consecrated palm leaves."

2. [TN.] This is a member of the zither class of musical instruments. I have heard it called a plucked dulcimer to distinguish it from one that is played with hammers. It is a kind of *psaltery*, a word derived from the same Latin word as the Spanish name for the instrument, *salterio*. The instrument, a sound board over which as many as a hundred strings are stretched at different levels on frets, is played resting flat on the lap. The strings are plucked by plectrums on the first three fingers of both hands. They are made in the Mazatec mountains in the town of Mazatlan. At dances the person who plays the zither is sometimes accompanied by one who plays the guitar and another who strikes the triangle.

CHAPTER 17

1. María Sabina is referring to people from foreign countries (the United States, Italy, Argentina, France, and Japan) and from Mexico.

2. *Mushroom Ceremony of the Mazatec Indians of Mexico*, Folkways Record recorded by V.P. and R.G. Wasson at Huautla de Jiménez, Oaxaca, Folkways Records and Service Corporation, NYC, U.S.A., FR 8975. The chants on the record are translated above.

3. [TN.] Leaves of the Shepherdess: *Hojas de la Pastora, salvia divinorum*. Seeds of the Virgin: *Semillas de la Virgen*, the ancient Aztec *ololiuhqui, rivea corymbosa*, and the related morning glory seeds, *ipomoea violaceo*. See Richard Evans Schultes and Albert Hoffman, *The Botany and Chemistry of Hallucinogens*, (Springfield,

Illinois: Charles C. Thomas, 1973), pp. 144-47 and 159. Also see R. Gordon
Wasson, "A New Mexican Psychotropic Drug from the Mint Family," Botanical
Museum Leaflet (Cambridge, Mass.: Harvard University, 1961), 20:77-84; and
R. Gordon Wasson, "Notes on the present status of ololiuhqui and other
hallucinogens of Mexico," Botanical Museum Leaflet (Cambridge, Mass.: Har-
vard University, 1963), 20:161-193.

4. The Woman of the Flowing Water (Chjon^{42}nta^{1}ve) is a person of Mazatec
mythology. It is said that she is the wife of Chi^{3}con^{3} ni^{3}nto^{3}.

5. See chap. 10, note 4, p. 199.

CHAPTER 18

1. The Hippies of the 1960s.

2. Some Mazatecs are known to have remained traumatized for a long time,
two years for example, as a result of a "punishment" by the mushrooms.

3. Starting in the summer of 1967, army and federal authorities intervened in
Huautla to expel the young foreigners and Mexicans who had made the place a
center of psychedelic experimentation. The conduct of the young Mexicans,
among whom were delinquents and not a few children of the rich in search of
adventure, was lamentable. The presence of the young foreigners was not scandalous but notorious. This irresponsible intrusion of young outsiders into Huautla
encouraged the Mexican authorities to prohibit the hallucinogens—their traffic
and use—by including them (January 1971) in the Health code of the Republic of
Mexico at the initiative of President Gustavo Díaz Ordaz. Federal surveillance
over the area continued until recently, when the youthful visitors in search of
drugs ceased to be so numerous. At present the municipal authorities are in
charge of the local situation.
    The fame of Huautla, become worldwide, attracts a small but constant number
of tourists each year. Embroidery, the work of the women is something the
visitors especially prize.

4. Federal agents of the State of Oaxaca.

5. [TN.] The Instituto Nacional Indigenista is a government agency whose aim
is to further the integration of the Indian sectors of the Mexican population into
the modern life of the nation. It establishes schools in predominantly Indian rural
regions, where the people speak only their native language, to teach the children
Spanish; and it stimulates the economic development of the remote indigenous
areas by promoting the construction of roads and by finding means to get the
local crops and handicrafts to market. The agency was founded in 1948, during

the administration of President Miguel Alemán, by Dr. Alfonso Caso, the excavator of Monte Alban and the decipherer of the ancient Mixtec codices.

6. The late José Natividad Rosales, a well-known Mexican journalist, in an interview with María Sabina published in the influential *Revista Siempre* in 1969 (no. 830) asked Professor Victor Bravo Ahuja, the then governor of the state of Oaxaca, to leave in peace the "most famous shamaness in the world, whom anthropology and escapism have ruined." [the author acted as interpreter between him and the Wise Woman.]

7. María Sabina means the Museo Nacional de Antropología in Mexico City. In the display devoted to the Mazatecs of Oaxaca, the Folkways record of her singing is played over and over again.

8. [TN.] The *Guelaguetza* or Monday of the Mountain is a festival at which delegations from the seven linguistic ethnic regions of the state of Oaxaca gather together in Oaxaca every July to dance their regional dances. The name means "The Time When Gifts Are Exchanged" in Zapotec and refers to a Zapotec custom of reciprocal exchange in which donations to a baptism or wedding have to be returned in kind on another such occasion.

CHAPTER 19

1. Aguirre Beltrán has written that the Indian doctor did not exactly look for knowledge of the pharmacological properties of the hallucinogenic plants, but rather for two aspects that impressed the magical way of thinking of the Indian: (1) the mystical force that the magic plants provoked in the mind of the native doctor; and (2) the diagnostic power, more than the supposedly therapuetic virtues, contained in the hallucinogens.

Beltrán writes: "One more circumstance, of great importance, should be considered. The sacred herbs, deities in themselves, act by virtue of their mystical properties; that is *it is not the herb itself that cures but the divinity, the part of the divinity or the magic power with which it is imbued*. In order for this power to remain in the plant a complicated ritual is indispensable as much in its harvest as in its preparation and use; *if this is not done, its employment is completely inefficacious*, since it is not the pharmacological properties of the herbs that cure but their mystical properties" (Beltrán, *Medicina y magia* p. 123).

Without doubt María Sabina refers to this mystical power when she says that the mushrooms "have lost their force." The mysticism that for centuries surrounded the ingestion of the mushrooms in the Mazatec region "has now been lost..."

The author's interview in 1969 with old Apolonio Terán, who was considered in the community to be a powerful Wise Man, documented a series of ideas that parallel what María Sabina has told us:

Mushrooms that Speak

There exist in the Mazatec region Wise Ones of both sexes who are renowned in the community for their great mastery.

One October morning, in 1969, I went in search of a Wise Man who had attained unusual prestige in the region. I found him seated on a wooden stool at the center of his patio. Becoming aware of my presence, he lifted his old, sad, blurred gaze.

"Who are you?" he asked with difficulty.

"I'm the son of Evaristo Estrada," I answered.

"What do you want?"

"To speak to you about the mushrooms. About your wisdom. But first, what are you doing seated here?"

"I'm taking the sun. Inside the house it's cold."

"How old are you?"

"He-goats! I've been alive a long time. You know, I have only two years to go to be a hundred."

"How were you initiated in order to reach wisdom?"

"I initiated myself, alone, when I was twenty . . ."

"Were your parents or uncles Wise Ones like you?"

"No. My wisdom wasn't hereditary, though in some it is."

"The people who know of you in Huautla say that your ritual Language is very elevated. How did you learn it?"

"There is no mortal who knows or could teach such wisdom. The mushroom taught me my Language."

"Could you give me an example of your Language now?"

"No, the Language comes only if the mushroom is inside the body. A Wise Man doesn't memorize what he should say in his ceremonies. The sacred mushroom is the one who speaks, the Wise Man simply gives it voice."

"Do you know of anyone who has gone crazy from eating mushrooms?"

"No, no, the mushroom doesn't drive you crazy, but it does punish bad people by making them vomit frogs, snakes, cockroaches, or worms . . ."

"Are the Curers rich in money?"

"Yes, they are rich, but in wisdom, and poor in material goods. The merchants, like those up there, those in the center of Huautla, live in big, fine houses; the Curers live in huts, like their ancestors . . ."

"Why is the mushroom sacred?"

"Because it cures the sores of the body and the spirit, because God inhabits it."

"At your age could you give a ceremony?"

"Not anymore. Not just because of age, though, which has vanquished my physical force so that now I probably wouldn't be able to stand the ritual activity which lasts from four to five hours. What is terrible, listen, is that the divine mushroom no longer belongs to us. Its sacred Language has been profaned. The Language has been spoiled and it is indecipherable for us . . . ."

"What is this new Language like?"

"Now the mushrooms speak $nqui^3le^2$ ('English')! yes, it's the tongue that the foreigners speak . . . ."

"What is this change of Language due to?"

"The mushrooms have a divine spirit; they always had it for us, but the foreigner arrived and frightened it away . . . ."

"Where was this divine spirit frightened to?"

"It wanders without direction in the atmosphere, it goes along in the clouds. And not only was the divine spirit profaned, but that of ourselves (the Mazatecs) as well."

2. Zárate Aquino visited Huautla in August 1974 during his campaign as the Institutional Revolutionary Party (PRI) candidate for governor of the state of Oaxaca.

CHAPTER 20

1. To give the reader an idea of how other Mazatec shamans speak, here are selections I have translated from the Language of the Wise Man, Roman Estrada, sixty years old, who was initiated through the teachings of a Wise Man of the little town of San Lucas named Juan Manuel, who lived to be one hundred and twenty-two years old. Juan Manuel's father supposedly lived more than a hundred and thirty years.

Roman's Language, in accordance with the concepts of María Sabina, is addressed to the Lords of the Mountains, despite the inclusion of Christian deities due to the influence of the Church.

The recording was made in the autumn of 1969.

The Wise Man chants in a trance which can last from four to five or six hours.

[TN.: This is the same shaman who is studied by Henry Munn, "The Mushrooms of Language," in *Hallucinogens and Shamanism*, ed. Michael Harner (New York: Oxford University Press, 1973).]

Shamanistic Songs of Roman Estrada

Medicinal herb, remedial herb
Cold herb, Lord Christ
Free this person from his sickness
Where is his spirit trapped?
Is it trapped in the mountain?
Is it enchanted in some gully?
Is it trapped in some waterfall?
I will search and I will find the lost spirit
Ave María!
I will follow his tracks
I am the important man
I am the man who gets up early
I am he who makes the mountains resound
I am he who makes their sides resound
I am he who makes the spirit resound
I make my tracks resound
I make my nails resound
Christ Our Lord
Lord Saint Martin is present
The Lord of the Dry Tree is present
The Lord of the Lake is present

Santa María Zoquiapan
I am the dawn
I am he who speaks with the mountains
I am he who speaks with the echo
There in the atmosphere
There amid the vegetation
I will make my sound felt
Father Saint John the Evangelist
We see how the dolls and the eagles
Already play in the air
Already play on the mountains
Already play between the clouds
Whoever curses us won't do us any harm
Because I am the spirit and the image
I am Christ the Lord
I am the spirit
The serpent is present
It is coiled up
It is alive
I give relief
I give life
I am the tall and handsome one
I am Jesus Christ
I am Lord Saint Martin
I am Lord Saint Mark
In whose dominions there are tigers
Whoever curses us has no influence on us
I give strength to the sick
I am the medicine
I am the damp herb
Come back lost spirit
I will whistle to guide you

[He whistles]

Return!
May there come with you
Thirteen deer
Thirteen eagles
Thirteen white horses
Thirteen rainbows
Your steps move thirteen mountains
The big clown is calling you
The master clown is calling you
I will make the mountains resound
I will make their abysses resound
I will make the dawn resound
I will make the day resound
I will make the Jar Mountain resound
I will make Mount Rabon resound
I will make the Stone Mountain resound
I will make the Father Mountain resound

I am the big man
The man who gives relief
The man of the day
It is time for the sick one to recuperate
It is time the miracle happens
The miracle of the Holy Trinity
Like the miracle of the creation
Like the miracle of lunar light
Like the miracle of the starlight
Of the Morning Star
Of the Cross Star
The dawn is coming
The horizon is already reddening
There is nothing bad outside
Because I am he who gives relief
I am he who gives the dawn
Santa Maria Ixtepec speaks
Santa Maria Ixcatlan speaks
There is the drought and the thorn

This is only a small part of the long chant of the Wise Man. He has told me that the day his initiation ended—Roman explained this in Spanish—he received a diploma from the hands of the Principal Ones.

2. *Arosio* is an indecipherable word. Maria Sabina says that it is "the name of a place in the mountains".

CHAPTER 21

1. This is an abundant fruit in the Mazatec mountains. Because of its function in Mazatec customs it is called to^3-le^4 $c\text{?}en^3$: "ball of the dead."

NOTES TO THE CHANTS

The Folkways record of the 1956 session is accompanied by an English translation done for R. Gordon Wasson by two American missionary linguists fluent in everyday Mazatec but with little understanding of the sacred language of the mushroom ceremonies. Aware of the inadequacies of the translation and its many gaps where the missionaries had no idea of what the shamaness was talking about, I had the record translated for me into Spanish by a bilingual speaker of Mazatec, Sra. Eloina Estrada de González, in 1970. When he came to write the life story of María Sabina, Sra. González's brother, Alvaro Estrada, did his own Spanish translation of the record without refrence to his sister's translation and published it with his *Life of María Sabina*. The discrepancies between the two latter translations, which in most lines were otherwise identical, pointed up the passages of difficult interpretation and led me to listen to the session over again with both translators. In some cases the sister had heard better than the brother; in others the brother had heard better than the sister. The translation from Mazatec into Spanish, therefore, is the work of both Alvaro and Eloina Estrada.

Besides the two sessions included in the present book, the only other translation of a shamanistic session given by María Sabina is that published by R. Gordon Wasson in his book, *María Sabina and Her Mazatec Mushroom Velada*, (New York: Harcourt Brace Jovanovich, 1974). I shall refer to that session in what follows as "the 1958 Session," or *Velada*. It was translated by the linguists George and Florence Cowan. Every student of Mazatec must be especially grateful to the Cowans for their pains-taking transliteration of the Mazatec. It has enabled me to write the Mazatec words in these notes and provides a basis for the correction of their own translation where they are in error. Selections from that session are readily available for comparison in Joan Halifax, *Shamanic Voices* (New York: E.P. Dutton, 1979).

The Mazatec shamans, inspired by the mushrooms, all sing in more or less the same manner: in short enunciations, often in the first person singular, ending with the word tso^2, it says. (See above, chap. 12, note 1, p. 201.) For them it is the mushroom that speaks through them: they are merely the mouthpieces of a meaning greater than themselves. "In the unconscious," says the French psychiatrist Jacques Lacan, "which is not so much profound as simply inaccessible to conscious apprehension, *it* speaks: a subject in the subject, transcendent to the subject, poses its question to the philosopher since the science of dreams." (Jacques Lacan, "La psychanalyse et son ensignment" in *Ecrits* [Paris: Editions du Seuil, 1966], p. 437.) It is to this *id*, this *it*, this anonymous impersonal subject of speech, that the "says" at the end of each utterance points to. Often, however, María Sabina and her niece use the *tso* even when they are obviously speaking for themselves. In such places it doesn't sound right to say, "it says"; the reference is much more unspecific. Therefore I have translated the verb without any pronoun to give an idea of how the Mazatec shamans use it as a vocal stop, a mark emphasizing the act of enunciation that punctuates the flow of the chant.

Two key words in María Sabina's chants are the adjectives nai^3 and chi^3con^3.

She says: "I am an eagle woman nai^3, I am an eagle woman chi^3con^3; I am a clown woman nai^2, I am a clown woman chi^3con^3; I came forth nai^3, I came forth chi^3con^3"; or "I am a woman who sounds forth nai^3, a woman who sounds forth chi^3con^3." Estrada translates nai^3 as "*dueno,*" "Lord" or "Master." It is a term of respect used whenever one addresses an elder. Nai^3 means "principal" or "first." It has the connotation of age and therefore of what is worthy of respect. Sra. González remembers once overhearing a woman say to another: "Your mother's grandmother is a hundred and forty." "Poor grandmother," the other replied, "she's getting nai^3. In other words ancient. Asked whether nai^3 means old, the medicine woman, Irene Pineda answered: "Yes, it is what comes from the root." It has the sense of what is primordial. I have translated it sometimes as Lord ("Lord eagle woman"), sometimes as principal (as in "principal medicinal berries"), and at other times as important (as in "woman who came forth important"); and, where it refers to sound, as grandiloquent.

The Lord of the Sacred Mountain is known as Chi^3con^3 $To^4co^2xo^4$. Each mountain has its lord, its "chi^3con^3 ni^3nto^3." (See above, chap. 2, note 1, p. 197.) Each well or spring has its deity, its "chi^3con^3 nta^1." $Chjota$ chi^3con^3, the Mazatecs call men in government, people with authority. It means important people, high class people, people with power. Because in modern times such people are usually white, in contemporary Mazatec the word "chi^3con^3" has come to mean *guero,* "white"—a recent corruption of the original meaning of the word. In a similar way, since the conquest, the idea has grown up that Quetzalcóatl was white and in recent versions of the Mazatec legend about Chicón Tocosho, he is said to be white. Chi^3con^3 means "Lord" in a religious, transcendental sense. In Mazatec the word for godfather is the word for father with chi^3con^3 added to it, the word for godchild is child with chi^3con^3. Xca^{42} (leaves) qua (things) chi^3con^3 are leaves that have been blessed. Nta^1 (water) qua chi^3con^3 is holy water. $Quachi^3con^3$ alone means "religious doctrine, divine things." Estrada translates chi^3con^3 as "sacred." I have folllowed him. Cowan translates the word in the 1958 session as "important," "chief," "blessed," or "holy."

One of the difficulties in translating María Sabina's chants is that her words, drawn from the treasure troves of the tongue, are often incomprehensible to the contemporary Mazatec. When you ask people what her words mean they are liable to dodge their ignorance by saying that she doesn't know what they mean herself. The truth is that the vocabulary used by the shamans in these conditions of linguistic inspiration differs from ordinary everyday language, as does any literary, poetic, or philosophical language. "Who knows where the old lady gets her words from!" a Mazatec man of great sophistication, versed in the language, once exclaimed to me. "The poetic vocabulary of a Yakut shaman contains twelve thousand words, whereas the ordinary language—the only language known to the rest of the community—has only four thousand," notes Mircea Eliade in *Shamanism: Archaic Techniques of Ecstasy,* trans. Willard R. Trask, (Princeton, N.J.: Princeton University Press, Bollingen Series 76, 1964), p. 30. She herself, says Estrada, refuses to explain her words and even seems at times to take delight in their obscurity. On one occasion she told the translators of the 1958 session that an inexplicable phrase was "mushroom language." One is reminded of the

Nahuallatolli, the "hidden or magic language" of the ancient Mexican medicine men described by Jacinto de la Serna: "In all of these spells, the sorcerers use vocables that are so metaphorical and syncopated, that not even they themselves understand them, and asked what they signify and where they come from, they have no other explanation than to say that so they were taught by their ancestors." (Jacinto de la Serna, *Manual de Ministros de Indios, para el conocimiento de sus idolatrias y extirpación de ellas* [Mexico, D.F.: Ediciones Fuente Cultural, 1953], p. 263.)

Two of these difficult, esoteric words are the ones I have translated as "Whirling woman of colors/Woman of the networks of light." (See below, p. 220.)

Throughout her chants she says many words in pidgin Spanish. They are "saint," "saintess," "spirit," "clock," "book," "labor," (Estrada and Cowan translate it as "wolf" but since she usually says it after she has stated her function as a shaman it is more likely that it is "labor" than "lobo"), "justice," "government," "lawyer," "transactions," "general," "sergeant," "corporal," "commander," "violin," "drum," "medic," "mine," "launch," "number," "people of reason," "pound," "ounces," "archbishop," "nun," "scribe," "letters," "shepherdess," "communion wafer," "head," "beer," "fire," and fragments of church prayers, e.g., "in the name of the Father, the Son, and the Holy Spirit." The inclusion of Spanish words in her songs reflects her situation as a speaker of Mazatec in a Spanish-speaking country; but shamans have always spoken in different languages. A Conibo shaman whom I recorded in the Ucayali River region of Peru used words in his *yaje* chants taken from the languages of neighboring tribes. (Henry Munn, "The Painted Air," *Journal for the Protection of All Beings: The Coevolution Quarterly*, Sausalito, Calif., no. 19, Fall 1978.) According to Eliade, the Northwest Coast shamans did the same. Shamans are adepts at communicating with the spirits and talk "in tongues." They are polyglots who understand the language of the birds and animals as well as those of other men.

Coleridge held the imagination to be "the living Power and prime Agent of all human Perception and as a repetition in the finite mind of the eternal act of creation in the infinite I am," — a statement that illuminates María Sabina's succession of assertions in the first person singular. The "I," the French linguist, Emile Benveniste has pointed out, "refers to the act of discourse itself, to the enunciator of the enunciation (Emile Benveniste, *La nature des pronoms*, and "De la subjectivité dans le language," in *Problemes de Linguistique Générale*, vol. 1, Paris: Editions Gallimard, 1966.) The "I" here is simply the grammatical armature of articulation. If she is the moon, the sea, a spider, a hummingbird, an eagle, and an opossum, it is evident that the "I" of her affirmations is not the individual, personal, particular, egocentric "I," but the "I" of the transcendental ego, an "I" created by the grammar of language, the impersonal, abstract, universal, generic subject of speech by which she assumes the being of everything in the universe by turn. Her predications are not metaphors but identifications: they are like the masks of different beings that the Tlingit shamans put on and took off. In a set of eight such masks in the American Museum of Natural

History, New York City, each one representing one of the shaman's personae, there is a mask of the bear spirit, of the deer spirit, of the moon, of the kingfisher, of the spirit of the raven, of an eagle spirit, of an old woman's spirit, and of a spirit living in the clouds. Maria Sabina becomes what she names and at the same time her listeners are led by her words to feel their own egos extended beyond themselves to become all things.

FOLKWAYS SESSION: NOTES

The notes contributed by Alvaro Estrada are marked [A.E.]; The other notes are mine. The breaks in the text indicate the bands of the record.

p.105

[A.E.] *"Our Ustandi woman..."* Another name that María Sabina gives to Saint Peter.

For the Mazatecs, Saint Peter and Saint Paul are the deities of tobacco, the tutelary Gods of medicine. (See above, chap. 3, note 2, p. 197; and chap. 10.)

"...*shooting star woman...*" The chji^4 njon^3, I have been told, "is red light like a comet." The Mazatecs believe that some people have the spirit of a shooting star. "One realizes it when the spirit begins to function. The person comes out of the house where he or she lives in the form of a shooting star and plunges into a mountain or comes out of a mountain to return home. It goes into the mountain to find money or luck or whatever the person wants. People who are shooting stars are successful but tend to be sickly." The idea is associated by the Mazatecs with wealth. If one happens to see a comet zoom out of a house at night and dive into a mountain, then emerge from the mountain and whiz back to the same house, one shouldn't say anything about it because if it gets to be known that a person changes into a shooting star the person is likely to die.

María Sabina usually mentions the shooting star in association with Saint Peter. The connecting idea is fire. The tobacco is said to burn like a light and to heat up the body. The full name of the shooting star is chji^4 njon^3 li. Li means fire. María Sabina leaves off the ending of the word to fit it into the melody of her chant, but the image of fire is there in the image of the meteor streaking through the sky.

p.106

"...*well-prepared woman...*" She means she is a woman who has been trained to do what she does.

"...*well-prepared soul...*" The word I have translated as "soul" means literally "one's appearance." The meaning of the Mazatec word is the same as the Nahuatl use of "face" in such expressions as "It will pain your faces, your hearts," or "Reverence to your faces, to your hearts." Miguel León-Portilla explains: "The face is, then, for the *tlamatinime* (the Aztec Wise Men) the manifestation of a self that has been acquired and developed by education. 'Your face, your heart,' in Nahuatl thought defines people. It is the equivalent of what, according to our Western way of thinking, we call "personality" (Miguel León-Portilla, *La Filosofia Nahuatl*, [Mexico: Universidad Nacional Autonoma de México, 1966], p. 190, 191). Just as for the ancient Aztecs, for the Mazatcs the character of somebody, their soul, is manifested by their physiognomy.

p.107

"*...woman fallen into the world...*" She doesn't actually say "world." She simply says that she fell out. The Mazatec women have their babies kneeling rather than lying down. The sense of the word is close to the "slip" or "slide out" (*escurri*) used for birth in the Nahuatl invocation of the Lord and Lady of Duality recorded in the Codex Matritense: "The celestial god is called the Lord of Duality/ And his consort is called the Lady of Duality, the Celestial Lady/ Which is to say, over the heavens, he is Lord, is King/ From there we receive our life, we humans, from there falls our luck, when it is placed (in the womb), when the baby slides out, from there it gets its being and its destiny, it is placed in its insides, the Lord of Duality dictates it."

Her phrases go together in pairs, in couplets. The binary structure of her chant exemplifies what Angel María Garibay called the "diaphrasism" characteristic of ancient Nahuatl poetry: "...a procedure that consists in expressing the same idea by means of two words that complement each other in meaning, whether because they are synonymous or adjacent." These double expressions reflect, as León-Portilla has pointed out, the underlying dualism inherent in Mesoamerican thought (*ibid.*, p. 143).

"*...woman who gives life/ ...woman who reanimates...*" Literally she says: "Woman who sits down, woman who stands up." Estrada notes that "those are movements that signify a person is alive." This is an idiomatic expression. I have translated it as Eloina Estrada understood it, as referring to María Sabina's function as a woman who makes the sick sit up and get on their feet again.

"*...Old One...*" The word she uses is *Tata*, a respectful, affectionate term for father used by the Indians throughout Mexico for important elders. In the Mixteca, for instance, Lazaro Cardenas, the former president of Mexico was called "Tata Cardenas."

"Green Mother..." The word *xcoen¹* which I have translated as "green," means a plant that is not yet ripe. The word for the color green is *sase*. *Xcoen¹* could be translated as "tender," but it doesn't denote a sentimental attitude either. Cowan translates it in the 1958 session as "fresh," and I do as well where it seems appropriate as on page 115, where she uses it to refer to water.

"*Yo⁴ va²*," which I have tranlated as "clarity," Estrada in a personal communication tells me means "transparent." "It is the translucence of the young leaves seen against the light at sunrise. The shamans refer frequently to what occurs and is observed at dawn: the clouds, the freshness, phenomena, etc."

p.108

"*...woman who looks into the insides of things/ ...woman who investigates...*" In Mazatec: "*Chjon⁴² (woman) nca³co³ya³nia¹³, chjon⁴²nca³co³t?a³nia¹³.*" This is one of those pairs of words that go together in her chants not only because of their complementarity of meaning, but also because of the similarity in sound between them. *Co³ya³* means to look inside of something. The mushrooms make her clairvoyant. She is a woman endowed with insight. $Co^3t?a^3$ means "to observe from the outside, to probe." Estrada translates it as "examine." What she is referring to is how she examines her patients to arrive at a diagnosis of their ills.

p. 109

"...woman of the great expanse of the waters..." The word she uses here, nta^1 (water) ts jon^1, is an obscure one. Estrada understands $tsjon^1$ as "to kick" and thinks the expression means "to swim," literally "to paddle in the water." He translates this passage as follows: "I am the woman who knows how to swim, says/I am the woman who knows how to swim in the sacred, says; Because I can go up to heaven, says/Because I can swim over the water of the sea, says..." I don't believe that she actually says she swims in the water. There is no verb in Mazatec that means, literally, "swim," since it is very uncommon for them to swim. They say somebody "knows how to go into the water." When she says she goes through the water, as she does in 1970, p. 140, she uses a verb that means "traverse the water," as in fording a stream. Moreover she uses the word as a noun, not a verb: she says, '$chjon^{42}nta^1tsjon^1nai^3nia^{13}$, $chjon^{42}nta^1tsjon^1chi^3con^3 nia^{13}$ just as she says, "$chjon^{42}ja^4tse^3nai^3 nia^{13}$, $chjon^{42}ja^4tse^3 chi^3con^3 nia^{13}$"—"I am a Lord eagle woman, I am a sacred eagle woman." One could translate it as swimmer; then it would be: "I am the Lord swimmer woman, I am the sacred swimmer woman," but then she says she can go over the nta^1tsjon^1. The Mazatecs call the sea, $nta^1chi^3con^3$, "the sacred waters", just as the ancient Mexicans called the sea that surrounded their land the "divine waters." The expression, "$nta^1tsjon^1nai^3$, $nta^1tsjon^1chi^3con^3$" is associated in her mind with the idea of going up to heaven. It occurs once in the course of the 1958 session (p. 137) after she says: "Look, I feel that I am going up to heaven." Cowan translates it there as: "I am a woman lord of the sea which ends, I feel/Woman who came blessed am I, I feel." One person I asked told me that she is saying "woman above the water." $Tsjon^1$ means "a plain, a flat place." I think that what she says is that she is the woman of the expanse of the waters, the expanse of the sea. In a letter to Wasson from Huautla in 1953, Eunice V. Pike, the linguist, talking about what the Indians say about their mushroom experiences, wrote: "Most of them agree that the wisemen frequently see the ocean and for these mountain people that is exciting."

"Calmly...without mishap..." This is something that is said when people go on a trip, a wish for them to arrive safely at their destination. The expression means literally "calmly and on the ground." In the 1958 session, she says over and over again: "Calmly, without mishap/With sap, with dew/With tenderness, with clarity." One is reminded of the Navajo prayer: "On the trial marked with pollen may I walk/ with grasshoppers about my feet may I walk/ with dew about my feet may I walk" (Washington Matthews, *The Night Chant: A Navajo Ceremony*, Memoirs of the American Museum of Natural History, vol. 6, New York, 1902).

p. 110

[AE.] "*Mother of the Sanctuary/...Father of the Sanctuary...*" Otatitlán, Oaxaca. The Christ of Otatitlán.

...*"Baby Water..."* The name of a place in the Sierra Mazateca.

p. 111

"*My clean staff...* Many of the figures in the ancient Mexican codices are walkers with staffs. The Huichol goddess of growth, Nakawé, has a magic staff symbolizing a snake. Decorated staffs are leaned against her effigy. "Sticks similar to the batons of Grandmother Growth, called by the same name, *Nakawé Kwalele* or *Nakawé itzu*," writes Lumholtz, "are in common use among the Huichol and symbolize the power and old age of Grandmother Growth. They are deposited in the cave of the goddess as prayers for health and long life and generally, a large pile of them may be seen there..." (Carl Lumholtz, *Symbolism of the Huichol Indians*, Memoirs of the American Museum of Natural History, vol. 3, [New York, 1900], p. 50).

"*They are important people...*" Here she is apparently talking about the host, Cayetano García, and his wife, Guadalupe, in whose house the ceremony was taking place. Cayetano is the *síndico* of the town she talks about in her life story, chap. 14.

p. 111

"*I know how to speak with the judge...*" Two years later in the 1958 session, almost the same words recur (p. 19): "I am a woman of justice/ I am a woman of the law/ Because God knows me/ the Saints know me/ Cross Star woman am I/ Because I go up to heaven." This is a description of the shaman as an intermediary between the community and the supernatural, transcendental world of the spirits, where she is known because of her frequent visits on behalf of her people. "I am a lawyer woman," she states in 1970 (p. 153), using the Spanish word *licenciada*, "I am a woman of transactions." The lawyer is one who arranges a person's affairs with the law, and in archaic communities, where sickness does not have natural but spiritual causes and can often be the consequence of transgressions, that is precisely the funciton of the shaman: to intercede for the patient and argue his or her case with the powers that govern life. "And I go to render account to the Judge/ And I render accounts to the Government," she says in 1958 (p. 85).

I have been told that Toribio García, another shaman, long since deceased, whom she mentions in her autobiography as living down the hill from her (above, chap. 12), also spoke of appearing in the Courts of Heaven and going to the Table of Justice to inquire about the case of his patient. "I have been to the Offices of Government," he is rememberd as saying, "I have been to the Golden Table and looked through the Book of the Law. There is nothing registered in the Archives of Heaven against this man. He will grow old and use a staff and have many grandchildren." The theme of justice and law in María Sabina's chants, therefore, is not unique to her, but is a part of the traditional rhetoric of the Mazatec shamans. This is an example of how their figures of speech are drawn from a communal, shared repertory of images.

p. 112

"It is not anything salted..." "Salted" is a Mazatec expression for something that has been hexed.

"hmm hmm hmm/so so so si..." Throughout María Sabina's sessions there are passages like this of nonsemantic expressions, where she hums and claps, utters meaningless syllables, and whistles. The mushrooms, by a profound modulation of the nervous system, attune one to Being in a more primordial way than usual. The body begins to vibrate, hence her humming, a mode of tuning herself in to the energy flowing through her. The intensified pulse beat of existence expresses itself in percussion and ecstatic, phonemic, articulatory sound play. This dynamic, rhythmic syllabification of impulses goes back to the babble of infantile orality, as appears vividly earlier in this session on p. 109 in her "...ma, ma, ma, ma mama who art, art, art, art in the house of heaven," where the bilabial articulation of the "m's" reproduces the movements of the mouth sucking at the breast. It is as if she were playing with the raw, phonemic antecedents of words. Wasson intuits this primitive, phonological level of vocal expression anterior to verbal semantic speech, when he says of what he calls her "glossolalia," that it is "as though the syllables were groping for the respective slots to slip into place, thus shaping 'the Word'" (*Velada*, p. 276).

The syllables she utters the most frequently in this session and the 1958 session are "si," "so," and "sa": a sibilant with a sharp aspirated vowel, a rounded vowel, and an open vowel that run through the principal positions of vocal articulation. This choice of syllables comes from the common exclamation of Mazatec women: "Jesusi." She breaks down "Jesus" into its component parts and recomposes the name from them again as on page 109 in this session. At a later moment p. 119, she introduces "ki," "ko" and "ka" sounds, using the same vowels with the occlusive "k" as with the sibilant "s." The "ki" sound is the beginning of "Christ," which she pronounces, *Kristo.*

The fact that she calls herself a woman saint and a woman saintess, as on p. 106 of this session, led the eminent Mesoamerican ethnologist Roberto J. Weitlaner, in a comment on the 1958 session, to say that it reminded him of the bi-sexuality of some Gods in the calendar of the Zapotecs, another people of Oaxaca. Beyond the fact, however, that when she mentions the saints she mentions them all, as she says herself here, p. 117, I think that the explanation is that the words *santo* and *santa* have the same endings as the "so" and "sa" of her meaningless syllables. The alternation of sound is what she likes, the contrast of "to" and "ta." That the binary pulses also signify male and female is a further expression of the duality that runs through her chants as it does through nature.

"*Woman who resounds...*" She is referring to how, under the effect of the mushrooms, she becomes reverberant. Cowan translates this verb as "thunder," which leads Wasson to remark on the connection between mushrooms and thunder (*Velada*, p. 82). If she were referring literally to thunder, however, she would say *chaon fa³ne³je³. Tjo³tsin³*, the word she uses, is said of rockets exploding at fiestas. She says in the next line just "torn up" or "picked," identifying herself with the mushrooms. I've added "ground" to go with "resound" in order to give an idea of the consonance of sound between the two words she uses: *tjo³tsin³* and *tjo³ne³.* She often says she is "...a woman who resounds/...a woman torn up out of the ground..." together with the statement that she is "...a woman wise in medicine/...a woman wise in herbs," as on p. 108 in this session and on p.145 in the 1958 session.

"*Woman of the principal medicinal berries...*" "*To¹xqui³nai³/To¹xqui³chi³con³.*" *To¹* means "berry or tuber." There are a number of tubers and berries used medicinally whose names all begin with *to¹*, as the names of the edible mushrooms all begin with *tjain³*: there is *to¹vow*, "hot tuber," a root used for stomach ailments; *to¹na⁴tse¹chzin*, "mute rabbit tuber," which is used to cure diarrhea; *to¹nyon*, a purgative; and *to¹zui³*, green berries that are used to wash children when they have the measles, and women after childbirth. *To¹* ("berry") *xqui³* ("medicine") is therefore a *generic* name for all of the tubers and berries used as remedies. From what I have been told, "Woman of the principal medicinal berries/ woman of the sacred medicinal berries," is a magical formula like "In the name of God the All-Powerful," or "Saint Peter and Saint Paul and all the Saints," recited in the course of doctoring, especially when pressing the sick person's stomach. Most of the different tubers and berries that come under the *to¹* category are for stomach ailments.

p. 113

"*Work, work...*" Cayetano urges her on in the same spirit as people listening to jazz sometimes yell out enthusiastically: "That's it. Tell it like it is." The tone of voice in which she begins this passage is definitely playful and at one point the man laughs with pleasure at her song. He thanks her for the beauty of her words.

"*Lord clown woman...*" The idea of being a clown woman appears throughout her chants from session to session. It is often associated with water. Two years later, in 1958, she sings: "I am the Morning Star woman/ I am the God Star woman/ I am the Cross Star woman/ I am a launch woman/ I am a lord clown woman" (p. 117). All of the Mazatec shamans in their chants call the mushrooms clowns and children. The reference here is to the hilarity characteristic of these emotional, cathartic experiences during which people laugh and cry. When the shamaness calls herself a clown it is an expression of her good humor and euphoric exuberance. But she is not a silly clown, she is a Lord clown, a sacred clown. The Trickster is a figure who plays an important role in the mythology of the North American Indians. "The reaction of the audience to both him and his exploits is prevailingly one of laughter tempered with awe," says Radin (Paul

Radin, *The Trickster: A Study in American Indian Mythology,* [New York: Schocken, 1972]). He is called "First born" or "Old Man." In the same way María Sabina speaks of the clown as *nai³,* a word which not only means Lord, but has the connotation of ancient, primordial, elder. (See p. 211.) "First-born you are the oldest of all those I have created," says Earthmaker to Trickster, who makes fun of everything sacred at the same time as he is represented as the creator of the world. According to the origin myth of the Winnebago Medicine Rite, he was created to free men from evil spirits. Radin says he is "a divine culture hero and a divine buffoon." That is exactly what María Sabina calls the clown. She says she is a holy clown woman, a divine clown woman. In many of the sacred ceremonies of the American Indians, for example among the Huichol, there are clowns who give expression to the blasphemous thoughts that always contradict the sacred in the antithetical workings of the mind. It may be, though, that the idea of the clown in Mazatec thought, handed down from shaman to shaman, is a vestige of the ceremony, described by Sahagún, celebrated by the Aztecs every eight years to renew the edible plants—a festival at which they fasted and dressed up in costumes like butterflies and animals in an efflorescence of oneiric fantasy (one person carried a sleeping man on his back and said he represented Dream)— and people they called Mazatecs swallowed snakes and frogs alive, uttering "pa, pa," as they gulped them down without touching them with their hands. (Fray Bernardino Sahagún, *Historia General de la Cosas de Nueva España,* Book 2, Appendix I [México: Editorial Porrua, 1969].)

The fact that this ceremony was obviously concerned with the rain, since frogs and snakes are animals of the water, relates it to María Sabina's connection of the clowns with water. Soustelle, whether because of the mention of Mazatecs acting as clowns at the festivities or on the basis of other information, asserts that the Aztecs adopted this festival from the Mazatecs, who celebrated it every eight years in honor of the Morning Star (Jacques Soustelle, *The Daily Life Among the Aztecs,* [New York: Macmillan, 1962]). In that light, one wonders at her connection of the Morning Star and the clown in the passage from the 1958 session quoted above.

p. 114

"*Whirling woman of colors/ Woman of the networks of light. . .*" Estrada translates this as: "Whirlwind woman, whirlwind woman/ woman of the big town, Big town woman." The Mazatec is: "*Chjon⁴²nca³ts?o¹tji³/ Chjon⁴²na⁴jncha⁴?no¹.*" The *ts?o¹tji³* woman is an atmospheric, optical phenomenon that appears in the mist at sunrise. Everybody I have talked to about it describes it in the same way. Many people, especially men who are accustomed to being on the path before dawn, have seen it. It looks like a woman in a huipil who goes along beside one through the mist, spinning around, her dress billowing out, bell-shaped, decorated with all the colors of the rainbow. Everyone who described the phenomenon to me emphasized the colors. Therefore I have translated it as "Whirling woman of colors," rather than simply "Whirlwind," in order to present the image evoked in the Mazatec's mind by the word. There is another word in Mazatec for just whirlwind, *ski,* a word used frequently by María Sabina's niece in the 1970 session. Wasson says in a note in *Velada* (p. 63): "The word *ts?o'tji* is no longer used, and María Sabina did not recognize it though she made use of it in her singing." According to one of his informants, "It means 'woman of the round (*tji³*) huipil (*ts?o¹*),' that is, 'woman who whirls like a whirlwind when dancing.'"

The "whirling woman of colors" is usually associated in María Sabina's chants with the "woman *na⁴jncha⁴?no¹*," an esoteric word of difficult interpretation. An informant told Wasson the word refers to "a sacred, enchanted place beyond Chilchotla in the Sierra Mazateca." "This holy ground will be invoked repeatedly," Wasson writes referring to the 1958 session (*Velada*, p. 62). George Cowan translates this as: "Whirling woman of the whirlwind am I/ Woman of a sacred enchanted place am I!" There is a village near Chilchotla named *Na⁴jncha⁴? no* situated, so people have told me, in the midst of a rocky landscape, but I don't think it is what the Mazatec shamans mean by this enigmatic word. Estrada translates it as "big population woman," or "populous town woman," following information provided by his father, who said it means a "pueblo tupido," a town where the houses are closely packed together. The word is an ancient one, derived from the immemorial lore of the Mazatec shamans, and its meaning has almost been forgotten. The shaman Roman Estrada (see above, chap. 20, note 1, on p. 207), when I questioned him about the meaning of the word, which he also uses in his chants, told me: "*Na⁴jncha⁴?no¹* is something that comes out in the sky at midnight and it is one of those things that the mushrooms show and indicate. It's seen very clearly when the sky is clear." "What is it, a cloud or stars?" my interpreter asked him. "No," he replied, "they're things hanging up there in the sky at midnight." "Is it the Milky Way?" "Yes," he said, "that's what it is." "And is it the same as the *ts?o¹tji³*?" "No," he replied, "the whirlwind comes out in the morning when the sun starts to come out and when it's misty. They form a ring, that's why it's called a whirlwind and people say when one is walking where there is a whirlwind, it follows you and goes ahead of you along the path."

On the basis of this information, I suggest that both words are names of optical phenomena that occur under specific atmospheric conditions in the mountains and that they are used by the shamans in their chants as metaphors for the colors and lights that illuminate consciousness during the psychedelic experience. *Na⁴no* means "rope" and *no* alone signifies "knot". Eloina Estrada de González, the cotranslator, from her childhood memories of people talking about their mushroom experiences, has the idea that *na⁴jncha⁴?no¹* is a net with a fine meshwork like lace. High on the mushrooms, when one opens one's eyes, one often sees ethereal networks of light in the air—that may be what the word means in the language of the Mazatec shamans. Even Estrada's translation, "populous town" or "place where the houses are clustered together," reminds one of the small, densely packed designs one sees on the mushrooms, and many are the people who have seen fabulous architecture and mysterious cities on these mind drugs. The "populous town" translation is supported by the fact that people say they are going to the *na⁴ jncha⁴*, to the center, when they're going to the biggest town around.

These are words imbued with magical power, as Wasson says. When you ask the Mazatecs what they mean they don't define them, they free associate around

them. Here is what different people have told me about the $Chjon^{42}na^4jncha^4?no^1$:
"She is a woman who appears at the wells in the mist, dressed in white lace like a
bride, and who devours children"; "She is the millionaire woman"; "She is who
you invoke when you inquire into the destiny of a person." If the meaning of such
words were clear it would dispell the spell they cast.

"*Clock woman...*" Her clapping—no longer in time to her words but slightly
out of phase, creating a syncopated effect—sounds like ticking when she says she
is a clock woman. It can't be by chance that she should call herself a clock woman
at the end of this passage in which she has been marking time to her words with
clapping. It is as if the clock here, at this moment, is the biological time clock. As
K.S. Lashley, the psychologist, pointed out in his essay, "The Problem of Serial
Order in Behavior" in *Cerebral Mechanisms in Behavior*, ed. L.A. Jeffress, (New
York: John Wiley and Sons, 1967), there is an effector mechanism underlying the
synergisms of movement and articulation. It is this neurological "pace-setter," as
he calls it, that governs the metronomic measures of her song. Since she is a music
woman it is not surprising that she is also a clock woman.

In this session and the 1958 session, the idea of time, which Kant said is the
essence of human consciousness, is associated in her chants with the eagle, an
image for the transcendental nature of the mind. "I am a woman like a clock/ I am
a lord eagle woman," she sings in 1958 (p. 21); and later that same night, she says:
"I am a woman with a good spirit/ I am a lord eagle woman/ I am a clock woman/
I am a whirling woman of colors." She says "clock" in Spanish, *reloj*. At the center
of Huautla, opposite the church, the town schoolhouse has a tall clocktower with
the Mexican emblem of the eagle on it. That may be one of the sources of her
connection between the eagle and the clock. Throughout the day and night the
clock used to chime every quarter hour: one bell for quarter past the hour, two
for half past, three for quarter to, and on the hour, after chiming four times, it
would ring the number of the hour. In the silence of the night, the bells could be
heard all over the dark town, where until 1968 there were no electric lights.

This same image of the clock is used by Leary to describe the processes of
consciousness disclosed by LSD: "You feel yourself sinking down into the soft
tissue swamp of your own body, slowly drifting down dark red waterways and
floating through capillary canals, softly propelled through endless cellular facto-
ries, ancient fibrous clockworks—ticking, clicking, chugging, pumping relent-
lessly." (Timothy Leary, "She Comes in Colors," in *The Politics of Ecstasy*, New
York: College Notes and Texts, 1968, p. 137.) The image of the clock also
appears in the chants of the Conibo medicine man, inspired by *yajé*, whom I
recorded in the Ucayali area of Peru: "Our King gives contentment/ we are going
to heal the bodies/ ladder of heaven/ the good sounds/ the one that sounded was
like a brilliant clock/ I am going to cure the bodies, to cure them well." "There is
a clock bell/ it is ringing beautifully/ good sound/ with this I am going to clean
the body" (Munn, "The Painted Air"). For more about the meaning of the clock
to María Sabina, see note to p. 145 of the 1970 session, on p. 231.

p. 115

"Flower of the dew..." As Wasson points out, María Sabina often refers to the mushrooms as flowers. "The Nahuatl spoke of *temixoch,* 'the flowery dream,'" he says, "'the dream caused by magical means,' according to Ruiz de Alarcón; by which he obviously meant the hallucinogenic trance. For it seems that flower in Nahuatl carried the metaphorical sense of an hallucinogen." *Velada,* p. 274). The Huichol, too, call peyote a flower and often depict the cactus as one. But one must avoid letting the drugs, which induce these conditions of poetic inspiration, get in the way of a wider interpretation of the images that appear in the shamans' chants. First and above all for the ancient Mesoamericans, flower was a figurative expression for poetry, which they called "flower and song." "Priest, I ask you, from where do the flowers that intoxicate men come?/ the song that intoxicates, the beautiful song?" The answer reminds one of this very passage: "They only come from his house from the interior of heaven/ only from there do the various flowers come/ from where the water of flowers extends." The verses of Nezahualcóyotl, the mystic poet of Tezcoco, give us an idea of the source of flowers in María Sabina's poetry: "You only distribute/ flowers that intoxicate/ precious flowers/ you are the singer/ in the interior of the house of spring/ you make people happy." (León-Portilla, *La Filosofia Nahuatl;* and *Trece Poetas del Mundo Azteca,* [México: Universidad Autonoma de México, 1967]).

p.116

"Mine that is increasing..." See note to p. 173 of the 1970 session, on p. 237, where this theme is taken up by her niece.

"There is no wind, there is no spit, there is no garbage, there is no dust..." In the conjurations of the ancient Mexican Sorcerers, collected by Ruiz de Alarcón and recently retranslated and commented on by Alfredo López Austin, the expression, "bath of others' garbage," means problems caused by contact with people who had committed sexual transgressions. In their exorcisms, "garbage" refers to sexual abuses. "Come you gods of garbage," they sang, "stand up and look at me, red garbage, white garbage, green garbage." (Alfredo López Austin, "Conjuros Medicos de los Nahuas," in *Revista de la Universidad de México,* vol. 24, no. 11, July 1970. Wasson is the first person to have pointed out the parallels between these conjurations and María Sabina's chants. See his retrospective essay to this book and the introduction to his *Velada.*)

For the Mazatecs garbage, dust, whirlwind, and bad air are figures of speech for witchcraft, gossip, arguments, and evil. The word for whirlwind used in this context is not the same word as that for the "whirling woman of colors." What they mean by whirlwind are quarrels and disputes that disrupt a household like the dust the wind lifts up and spins around in the mountain paths during the times of heat. When she says, "That is the work of my saints, that is the work of my saintesses," she means that it is the function of the mushrooms to clear away the bad air, to purify, to undo witchcraft, and restore peace.

"a man of cacoa now, you are a man of money, a man with a green staff, a staff of clarity..." She is speaking of Cayetano. This is an example of how truly pre-Hispanic her words are even four hundred years after the Conquest. In ancient Mexico, the merchants, the traders in cacoa, who carried their goods on their backs to distant places to exchange them for other valuables, were distinguished by their staffs and celebrated rites that had to do with staffs. (J. Eric S. Thompson, *Mexico Before Cortez,* Charles Scribner and Sons, New York, 1933, p. 127).

p.117

"Thirteen lord eagles, thirteen lord opossums..." Why thirteen? Roberto Weitlaner, cited by Wasson in a note to his Velada book (p. 17) suggests that thirteen is a lucky number for her because four times thirteen is fifty-two, the number of years in the ancient Mexican century. It is noteworthy in this connection that the ancient Meso-american calendar consisted of twenty day signs—the Mazatecs still think in terms of a twenty day month—which were combined with the numbers one through thirteen. The magical significance attributed to the number thirteen is not particular to María Sabina but prevalent in Mazatec culture generally. The number thirteen also appears in the chants of Roman Estrada (above, Chap. 20, note 1, p.208).

p. 118

"Our doll Virgin who holds up the earth..." Wasson thought that this same word in the 1958 session, translated by Cowan as "detiene el mundo," "woman who stops the world," is related to the teachings of Don Juan, in the books of Carlos Castaneda, about "stopping the world." It seems, though, that this word she uses does not mean "stop the world," but "hold or support the earth" (literally: "beneath the earth"), like the statues of Virgins who sometimes hold a globe in their hands. This statement always goes together in the 1958 session as it does here with the words, $Chjon^{42}chjoa^4ca^3ma^3$. Wasson notes about $chjoa^4ca^3ma^3$: "From an elderly informant we learned that it means, 'a legendary woman who knows how to cure; she directs the hands of the skillful physician'" (*Velada,* p. 57). There is a passage identical to the present one in the 1958 session, p. 111, where the words $se^1nqui^3?nte^3$ ("beneath the earth"), $chjoa^4ca^3ma^3$, and $xon^4nti^4jin^2$ occur together. These form a group of related ideas in her mind. Cowan translates the passage: "Woman who stops the world am I, legendary woman who cures am I/ Woman of paper, of smoke am I." "There where my little prayers are," she goes on, "And where my little nuns are." The association of ideas is almost the same as here. $Chjoa^4ca^3ma^3$ means "a woman who has been marked, designated". Xon^4 ("paper") nti^4jin^1 ("smudged") means "paper blackened with charcoal." When the Mazatec ladies embroider their huipils, they first put a paper with the pattern punched out on it with holes over the cloth, and then rub charcoal dust over the stencil to draw the design. What María Sabina means is that she is a woman stencil through which designs are drawn on the world. Sra. González understood this as "woman covered with writing." María Sabina is referring to her destiny.

p. 120

" . . .*the lordly one with the vibrant wings*. . ." Estrada translates this passage as follows: "Because that is the work of my lord sucker, of my sacred sucker/ Because that is the work of my hummingbird/ Because that is the work of my hummingbird/ Because that is the work of my sucker/ Lord sucker, sacred sucker." As he suggests here, the medicine woman uses suction to draw the illness from her patients as the hummingbird draws nectar from flowers. The usual verb for "suck," however, is not the obscure word, *ntsi⁴ca¹*, which he translates as "sucker." The word, when she uses it, always complements the word for hummingbird, and one of his informants, says Estrada, told him that it is another word for hummingbird. María Apolonia, her daughter, uses the same word in the 1958 session, p. 153, where Cowan translates it as "bird," but the word for bird is *ni⁴se³*. According to him she says: "Go with thirteen hummingbirds/ lord of the birds/ lord of the sacred birds." The cotranslator, Eloina Estrada de González, broke the word down into its component parts: "*ca¹*", she thinks, is "wing," *jnca³*; and she suggests that the *ntsi⁴* which precedes it is an onomatopoetic sound imitating the "tsing" of the hummingbird, the word for which ends itself with the particle *ntsin⁴*. People in Huautla say the hummingbird's wings go "*tsin*." The word when she uses it with *nai¹* and *chi³con³* would thus mean: "lordly one with the vibrant wings/ sacred one with the vibrant wings." Estrada is certainly right that the hummingbird, which Sabina usually evokes in connection with flowers as one would expect, is associated in her mind with the idea of sucking out illness, but the sound the bird makes is also present in her mind. The colloquial Spanish word for hummingbird, *chupamirto* or *chuparrosa*, places the emphasis on sucking, but it appears that the Mazatec word, like our "hummingbird," distinguishes the vibrant sound of the little bird as it hovers in the air, its wings beating. The word I have translated as "resound" is *tjo³tsin³*. Except for a slight tonal difference of a register, it has the same ending as *to²ntsin⁴*, hummingbird.

The shamans in these vibrant conditions of vitality literally hum and buzz with energy — that is another reason why they identify with hummingbirds. "Jonathan Koshiway, the Oto peyote teacher said: 'The peyote spirit is like a little hummingbird, when you are quiet and nothing is disturbing it, it will come to a flower and get the sweet flavor. But if it is disturbed it goes quick'" (Weston LaBarre, *The Peyote Cult* [New York: Schocken Books, 1968]). María Sabina's "our hummingbird children," reminds one of how the Huichol shamans at the Festival of the Drum transform the children, imaginatively, into hummingbirds and sing them to Viracota, the sacred land where the peyote grows (Peter T. Furst, "To Find Our Life: Peyote Among the Huichol Indians of Mexico," in *Flesh of the Gods* [New York: Praeger, 1972]). In Huichol mythology the hummingbird is "the father of the sun." Lumholtz says: "This is a sun bird and it is generally represented in pairs sipping a flower" (Lumholtz, *Symbolism of the Huichol Indians*). The name of the Aztec sun god, Huitzilopochtli, the war god, means literally, "Left-handed Hummingbird," from the Nahuatl *uitzitzilin* for hummingbird. *Opochtli* refers to the left side of the sun, the south.

The hummingbird also figures in the *yajé* songs of the Conibo medicine man I recorded in the Ucayali region of Peru: "From up above comes the doctor with a ladder/ Painted hummingbird/ With this going to heal the body" (Munn, "The Painted Air").

In this passage the children and the flowers María Sabina is talking about are definitely the mushrooms.

"It is the same as the Mountain of Medicine, the Mountain of Herbs . . ." Here she refinds the phraseology of the ancient conjurations which come down to her from pre-Hispanic times, like her language itself that was spoken in her land long before the Spaniards ever reached its shores. "I will give the sick one the priest from the place of medicine to drink," they said. The locution, "the priest from the place of medicine," thinks Lopez Austin, "may be the generic name of the medicines" (Austin, *Conjuros Medicos de Los Nahuas.*).

". . . Thirteen doctors . . ." She says the Spanish word, "medico."

p. 122

"It is your blood. . ." The Mazatecs say Christ walked through their mountains carrying his cross. From where his blood dropped the mushrooms sprang up. They are the "blood of Christ." The idea of following in the footsteps of Christ, along the stations of his way, is a common idea in her chants. Aside from its Christian reference, it is a native American idea. In the Night Chant of the Navajo, the patient on the first night has to enter the medicine lodge and walk on the footprints of Hastséyalti, "the Chief of the Gods," drawn on the floor, to the center of the sand painting. The patient "it is said must walk exactly in the footsteps of the God if he would recover" (Matthews, *The Night Chant*).

p. 123

"I am going to receive the bewitched spirit. . ." The Mazatec shamans conceive of themselves as following the tracks of the extravagated spirit of the sick. Their function is to find the lost spirit and bring it back. They whistle for it, they call it, they entice it to return. An almost identical passage to this occurs in the 1958 session, p. 59, as she is attempting to cure the sick boy Wasson brought her (see above, chap. 14): "I am going to the meeting/ I am going to disenchant him/ I am going to bring air/ Because I am a doctor woman."

p. 125

". . . eagle woman/ . . . oppossum woman . . ." See note to p. 149, 1970 Session, on p. 232.

1970 SESSION: NOTES

Throughout this evening, María Sabina and her niece, María Aurora, take turns singing as she and her daughter, Apolonia, did in 1958, the younger woman relieving the old lady of seventy-six so that she can rest. This night her words are not nearly as vibrant and melodic as in the session fourteen years before—her age makes itself felt.

The session was called primarily to poetize. I don't know what pretext my friend, Celerino Cerqueda, used to invite her to his house to give a ceremony; but there are always troubles in a house: the husband and wife quarrel, there are problems with the neighbors, and they have enemies. The two women go about curing the household and the children. They ask for the well-being of their hosts and at one point they symbolically remarry them (p. 162).

p. 128

"...*the Woman of the Flowing Water...*" The *Chjon*[42]*nta*[1]*ve*, who she says in her autobiography she sometimes becomes, is the most important female figure in Mazatec mythology (see above, chap. 17, chap. 20). She is either the daughter-in-law of Chicon Tocosho, the Lord of the sacred mountain, or his wife; in some versions she is the wife of the son of the old *Cojon*, a God whose dwelling is Mt. Ladder of Water—maybe a rain god because he is said to care for the crops. Whatever the version, however, what is important is that she is a daughter-in-law. Her mother-in-law, according to the story, tells her to go to the cornfield to pick some ears of corn. She comes back with a full sack. The mother-in-law reprimands her for having picked all the corn and the daughter-in-law insulted, leaves the house of her in-laws, taking all her animals and possessions with her. When they go to the cornfield, expecting to find all the corn picked, they are surprised to find that she had hardly picked any ears of corn at all. The Woman of the Flowing Water is the Goddess of Abundance. Whereas the mother-in-law is parsimonious as befits an economy of scarcity, the daughter-in-law is lavish, prodigal, generous. She embodies the inexhaustible fertility of nature.

The myth is about marriage. Its message is: be careful with daughter-in-laws, treat them nicely or they'll leave the household and if they do you'll miss them. In Mazatec society it is customary for a newlywed girl to go and live in the house of the husband's parents, where she is expected to follow the orders of her mother-in-law. "The Woman of the Flowing Water was so mad [at the accusation she had picked all the corn]," the shamaness Irene Pineda told me, "that she left the house taking her pig with her, her salt, her chilis, and that's why, at times, daughter-in-laws are very touchy, they get upset for the slightest thing, because the Woman of the Flowing Water set the example, Our Mother Mistress of the World...She, the daughter-in-law of the Old One of the Mountain, is the one who should be present when any daughter-in-law leaves the house from bitterness."

The things that happen to her on her peregrinations through the mountains after she leaves the house of her in-laws give their names to places. "Where it is called *Xinda*," related Irene Pineda, "there they castrated her hog; where it is called Much Mud is where her hog was tied up; where it is called Soft Stone is where she made her tortillas; where it is called Steambath is where she took a steambath; on Chili Hilltop is where she spilled the chilis she was carrying." She finally arrives at a place called *Nta¹chian*, "Cold Water," where a stream of clear water, welling up from an underground spring, flows out from underneath a rock into the Rio Quiotepec, the largest river in the mountains which divides the territory of the Mazatecs from that of the Mixtec and Cuicatec-speaking peoples on the other side. Here she settles down, where two streams join as two lives are joined in marriage, and according to legend can sometimes be seen washing her clothes on the banks of the river. She is the Mazatec equivalent of Chalchiutlicue, the ancient Mexican goddess of the flowing water, "She with the Skirts of Jade."

p.128

"...*woman whose palms are like spoons/...woman with hands of measure...*" "*Chjon⁴²chaá zae/ chjon⁴²chaá za.*" *Chjon⁴²* is woman; *chaá* is a wooden spoon; *zae* is the palm; *za* the whole hand. The Mazatecs understand that what is meant by spoon is a measuring spoon. A woman with hands of measure is a woman who knows exactly the right amount of ingredients to put into her cooking; she is a woman whose meals are bountiful: no matter how many guests there are for a meal there is always enough to go around. The Woman of the Flowing Water is the Goddess of women's work, the deity of the kitchen and cooking. She scoops up chilis or spices in her hands in fistfuls.

All of the Mazatec shamans refer to her in the same terms. Irene Pineda says: "The Woman of the Flowing Water is the woman of measures, says/ The woman with fists of measure/ The woman who gets the most out of things, who makes a lot from little/ May his business and his well-being progress and prosper," she sings, praying for her patient, "may the little beans and gourds grow and develop/ As the Woman of the Flowing Water did/ As the Woman whose palms are like spoons did/ As the Woman with hands heaped with plenty did." And the same shamaness explains why this deity is invoked, referring to the myth about her: "Later she left on foot taking her animals, her hog and her chickens. She took everything and that is why we call on her for our animals, our pigs, chickens, all our domesticated animals, our goats, to grow and multiply, and for our businesses too, for them to go well and progress with cacao."

"*Fresh Father...*" This cluster of words is usually composed of "sap," "dew," "greenness (or tenderness)," and "clarity." Here she substitutes the word *chian* for *xcoen*. It means, literally, "cool," and is the same word she uses in the Folkways Session when she says: "Let us go with freshnes" (p. 120).

p. 130

"*Benito Juárez...*" The first president of Mexico after the expulsion of the French (1867) and the promulgator of the Mexican Reform laws whose main aim was the separation of Church and State. He was an Indian from the State of Oaxaca like herself and is the one historical person she mentions in her chants. She often invokes him after declaring that she is going to demonstrate her courage, as if the valor she has in mind is eminently civic.

"*Constellation of the Sandal/ Hook Constellation...*" See above, chap. 12, note 3, p. 201.

It is interesting that here she connects the stars, time, and writing. The glyphs on the carved bones found in the tombs of Monte Alban in Oaxaca are dates, and astronomical observations were of course at the basis of the Mesoamerican calendar.

p. 131

"*...music woman...*" Chjon^{42}chji^{4}ne^{4}chjao^3, literally wise (or proficient) in trumpet playing. It is the generic term the Mazatecs use for music. When they hear music they say, "The trumpet is sounding." Estrada (above, Chap. 16) translates it literally. I usually translate it as "music," but here I also translate it as "trumpet" to give some variation. The session is characterized by music as much as by verbal expression. What cannot be translated is the melody of her words whose power to heal lies in the ability of music to uplift and transport the soul. It is interesting that the mushroom ceremony depicted at the center of the Codex Vindobonensis, an ancient Mixtec pictographic book, first attracted the attention of musicologists, not mycologists, because of the curious musical instrument Quetzalcóatl is shown playing, sitting in the midst of a gathering of Gods and Goddesses, with the volutes of song issuing from his mouth: an *omichicahuaztli*, a rasp with a human cranium for resonator. It was only when Alfonso Caso identified the objects in the hands of the assembled Lords and Ladies as mushrooms that it was realized that Quetzalcóatl is pictured here officiating at a shamanistic session (Alfonso Caso, *Representaciones de hongos en los codices, Estudios de Cultura Nahuatl*, vol. 4, Mexico, 1963).

In the past the Mazatec shamans undoubtedly used drums, but the custom has been lost. María Sabina uses her hands, marking time to the tempo of her words by clapping. She doesn't actually play the violin either, but the idea aptly evokes the resonant emotionality of her songs. It is curious that she should say she is a violinist (drum and violin are both said in pidgin Spanish), an instrument rarely played in the mountains except in the town of Mazatlan, but never call herself a zither woman, an instrument which, as she says in her life story, she likes and even once owned. Is the choice of the violin over determined by a memory, passed down in tradition, of the pre-Hispanic rasp, played by rubbing one bone against another as the bow is drawn over the strings of the violin? The violin is the favorite instrument, next to the drum, of the Huichol shamans.

"*...little woman...*" Throughout her chants she often uses the diminutive article, nti, and later the affectionate, diminutive form of the verb "says," *shotze*, "the little one says." The Mazatecs like to use the diminutive in such expressions as *trabajito, frijolito, mamacita*, etc.

p. 133

"*Woman of the great Sun Stone...*" This is an expression Estrada took down from her lips (see above, chap. 20, p. 96). Where does the image come from?

Maybe it comes from the picture of the Aztec calendar stone on the Mexican ten peso bill. It could, though, refer to the place where the Old Cojon lives. See note to p. 173, on p. 237.

p. 136

"...*the person with the staff and the baton of authority*..." For the significance of the staff see the notes to p. 111 and 116 of the Folkways Session, on p. 217 and 223 respectively. The municipal authorities in Huautla have batons of black polished wood tipped with silver as insignia of their public office.

"*The tracks of his hands and his feet*..." This means what one does, where one goes. The Mazatec shamans consider themselves to be hunters on the track of the extravagated spirit of the sick.

p. 137

"...*our bond and our root*..." The root is a trope for ancestry and tradition. See Folkways Session, p. 119. In the 1958 session published by Wasson, there is a beautiful passage where she sings: "I am a root woman beneath the water/ I am a fresh root woman, a root woman of clarity/ I am a woman begonia" (p. 61).

"*Man, Lord of the door and the dooryard*..." It is María Aurora (this night), who takes upon herself the task of speaking for the young couple in whose household the ceremony is being conducted. Wasson, with his customary perspicacity, noted that "a standard feature of the ceremony" is what he aptly describes as "the elaborate homage paid to the hosts in whose house the performance is given" (*Velada,*). Its purpose is to talk for them, to make them feel good, to enhance and exalt them, to renew and reinforce their sense of themselves. María Sabina does it briefly in the Folkways Session (p. 111) for the host, Cayetano García and his wife. In 1958 (p. 139-41) she says of the same couple: "The principal person of my house, the chief of the shade now/ Cayetano García is his name/ Mother Guadalupe, who thunders, who plays music/ Head of the house, chief of the shade, manager of the wind, chief of the thunder/ With calmness, Cayetano García/ Mother Guadalupe, Mother princess/ Admired woman, brilliant woman/...Woman of the house, woman of the shade." The word Cowan translates as head or chief of the house is the word "*chi³con³,*" which I discuss above, p. 211. I translate it here as "Lord" as in Chicon Tocosho.

p. 142

"*Then the plains and the hollows hardened*..." The sense here is of dough that hardens. The evocation of the creation of the world is a constant theme in the chants of the Mazatec shamans. See what María Sabina herself says about how the mushrooms take her back to the origin of all things (above, chap. 9).

p. 143

"*If anyone is criticizing us/ . . . anyone watching us . . .*" She is paranoid that others may hear them giving the ceremony and think that they're doing witchcraft.

p. 145

"*That is your number. . .*" Number is said in Spanish, "numero." It has the connotation of luck as in the number of a winning lottery ticket. Once when a Mazatec friend of mine who is a public accountant and works as an executive in Mexico City ate the mushrooms with María Sabina, she said: "Son, you have clocks all over you." "No," he said, "I only have one." He meant his wristwatch. "What she means," explained the young man's mother, "is that you have lots of time, that you have lots of luck." The association in her mind between the clock and the idea of luck appears clearly in this passage.

p. 146

"*. . . Launch woman. . .*" Launch is another word she says in Spanish, *lancha.* Estrada says (personal communication) that she told him she saw boats in the Hot Country, the tropical lowland area on the Veracruz side of the Sierra Mazateca that was crossed by rivers before it was flooded to form a reservoir for the generation of hydroelectric power (see above, chap. 4, note 3, on p. 198). The idea that she is a launch woman is usually associated with the expanse of the waters and the stars as if she not only crossed the sea, but traversed the heavens as well in her boat, like the Sun and Moon who in certain South American and North American Indian myths are said to travel by canoe. (See Claude Levi-Strauss, "The Canoe Journey of the Moon and Sun," in *The Origin of Table Manners*, trans. John and Doreen Weightman [New York: Harper Colophon Books, 1978]). Twelve years before this, in the 1958 Session, she sings: "I am the Morning Star woman/ I am the God Star woman/ I am the Cross Star woman/ I am a launch woman/ I am a lord clown woman." The reader can see from this example and many others how her associations persist over the years as if they were written in her mind.

p. 147

"*. . . powerful their faces, powerful their day. . .*" She means by faces their entire personalities (see note to p. 106 of the Folkways Session, on p. 214). It could be translated, "their presences." The word for day in Mazatec also means destiny. In other words, the day of one's birth, whose sign determines one's fate.

"*. . . whose will shines. . .*" The San Pedro tobacco is connected with heat, fire, and light. One shaman told me that if one has a packet of tobacco in one's pocket, it will shine there like a light, protecting the person from harm.

p. 148

"*. . . The god of the house, with the god of the shade. . .*" The words I have translated as god here is *chi³con³* (see above, pp. 211 and 230). The *chi³con³* of the house is the household god, the spirit of the place. A Mazatec lady has told me that in one of her mushroom visions she saw a man in calzones and a woman in a huipil at the well near her house and then in the courtyard of the house. She was about to throw holy water at them to dispel the vision when she heard a voice, the voice of the mushrooms, telling her: "No, they won't go away, they are the Gods of the house." Elsewhere in this session there are places where I assume that when María Sabina or María Aurora speak of the man chi³con³ of the house or the woman chi³con³ of the house, they mean the actual master and mistress of the house.

"...*Gustalinia*..." This is María Aurora's pronunciation of her aunt's "*Ustandi.*" (See note, Folkways Session, p. 214.)

p. 149

"...*eagle woman/...Opossum Woman/...Woman who sees*..." She thinks in opposites: the eagle flies high in the sky surveying the earth from above; whereas the opossum goes along close to the ground. The verb she always uses in such passages is not that for looking into the insides of something nor for examining, but *cojónia*, which means "look or see." It is used, for example, when a person is said to look somebody up and down, from head to foot, scrutinizing them critically. When she identifies with the eagle and the opossum, María Sabina is referring to how she seeks for the source of sickness. In the 1958 session (p. 21) after calling herself an eagle woman and an opossum woman, she says: "I am a woman like a hunting dog," as if she imagined herself nose to the ground on the scent of something.

The opossum, because it carries its young in a pouch has a maternal connotation. "The *tlaquatzin*," says Sahagun (in modern Mexican, *tlacuache*), "lives in the cornfields, it makes a cave between the stones where it lives and where it raises its children...when anyone takes its children it screams a lot and cries for them. This animal eats corn and beans... The tail of this animal is very medicinal, it gets rid of anything that is in the flesh or the bones... women who are giving birth by drinking a little of the tail of this animal give birth right away afterwards." "It's also good for constipation," he notes, "because it opens and cleans the pores," and for coughing (Sahagun, *Historia General*, México: Editorial Porrua, 1969, book 11, chap. 1:4). There is thus good reason to include the opossum in a medicine chant, although I have never heard of the Mazatecs using the animal for medicine, but they may have in the past.

The Mazatecs say that opossums have many lives. It's impossible to kill them. If you hit one over the head and leave it for dead, as soon as you go away it will get up again, as in the expression "play possum." In Mayan mythology, the four gods who hold up the sky, the Bacabs, are called in the Books of Chilam Balam "opossum actors." "As opossum actors," says Eric S. Thompson, "they are prominent on the four pages of Codex Dresden which give the ceremonies and prognostications for the incoming year. Each wears the head of an opossum as a mask and has the prehensile tail of the same marsupial attached behind. Most important, each carries the image of the ruling god of the incoming year on his back, seemingly to indicate that his is the responsibility for the fate of the incoming year" (J. Eric S. Thompson, *Maya History and Religion* [Norman, Oklahoma: University of Oklahoma Press,1970]). The same opposition of sky and earth, mediated by the "opossum" Bacabs, occurs in María Sabina, since it is often after she calls herself an eagle woman that she calls herself an opossum woman. In a myth of the Apinaye Indians of Brazil, Star Woman change into an opossum (again the same shift from the high to the low) in order to show men the Tree of Life with corn growing out of it. They try to cut it down with a stone axe, but every time they take a rest the cut closes up. They go to get another axe and on their way back they eat an opossum and their hair turns white, which is said to be the reason why human beings only live a brief time. (See Claude Levi-Strauss, "The Opossum Cantata," in *The Raw and the Cooked*, trans. John and Doreen Weightman, [New York: Harper Torchbooks, 1969].) The Huichol Indians of Northern Mexico, in their myth about the origin of fire, say the opossum steals the fire from the first men night after night, until he almost gets all of it. They finally catch him and kill him, but he revives and they kill him again, they "knock him apart" and once more "he recomposes himself." Because of this indestructability, the myth concludes by saying that the animal's fat is good for ointment, without specifying for what. Zingg cites Lumholtz as saying that in every Huichol temple there is an effigy of an opossum in the rafters (R.M. Zingg, *Huichol Mythology*, Ms., Laboratory of Antropology, School of American Research, Santa Fe, New Mexico; and *The Huichols: Primitive Artists* [New York: Stechert, 1938], pp. 178 and 516). From these indications of the importance of the opossum in Amerindian thought, we can get an inkling of why it should appear in Maria Sabina's chants next to the much more spectacular eagle.

p. 150

"*Lord Patron Saint John...*" The Patron Saint of Huautla is Saint John the Evangelist, the author of the *Epistle According to Saint John*. There is a statue of him, brought there in the 1940s, standing in the Huautla church, with a golden goblet of communion raised in one hand and a quill pen in the other; a lectern is beside him in the form of an eagle, with a scroll draped over one of its shoulder on which is written in Latin: "In the beginning was the word." He is "Our Father scribe" on p. 150, and the statue explains María Sabina's association of the eagle with him. It may also be the source of the quill pen she speaks about in the Folkways Session, p. 111.

The invocations of Santiago, Saint Andrew, and Saint Michel cannot help but call up in her mind and in that of her listeners the nearby towns of San Andres, Rio Santiago, and San Miguel. She says, "He is Lord Santiago," as she says, "he is Benito Juarez," as if she were seeing personages and identifying them as they appear to her. The statues of the saints and virgins in the church and the pictures of them in the religious images the Indians have on the altars of their houses form the iconography of her visions, just as her ancestors must have seen the statues of their Gods in their visions. Santiago is always pictured on a horse and it is mounted that she speaks of him. Likewise, when she says, "doll Mother Magdalene" (p. 152), she means the idol of Magdalene in the church.

p. 151

"*Where our Principal Ones are*. . ." This is the only one of her recorded sessions in which she evokes her reunions with the Principal Ones whom she talks about at such length in her life story. *Gente de razón*, "people of reason," is how the Indians refer to people who speak Spanish and hold important posts. It is clear from what she says that the Principal Ones are ecclesiastical figures. She drinks beer with them as she says she does in her autobiography (chaps. 6 and 12). She says beer in Spanish, *cerveza*. Drinking beer is synonymous for the Mazatecs with social occasions; whether it be a wedding, baptisms, or simple gathering of friends, the tables are always covered with bottles of beer. I have also heard of cases of beer being left in caves as offerings to the gods. Her mention of beer is especially significant because it creates the same contrast between the mushrooms that have inspired her chant and an intoxicating fermented drink as appears in the Codex Vindobonensis, where a gathering of Lords drinking *pulque*, holding goblets of the frothing beverage up in their hands, is depicted next to an assembly of Lords (some of them the same as the *pulque* drinkers in the preceding scene) and Ladies eating mushrooms, holding them in pairs in their hands, at a ceremony presided over by Quetzalcóatl in honor of the Sun God, Piltzinticuhtli.

p. 153

". . .*beer*. . .*head*. . ." Both words are said in Spanish: *cerveza, cabeza*. She plays on the similarity in sound between them, doing the same thing that she does in Mazatec, as with co^3ya^3 and $co^3t?a^3$ (see note, Folkways Sessions, p. 108, on p. 214). In the Folkways Session (p. 109) she says *luna* ("moon"), then *labor*, one word engendering another by sound.

". . .*woman general*. . ." All of the military terms are said in pidgin Spanish. In the 1958 session, during which she felt beleaguered by enemies, she says frequently: "I am a woman general. . .Mexican flag/ I'm more than human/ Didn't the woman of war win? Wasn't it the woman of war who won the most?" The shaman in many archaic societies is thought of as a warrior who enters into battle with the forces of evil that cause sickness. In South America, they sometimes become jaguars; and in some North American tribes it was impossible go on the warpath until the shaman had given the word. "There's still no one who frightens me," she exclaims ferociously in 1958: "One still has to settle things with the woman of war," she threatens. "One still has to settle things with the woman of war, since she won by means of magic."

Her *soy más que hombre*, that night, which Cowan translates as "more than human," literally means: "I'm more than a man," in other words "more of a man than a man." In her chants, as in her profession, she transcends the inferior subservient position imposed on women in traditional Mazatec society. In that sense this woman doctor and poet is a liberated woman: she is not only a mother woman, she is a lawyer woman and a general woman. I once overheard some men in Huautla saying that the fame accorded to María Sabina puts into disrepute the wisdom of Mazatec men.

p. 154

María Sabina seems to be the only person who knows what she means here. Nobody else understands what she says. The same words, "Little woman," *nta[1] quichia*" occur again on pp. 154 and 187, where there are bracketed ellipses.

p. 155

"*We are going to greet our Lord Tocosho. . .*" Here she addresses the Lord of the Magnificent mountain that stands in front of the town of Huautla, whom she tells of meeting in one of her visions (chap. 1, note 7, on p. 195, and chap. 6 on p. 48). The Indians say that he sometimes appears mounted on a white horse along the paths of the mountain and gives money to the poor he meets trudging along beneath their burdens. At the summit of the mountain, known in Spanish as the Mountain of the Adoration, offerings are left to him in the form of turkeys and bundles of cacao beans wrapped in bark paper to bring a good harvest. She invokes him more amply later this same night (p. 171). He is the Mazatec culture hero, their variant of Quetzalcóatl. "Quetzalcóatl," says Seler, "is the priest who by his acts of self-sacrifice and penitence, by the cult that he renders to the Gods, assures abundance to the community, fecundity and the good development of plants. Quetzalcóatl is he who gives wealth. Of a man enriched in a short time, the Mexicans aid he was the son of Quetzalcóatl" (Eduard Seler, *Comentarios al Códice Borgia*, trans. Marian Frenk [México: Fondo de Cultura Económia, 1963]). In the 1958 session, María Sabina addresses him in exactly the same terms as she does in 1970: "As Lord Tocosho is ready/ Father of the Harvest, Rich Father/So is our Lord Tocosho" (p. 145).

p. 157

"*. . .with knees for hands, with knees for feet. . .*" This is a standard, stereotyped stanza in María Sabina's implorings. In the 1958 session (p. 141), she says: "I go on the knees of my thighs/ On my knees of tortillas, on my knees of water." She says exactly the same thing later in the present session on p. 170.

p. 164

"There is no problem nor any difficulty. . ." This is another way to translate the same expression that is given more literally elsewhere as "there is no resentment, there is no rancor."

p. 165

"*In your hands are the medicinal herbs. . .*" The Virgin Guadalupe, "Queen of Mexico," is a Christian transformation of the Aztec Goddes of the earth, Tonantzin, whose sanctuary stood at the outskirts of the ancient Tenochtitlán in the very place where the Basilica of the Guadalupe stands in Mexico city today. In the incantations of the ancient Mexican medicine men, "in your hands" meant "in the interior and beneath the protection of the earth; the place where the seed will germinate" (Alfredo López Austin, *Terminos del Nahuallatolli, Historia Mexicana* 65, El Colegio de México, vol 17, no. 1, July-Sept 1967, pp. 1-36).

p. 167

"*That is your book, my Father/ . . . That is your clock. . .*" Whereas in the Folk-ways session, the clock was associated with the eagle, in this session it is associated with the book, and it is no longer she who is a clock, the clock is God's clock. For her everything is written, predestined, foreordained. God has wound up the clock of existence and set it going, allotting to each his or her number of days.

p. 168

"*I who came from inside the stomach of my mother . . .*" The psychiatrist Stanislav Grof, who began his experiments with LSD in Prague and continued them in the United States at the Spring Grove State Hospital, Maryland, found from the reports of hundreds of subjects to whom he administered the psychedelic that one of the most common experiences of people was to relive their birth. Many had vivid visions of their life in the womb. María Sabina tells Estrada that she sometimes sees herself as "an illuminated fetus" inside her mother (chap. 17). Grof cautiosly leaves open to question whether such "perinatal experiences," as he calls them, are actual memories revived by the psychoactive effect of the drug, or symbolic products of the imagination (Stanislav Grof, *Realms of the Human Unconscious: Observations from LSD Research,* [New York: E. P. Dutton, 1976]).

At this moment, María Sabina is apparently tracing her ancestry back in her mind. The Peter she speaks of must be Pedro Feliciano, her grandfather, whom she says in her autobiography was a great shaman (chap. 8).

p. 169

"*. . .the principle broom is, the sacred broom. . .*" The herb she speaks of in the next line is the mushroom or any of the medicinal plants which get rid of sickness as brooms clean houses. The shaman Roman Estrada (see above, chap. 20, note 1, on p. 207) also speaks of having a broom in his chants: he says he is going "to sweep in the mountains of nerves" (Munn, "The Mushrooms of Language"). The Mazatec shamans sometimes clean people by brushing them with bunches of leaves. The Huichol shamans use fans of macaw and eagle feathers to clean their patients. Peter T. Furst says that "a broom was one of the principal insignia" of the Aztec goddess, Toci, Our Grandmother, the Mother of the Gods, one of whose forms was Tlazoteotl, the Goddess of fertility and medicine. "Ritual sweeping," he notes, "in honor of the Mothers, the goddesses of the earth, fertility and sustenance, is still an important part of Huichal ceremonial. . . and the altars on which the Quiche Maya in highland Guatemala make their offerings to the earth deity are called *mesabal*, 'Place of the Sweeping.'" (Peter T. Furst, "Morning Glory and Mother Goddess at Tepantitla, Teotihuacan: Iconography and Analogy in Pre-Columbian Art," in *Mesoamerican Archaeology: New Approaches,* Austin: University of Texas Press, 1974).

The Conibo shaman I have mentioned elsewhere in these notes also speaks of brooms in his *yajé* chants: "Bringing the brilliant broom, comes the man of medicine. . . I have a broom/ the body has a bad odor/ with my broom I am going to clean the body of the woman."

"*. . .woman fire. . .*" She says "*chjon*[42] *fuego*". Probably she means a woman who gives the command to fire. In 1958 she says several times, "I am going to burn the world" (p. 117).

p. 171

"*Let us go with tenderness, let us go with clarity...*" In this context I have translated the word xcoen[1] as "tenderness" rather than "greenness." (See note, Folkways Session, p. 107, on p. 215)

p. 173

"*...woman of the mine that is growing/...woman of the mine that is augmenting...*" "Mine" is said in Spanish: *mina*. The verbs she uses mean literally "to grow up and fill out." The counterpart of this image of wealth in the chants of Roman Estrada is the bank. (Munn, "The Mushrooms of Language"). María Aurora associates the idea of an inexhaustible source of wealth with the Woman of the Flowing Water, the Goddess of abundance. These conditions of overflowing, superabundant energy and spiritual plenitude naturally express themselves in visions of richness. Interestingly enough, among the Desana Indians in Colombia "taking *yajé*... is interpreted as a return to the cosmic uterus, to the 'mine,' to the source of all things." (Gerardo Reichel-Dolmatoff, *Amazonian Cosmos: The Sexual and Religious Symbolism of the Tukano Indians* [Chicago: University of Chicago Press, 1971]).

"*...elder master of the mountains woman...*": "Cjon[42] cojon nai[1], chjon[42] cojon chi[3] con[3]." The shamaness Irene Pineda says that the Woman of the Flowing Water was "the daughter —in — law of the old Cojon." In her relating of the myth, she says: "May he be freed from sicknesses, may he be freed from pains, may he be freed from all evil. That is what the old Father Cojon is for, where Cojon Water is, where the Mother of Medicinal Green Berries is, where our Father comes from, where Father Sun is, there where it is called Holy Cojon Water, there is where our sweet Chicon is, Chicon Tocosho." *Cojon*, therefore, seems to be an old Mazatec word for the Masters of the Mountains or for one of them. The same lady told me that the Cojon is a cultivator who looks out for the beans and cornfields of the campesinos. He may be a rain god. She says he lives on Mt. Ladder of Water near the Cliff of Green Berries, where the Sun comes out.

p. 175

"*...hot tongue...*" She is referring to the stinging effect of hot chili peppers. Later, p. 177, what she means by "plain" is insipid, without taste.

p. 176

"*Over there behind the mountain...*" They mean they are going to exorcise the evil and bury it. This is a spell. In the Nahuatl conjurations, the expression "I will have your hand, your venerable foot kept behind the wall," meant: "I will impede you using your malefic powers." "It is directed at sickness," explains López Austin, (*Terminos del Nahuallatolli*). We can get an idea of what Aurora means in the next line by "*Seven to the left.../ seven to the right,*" from the 1958 session when María Sabina asks the sick boy: "Did you kick those bullies in the butt? One to the left, one to the right?" (p. 127). Together with 13 and 53 (see this session, p. 147), seven is another magic number for the Mazatecs. It is noteworthy that such numbers are always odd numbers. According to Alfonso Caso, the ancient Mexicans put seven seeds in their rattles and the number seven stood for fertility.

p. 180

"*Admirable Book...*" The word *xcon¹* that she uses here I have translated elsewhere as "respected" or "awesome," but it also has the sense of "sacred." It means "something untouchable, something that inspires awe." Cowan translates it as "admired."

p. 181

"*...the rope of our personality...*" A Mazatec lady has told me that once when she ate mushrooms with María Sabina to be cured of an illness, she felt that the shamaness was pulling the sickness out of her with a rope that she coiled up on her shoulder with each measure of her chant.

p. 182

"*Little woman of the whirlpool in the lake...*" María Sabina calls herself this in the 1958 session, p. 107: "*Chjon⁴² jncho' v?a³ tji³.*" Cowan translates it as "Woman whirlpool in the lake am I," and it is followed by the statement: "I am a woman who looks into the insides of things." Wasson thinks it refers to a legendary lake on top of Mount Rabon, about eight hours walk from Huautla near the town of Ayautla, where there is supposed to be a gourd dish floating in the water "in the seven colors of the rainbow" (Wasson, *Velada*, p. 106). She says this again on p. 187. The next statement sounds like a form of the verb "look," but I am uncertain as to its meaning.

p. 185

"*Our woman shepherdess...*" The Mother Shepherdess María Sabina invokes so many times in the Folkways Session seems to be replaced in this session by The Woman of the Flowing Water. From what María Aurora says here it seems probable that they are the same person. The shamans, like shepherds, have the duty of bringing back the spirits of those who have eaten mushrooms under their care to everyday life again when the session is over.

p. 187

"*...spider woman...*" It is interesting that she should call herself a spider woman in light of the fact that in Navaho mythology it is Spider Woman who taught humans the art of weaving. Spider webs are a common symbol in Mixtec codices. The idea of spinning may be in the back of her mind, but the spider is also suggested to her by the similarity in sound between the word for spider, *to³ntso²2²* and for hummingbird, *to²ntsin⁴*. In a passage in the 1958 session (p.144), she says: "I am a woman who resounds, I am a woman torn up out of the ground/ I am a spider woman/ I am a hummingbird woman," using all similar sounding words: *tjo³tsin³*, *tjo³ne³*, *to³ntso²?o³*, and *to²ntsin⁴*. When she mentions the spider it is always together with hummingbird: they form one of those couples of words which recur throughout her chants, whose euphony is based on the repetition of similar sounding words with only slight differences between them, rather than on strict rhyme.

A NOTE ON THE BOOK'S DESIGN

In June 1960 I went to Huautla de Jiménez with some friends.
This was a few years after Wasson had rediscovered the traditional
use of the hallucinogenic mushroom in contemporary Mazatec ceremony.
I was intensely interested in the ethnology of Mexican cultures
and their relation to Pre-Hispanic traditions.

Omitting the adventures we encountered reaching Huautla,
after three or four days and with some negotiations we met
with María Sabina. A few days later she performed the Velada
with us as participants. It was everything I could have ever
imagined from my bookish ethnological travels.

Now, 20 years later, by some kharmic "bottom line" I find
myself confronted with her book. In all humility and fumbling with
my lack of a tradition such as has María, I have tried to present
her book in an appealing fashion. Simply as my personal appreciation
for what she gave me, once upon a time.

The designs on the cover, endpapers and title page are
directly derived from traditional Mazatec huilpil embroideries
(the style of Jalapa de Díaz).

—Fredrick Usher

A NOTE ON THE TYPE

The text in this book is set in Goudy Oldstyle,
a face designed by Frederic W. Goudy (1865-1947).
The type size is 11 on 12½ body.
The text was set by Jim Cook of A●Typical type
in Santa Barbara, California.

The book was printed and bound by
Burch Printing of Benton Harbor, Michigan